O9-BHK-045

A12900 373299

OF BOOKS AND HUMANKIND

OF BOOKS AND HUMANKIND

Essays and Poems Presented to Bonamy Dobrée

EDITED BY JOHN BUTT

Assisted by J. M. Cameron
D. W. Jefferson and Robin Skelton

Routledge and Kegan Paul
LONDON

First published 1964
by Routledge and Kegan Paul Ltd
Broadway House, 68-74 Carter Lane
London, E.C.4

Printed in Great Britain
in the City of Oxford
at the Alden Press

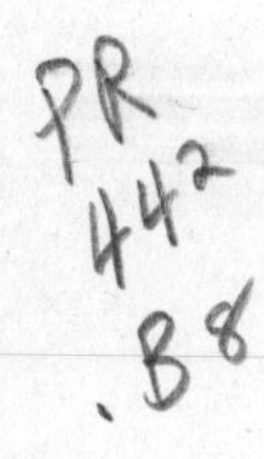

Contents

I. Essays

CONTENTS

CONTENTS

III. Personalia

Preface

ONE volume would not be extensive enough to contain the tributes of all the admirers of Bonamy Dobrée. The contributors to this volume are well aware that they form part only of a far larger group of his pupils, colleagues and friends, but they hope that few as they are they have succeeded in reflecting his manifold interests.

Though he has been 'sworn to no Master', his published works show that he is fondest of that period of our literature which extends from 1660 to the end of the eighteenth century; accordingly it has seemed appropriate that most of the contributions from his academic colleagues should have some bearing on authors whose work he has done so much to illuminate.

Above all a scholar and a man of letters, Dobrée has also been a patron of artists and poets. At the University of Leeds no one has shown more enthusiasm and practical concern for the development of the fine arts in the life of the University. This enthusiasm and this concern found a happy expression in the part he played in the foundation of the Gregory Fellowships in painting, sculpture, music and poetry and in the establishment in Leeds of a department of Fine Art. During his tenure (of nearly twenty years) of the Chair of English Literature he added further distinction to the tradition associated with such names as C. E. Vaughan, George Gordon, Lascelles Abercrombie and F. P. Wilson. Diversity of opinion and approach among teachers and students alike was vigorously encouraged. During these years the Leeds department was known for the breadth and humanity of its teaching and scholarship. These were for Dobrée years of intense activity in the University; but he continued to be remarkably productive in several fields of literary scholarship; and it was during these years, too, that he was occupied with the editorial work connected with the Oxford History of English Literature and in the preparation of his own volume, on the early eighteenth century, in this series.

A man so various in interest and accomplishment is a rarity in academic life. This variety is in some degree reflected in these pages. Scholars, poets, artists, colleagues, pupils, friends—and these are not of course exclusive categories—here combine to represent in their many ways the fields of interest of this many-sided man.

This book will not be worthy of its aim if it does not convey some of the joy in the arts which Dobrée has so abundantly expressed. The contributors offer him this tribute in gratitude and affection. They hope that he may find pleasure in reading it, and that he will long continue to enjoy the activity that has marked the years of his retirement.

We wish to express our thanks to the Publications Committee of the University of Leeds for their generous grant in respect of the expenses of publication.

J.B.
J.M.C.
D.W.J.
R.S.

I
Essays

Was Clytaemnestra a Liar?

A. NORMAN JEFFARES

I

WE know how many children Clytaemnestra had. One of them, Iphigenia, was sacrificed by her father Agamemnon at Aulis: 'to further a war waged to avenge the loss of a woman and as a preliminary offering for the fleet's voyage',[1] and because Agamemnon was his daughter's sacrificial murderer Clytaemnestra had an excuse for murdering him on his homecoming from Troy. Of course, the whole material of Aeschylus' great *Oresteia* trilogy, the *Agamemnon*, the *Libation-Bearers* and the *Eumenides*, carries complications. The killing of Agamemnon, as John Jones has recently pointed out,[2] is not a mere outrage like the murder of Duncan in *Macbeth*, because Agamemnon is not innocent in relation either to Clytaemnestra or to Aegisthus. Agamemnon's father Atreus killed some of the children of Thyestes, the father of Aegisthus, and served them up to him at a banquet.[3] Aegisthus therefore sees himself as an instrument of revenge, as does Clytaemnestra. This, however, could not excuse either the murder or the liaison between Clytaemnestra and Aegisthus.

[1] Aeschylus, *Agamemnon*, ll. 226–227.

[2] Jones, *Aristotle and Greek Tragedy* (1962), p. 74.

[3] To add to the complexity of the story, this was done in revenge for the adultery committed by Thyestes with the wife of Atreus.

Mr Jones makes many illuminating comments on the trilogy and argues that critics, particularly Anglo-Saxon commentators whom he sees as moralizing in a vacuum, have sealed off the principal figures—husband, wife and son—from the atmosphere of lyric commentary in which they live. He is concerned to stress the central importance of the οἶκος, the household, in the trilogy. And he explains that, like the murder of Agamemnon, the sacrifice of Iphigenia had also been no mere outrage. In so doing he is attacking, in part, 'the modern reader's distress at being unable to make sense of Agamemnon', and he offers us some new and subtle explanations of Agamemnon's dilemma in the process, stressing the double standards applied to the sacrifice of Iphigenia and the Trojan war in the play.[1]

He says we have no reason to think Clytaemnestra insincere when she says death is Agamemnon's desert and asks Zeus to fulfil her prayer for vengeance.[2] He argues that Agamemnon's first desire and duty on his homecoming is to return to his own hearth:

> No word of Clytaemnestra. The focus is the *focus*—the socio-religious hearth of Indo-European societies and a living force to Aeschylus and his audience now to be approached after long absence by the household's master who is also its priest. To feel the moment in this way is the first step towards a just reading of the carpet scene. The carpet lies between Agamemnon and his hearth: this is the situation which commentators have obscured in two closely related ways, by psychologizing the meeting of husband and wife into a process of temptation and by spiritualizing a quarrel about treading upon a carpet into something supposedly more exalted. Their joint effect is to reduce the carpet to a physical pawn in a mental conflict.[3]

Yet the meeting between Agamemnon and Clytaemnestra does possess significance. This can be erotic, as Mr Jones points out; but he is concerned to stress the kind of view we might imagine an Athenian fifth-century audience would take of it. He regards Clytaemnestra as hubristic in her wasteful use of the resources of the household and her view that the house is wealthy enough for it not to matter when she spreads the valuable carpets for Agamemnon and persuades him to walk on them. But she offends against society in other ways. She is a masculine woman who kills a man; she is blasphemous in her murder and her account of it; and she has asserted her sexual independence. She can argue that Agamemnon sacrificed Iphigenia, and that he has now brought Cassandra back with him as a concubine. Mr Jones

[1] Jones, op. cit., pp. 72–111. [2] *Agamemnon*, ll. 973. [3] Jones, op. cit., p. 85.

remarks that we are not told whether Agamemnon and Cassandra are lovers; he adds 'nobody shows the slightest interest in their sexual affairs—except Clytaemnestra who calls Cassandra Agamemnon's "bed-fellow" adding the plainly mendacious sneer that she is also a sailors' prostitute'. (Her jealousy of Cassandra is perhaps natural, and her own relationship with Aegisthus may, paradoxically, heighten it). Leaving aside the role of Cassandra, it is clear that Clytaemnestra's position—as avenger, yet adultress—causes problems. Pindar put the question about her character a long time ago, pointing out the extreme views which could be taken of her motivation:

> πότερόν νιν ἄρ' Ἰφιγένει' ἐπ' Εὐρίπῳ
> σφαχθεῖσα τῆλε πάτρας
> ἔκνιξεν βαρυπάλαμον ὄρσαι χόλον;
> ἢ ἑτέρῳ λέχει δαμαζομέναν
> ἔννυχοι πάραγον κοῖται;

> Was it indeed the thought of Iphigenia sacrificed on the banks of the Euripos far from her native land, that stung her so as to rouse her heavy plotting wrath or was it that, come to another man's bed, the adulterous embraces of the night beguiled her?[1]

Probably Clytaemnestra's vital offence was against the sexual norm. This is Mr Jones's view, to which the order of Pindar's alternatives may perhaps also have tended. Mr Jones sees, in the final confrontation of Orestes with Clytaemnestra in the *Libation-Bearers*, the sexual issue flaring into prominence, for 'at this great moment of the trilogy, the vital and dramatic fact is that sex has escaped from its proper place in the world of women'. This is, he thinks, a Hamlet-like situation of horror in the exceptional erotic sharpness of the dialogue between avenging son and guilty mother,[2] where Orestes expresses abhorrence at her regard for Aegisthus whom he has just killed.

II

There is a passage in the *Agamemnon* as yet not apparently fully commented upon by editors or critics which seems to throw more light on the significance of Clytaemnestra's behaviour and the view of it put forward by Aeschylus. These lines which Clytaemnestra speaks to Agamemnon on his return are somewhat baffling:

[1] *Pythians*, XI, 22. [2] *Libation-Bearers*, ll. 892–5.

τοιῶνδ' ἕκατι κληδόνων παλιγκότων
πολλὰς ἄνωθεν ἀρτάνας ἐμῆς δέρης
ἔλυσαν ἄλλοι πρὸς βιάν λελημμένης.

Because of adverse rumours such as these I often tied the noose above my head which others perforce took off.[1]

Why, we may ask, did she tell Agamemnon she had attempted to commit suicide in his absence?[2] Was this statement true or false? Why did she choose hanging? How does this statement fit into the framework of the trilogy? These questions may perhaps be answered by an attempt to view them in relation to other cases in Greek literature, and particularly in tragedy, where women commit suicide. Not all the cases to be mentioned will substantiate the theory to be put forward—in a very tentative way—as a means of explaining some of the striking similarities which emerge from the inquiry; but Greek mythology and the moral ideas behind the tragedies are not always clear to us and indeed can often seem almost contradictory—and may even have at times seemed so to the Greeks themselves. The examination is offered, then, because it seems to give an extra subtlety to a reading of the *Agamemnon*, in particular, which is not out of keeping with the view of Clytaemnestra put forward by Mr Jones.

In this passage it might appear that Clytaemnestra is ostensibly behaving as a true and noble wife when she tells Agamemnon how she attempted to commit suicide on hearing reports of her husband's death. Suicide did not seem morally base *per se* to the Greeks. Clytaemnestra could, for instance, be compared to Andromache who was a pattern of wifely virtue in the *Iliad* and contemplated suicide if Hector should die:

ἐμὸι δέ κε κέρδιον ἔιη
σεῦ ἀφαμαρτούσῃ χθόνα δύμεναι

It would be best for me to die if I lose you.[3]

It seems, however, that in Greek literature the suicides of women who hang themselves have a special significance. This was a form of

[1] *Agamemnon*, ll. 874–876. See note, *Agamemnon* (ed. Denniston and Page), 1957, p. 145, which translates the passage: 'Many nooses, up aloft, were loosed from my neck by others while they held me in their grip perforce.' See also note in Fraenkel's edition of the play, vol. II, 1950, pp. 394–5.

[2] The reason given in the text (ἐκ τῶνδε, 'for these reasons') is that Orestes has been sent away from home because in the words of Denniston and Page, op. cit., 'his mother might at any moment succeed in hanging herself'.

[3] *Iliad*, VI, l. 410.

death particularly associated with sexual irregularity. Indeed, the first mention of suicide in extant Greek literature illustrates the particular horror felt by public opinion about such irregularity. Homer is explicit about it:

> Μητέρα τ'Οἰδιπόδαο ἴδον, καλὴν Ἐπικάστην,
> ἣ μέγα, ἔργον ἔρεξεν ἀιδρείῃσι νόοιο,
> γημαμένη ᾧ̃ υἷι·ὁ δ' ὃν πατέρ' εξεναρίξας
> γῆμεν· ἄφαρ δ'ἀνάπυστα θεὸι θέσαν ἀνθρώποισιν.
> ἀλλ' ὁ μὲν ἐν θήβῃ πολυηράτῳ ἄλγεα πάσχων
> Καδμείων ἤνασσε θεῶν ὀλοὰς διὰ βουλάς·
> ἡ δ' ἔβη εἰς Αίδαο πυλάρταο κρατεροῖο,
> ἁψαμένη βρόχον ἀιπὺν ἀφ' ὑψηλοῖο μελάθρου,
> ᾧ ἄχει σχομένη·

> I saw the mother of Oedipus, fair Epicaste, who wrought an awful deed in ignorance of mind, marrying her own son. And he had slain his father and married her; and presently the Gods made it known to men. Then he in lovely Thebes endured sorrow and ruled over the Cadmeans by the grievous councils of the Gods. But she went to the house of Hades, fastening a high noose from the lofty hall, smitten by her woe.[1]

Epicaste committed an 'awful deed' in marrying her son. This is more shocking than the son's murder of the father described in the following line. The word ἀνάπυστα translated by 'made known' is used deliberately. It is the *mot juste* for the leaking out of some scandal. Stephanus, for instance, quotes examples from Suidas and Hesychius to demonstrate that ἀνάπυστος means not only ἔκδηλα (quite plain) and ἐξακουστα (heard, audible) but also ἀνεκλάλητα (unutterable) and ἄρρητα (unspeakable). And Herodotus uses the word for cases of scandal in VI, 64 and 66. Epicaste fled from the disgrace and the reproaches of the citizens.

The treatment of the story in the *Oedipus* of Sophocles is fuller and germane. In the tragedy Jocasta does not commit suicide until the real identity of Oedipus is on the point of being disclosed. Her one desire is to hush up the whole matter. During the interview with the Corinthian messenger she quickly realizes that Oedipus is her son and the main dramatic intensity of the play is concentrated into her efforts to stop Oedipus from making further inquiries about his birth:

> μὴ πρὸς θεῶν, εἴπερ τι τοῦ σαυτοῦ βιόυ
> κήδει, ματεύσῃς τοῦθ' ἅλις νοσοῦσ' ἐγώ.

[1] *Odyssey*, XI, l. 271 seq.

Oh, as you care for life, give up your search.
Enough the anguish I endure.[1]

These lines indicate that she then had no idea of committing suicide. Why should she? Oedipus provides the answer:

θάρσει. σὺ μὲν γὰρ οὐδ᾽ ἐὰν τρίτης ἐγὼ
μητρὸς φανῶ τρίδουλος, ᾽εκφανεῖ κακή

Be of good courage; though I be proved bondwoman's son, triply
A slave through three descents, your honour is unsmirched.[2]

It is only when she realizes that Oedipus is offended in his pride and stubbornly determined to track down the secret of his birth that she leaves him with a despairing farewell:

τοῦτο γάρ σ᾽ἔχω
μόνον προσειπεῖν, ἄλλο δ᾽ οὔποθ᾽ ὕστερον.

This is the last word I have for you
Henceforth I shall be silent for ever.[3]

Afterwards the messenger completes the story:

οὗ δὴ κρεμαστὴν τὴν γυναῖκ᾽ ἐσείδομεν,
πλεκταῖσιν αἰώραισιν ἐμπεπλεγμένην.

Then we saw the woman hanging there
A twisted noose about her neck.[4]

A. W. Mair, in commenting on Homer's story of Epicaste, points out that the essential points of this story are (1) suicide presents itself to Homer as the natural and fitting act when life has lost all that makes life worth living, and (2) no blame attaches to suicide itself.[5] The method of leaving life had, however, its special significance. We find, for instance, that Homer in a passage with clear commentary makes Telemachus go to the trouble of hanging those maid-servants who had slept with the suitors:

'μὴ μὲν δὴ καθαρῷ θανάτῳ ἀπὸ θυμὸν ἑλοίμην
τάων, ἅι δὴ ἐμῇ κεφαλῇ κατ᾽ ὀνείδεα χεῦαν
μητέρι θ᾽ἡμετέρῃ, παρά τε μνηστῆρσιν ἴαυον᾽
ὣς ἄρ᾽ ἔφη, κὰι πεῖσμα νεὸς κυανοπρῴροιο

[1] *Oedipus Rex*, ll. 1060–1061.
[2] Ibid., ll. 1062–1063. [3] Ibid., ll. 1071–1072. [4] Ibid., ll. 1263–1264.
[5] 'Greek Suicides', *Encyclopaedia of Religion and Ethics*, 1921.

κίονος ἐξάψας μεγάλης περίβαλλε θόλοιο,
ὑψόσ' ἐπεντανύσας, μή τις ποσὶν οὖδας ἵκοιτο

Heaven forbid that I should take these women's lives by a clean death, these women who have poured dishonour on my head and on my mother, and have slept with the wooers. With these words he tied the cable of a dark-prowed ship to a great pillar and flung it across the vaulted room, fastening it high that none of them might touch the ground with her feet.[1]

The significance of hanging emerges clearly in the *Hippolytus* of Euripides. Phaedra is introduced while trying to commit suicide by fasting. The reasons for her action are unknown, and the chorus says:

ἄσημα δ'ἡμῖν ἥτις ἐστὶν ἡ νόσος

We do not know what is afflicting her.[2]

A few lines later the chorus asks the nurse

πότερον ὑπ' ἄτης ἢ θανεῖν πειρωμένη;

Is this madness or a plan to die?[3]

The nurse replies:

θανεῖν· ἀσιτεῖ δ' εἰς ἀπόστασιν βίου

To die. She is fasting to make an end of her life.[4]

It is not until Phaedra has confessed her love for Hippolytus to the nurse that she adopts the idea of death by hanging. She has been trying to hide her adulterous passion and committing suicide by fasting will not cast a stain upon her honour. But suddenly the secret is out:

NURSE

τί φῄς; ἐρᾷς, ὦ τέκνον, ἀνθρώπων τινός;

What say'st thou? Child, thou lovest—oh, what man?

PHAEDRA

ὅστις ποθ' οὗτος ἔσθ' ὁ τῆς 'Αμαζόνος

Whatever his name—it's he—the Amazon's son.

NURSE

Ἱππόλυτον αὐδᾷς;

Hippolytus!

[1] *Odyssey*, XXII, l. 462. See note to *Odyssey of Homer* (ed. W. B. Stanford), 1948, II, 389: 'Telemachus takes leave to inflict a less clean death on them and proceeds to arrange for their hanging . . Hanging was always considered a dishonourable and shameful death by the Greeks.'

[2] *Hippolytus*, l. 269. [3] Ibid., l. 276. [4] Ibid., l. 277.

σοῦ τάς᾽ οὐκ ἐμοῦ κλύεις

PHAEDRA

Thou say'st it, not I.[1]

whereupon she hangs herself,

Βοηδρομεῖτε πάντες οἱ πέλας δόμων
ἐν ἀγχόναις δέσποινα, θησέως δάμαρ.

ATTENDANT

Run to the rescue, all ye nigh the house!
In the strangling noose is Theseus' wife, our mistress.

φεῦ φεῦ, πέπρακται· Βασιλὶς οὐκέτ᾽ ἔστι δὴ
γυνή, κρεμαστοῖς ἐν βρόχοις ἠρτημένη

CHORUS

Woe, woe! 'tis done. No more—no more is she,
The queen—in yon noose rafter hung up caught![2]

The reason for her suicide is given by the Chorus:

τεράμνων
ἀπὸ νυμφιδίων κρεμαστὸν
ἅψεται ἀμφὶ βρόχον
λευκᾷ καθαρμόζουσα δείρᾳ
δαίμονα στυγνὰν καταιδε—
σθεῖσα, τάν τ᾽ εὔδοξον ἀνθαι—
ρουμένα φάμαν, ἀπαλλάσ—
σουσά τ᾽ ἀλγεινὸν φρενῶν ἔρωτα.

disaster-oppressed
Over her bride-bower's rafters flinging
The noose, shall she cast the coil close-clinging
Round the neck that was whitest and loveliest,
Because that with shuddering shame she shrank from a loathed name,
And chose, instead, the stainless renown of a wife's fair fame
And, for anguish of love, heart-rest.[3]

This mode of death is described as unholy:

αἰαῖ τόλμας βιαίως θανοῦσ᾽
ἀνοσίῳ τε συμφορᾷ . . .

Ah for your desperate deed,
Dying by unhallowed violence . . [4]

[1] *Hippolytus*, l. 350. [2] Ibid., l. 776. [3] Ibid., l. 768. [4] Ibid., l. 814.

It appears, then, that once a Greek woman was discovered to be sexually dishonest, or impure, or irregular, conventional standards of morality demanded that she should hang herself.[1] So, since the idea of individual conscience did not prevail amongst the Greeks, we find that Phaedra had hopes of dying by some other means than hanging so that the reason for her death would be a mystery, but once the Nurse (who seems in this play to represent a kind of norm of public opinion, the opinion of a mean between Aphrodite and Artemis) knows of her love for Hippolytus, the only course of action left to her is to hang herself.

In the *Helen* of Euripides the heroine is particularly concerned to establish her purity[2] which Proteus honoured but which is now endangered by his son:

> εώς μὲν οὖν φῶς ἡλίου τόδ' ἔβλεπεν
> Πρωτεύς, ἄσυλος ἦν γάμων· ἐπεὶ δὲ γῆς
> σκότῳ κέκρυπται, παῖς ὁ τοῦ τεθνηκότος
> θηρᾷ γαμεῖν με.
>
> While Proteus remained alive I was left inviolate;
> Now he is dead, and his son is eager to marry me.[3]

After Teucer arrives to tell her that Menelaus is dead, she considers her future

> Τί δῆτ' ἔτι ζῶ; τίν' ὑπολείπομαι τύχην;
>
> Why do I then live on? What fortune awaits me?[4]

She considers the alternatives and her description of the two methods of suicide contemplated clarifies the view taken of hanging:

> γάμους ἑλομένη τῶν κακῶν ὑπαλλαγάς,
> μετ' ἀνδρὸς οἰκεῖν βαρβάρου, πρὸς πλουσίαν
> τράπεζαν ἵζουσ'; ἀλλ' ὅταν πόσις πικρὸς
> ξυνῇ γυναικί καὶ το σῶμ' ἐστιν πικρόν,
> θανεῖν κράτιστον. πῶς θάνοιμ' ἂν οὖν καλῶς;
> ἀσχήμονες μὲν ἀγχόναι μετάρσιοι,
> κἀν τοῖσι δούλοις δυσπρεπὲς νομίζεται,
> σφαγὰι δ'ἔχουσιν ἐυγενές τι καὶ καλόν

[1] For instance, there is the example of Mykerinos who hangs herself after she has been violated by her father, see *Herodotus*, II, 131. The daughters of Skedasos hanged themselves because the Spartans offered them violence, see *Pausanias*, IX, 13, 6.

[2] *Helen*, ll. 32–36. [3] Ibid, l. 61. [4] Ibid, l. 293.

> Shall I choose marriage as an escape from my ills?—live with a barbarian husband, sitting at his rich table? But when a loathsome husband lives with a woman she finds herself [*lit*, her body] loathsome too. It is best to die. But how would I die well? For hanging from a high rope is unseemly and it is disgraceful even for slaves. There is something noble and fine in death by the sword.[1]

The marriage which is repugnant to her, owing to her Greek dislike of a barbarian and harsh husband, or death? She is not sure that Menelaus is dead, so she chooses death as a way out of her difficulty. G. M. A. Grube seems to give only one of her reasons for dismissing hanging as her mode of dying, for he suggests that she disliked this procedure because it would spoil her beauty.[2] His argument covers the word ἀσχήμονες in line 299, but not the line

κἀν τοῖσι δούλοις δυσπρεπὲς νομίζεται.

And it is disgraceful [or shameful] even for slaves.

This clearly shows a definite idea of disgrace attached to suicides by hanging. There is some hesitation which adds to the tension of the play:

φόνιον αἰώρημα
διὰ δέρης ὀρέξομαι,
ἢ ξιφοκτόνον δίωγμα
αἱμορύτου σφαγᾶς
αὐτοσίδαρον ἔσω πελάσω διὰ σαρκὸς ἅμιλλαν
θῦμα τριζύγοις θεαῖσι . . .

I will twine the death dealing cord
around my neck
or drive the sword
through the flesh of my neck
plunging it into life's shrine
for a sacrifice to the three goddesses.[3]

But after this Helen chooses a noble form of death.

Another important reference occurs in the same play where Helen agree to die with Menelaus if they cannot escape together, and now there is no possible questioning of the means to be adopted:

τί φής; θανεῖσθαι κοὔποτ' ἀλλάξειν λέχη;

MENELAUS

How? Will you die ere deserting your lord?

[1] *Helen*, ll. 294. [2] *The Drama of Euripides*, 1941, p. 338. [3] *Helen*, ll. 353 seq.

ταυτῷ ξίφει γε· κείσομαι δὲ σοῦ πέλας.

HELEN

Yes, by this same sword. I will lie beside you.[1]

There are three references to the death of Leda, Helen's mother, in the *Helen*.[2] The last of these may have some bearing on the disgrace of irregular sexual behaviour. It runs:

οὐκ ἔστι μάτηρ. ἀγχόνιον βρόχον
δι ἐμὲ κατεδήσατο δύσγαμον αἰσχύνᾳ[3]

No mother have I. She bound up her neck for shame in the strangling noose, because of my ill-famed marriage.

This shows that Leda was ashamed of her daughter's behaviour. Once Helen was detected in her open love for Paris and her disloyalty to Menelaus she should have committed suicide by hanging. Perhaps Leda may have seen herself as a kind of substitute, or as taking the guilt of her daughter on herself? (All three references to Leda's suicide seem to show that it would not have occurred if Helen had behaved in the *Helen* in accordance with accepted custom.) This view, that Helen ought to have hanged herself, may perhaps seem far-fetched, yet it is born out by a highly interesting passage in the *Troades* of Euripides. In the *Troades* Helen's defence of her actions is ingenious. She tries to persuade Menelaus that she was innocent; she blames Cypris for misleading her; and asserts that she went to Troy unwillingly. Indeed, she says that she often tried to escape:

μάρτυρες δέ μοι
πύργων πυλωρόι, κἀπὸ τειχέων σκοπόι,
οἵ πολλάκις μ' ἐφηῦρον ἐξ 'επάλξεων
πλεκταῖσιν εἰς γῆν σῶμα κλέπτουσαν τόδε.

My witnesses are
the gate-warders and the watchers from the walls
who often found me letting my body down stealthily
to the ground from the battlements with cords.[4]

This defence of Helen's, that she was not deliberately wicked and was under constraint, introduces a new element of intention and action into the story, but Hecuba, who is on stage as a prisoner, neatly attacks Helen's plea and eagerly seizes on the lines quoted above to point out by means of a verbal ambiguity, what Helen's correct

[1] Ibid., ll. 836 seq.
[2] *Helen*, ll. 134–136, 200–203 and 686–687.
[3] αἰσχύναν can be read for αἰσχύνᾳ.
[4] *Troades*, l. 956.

course of action would have been. She affects to misunderstand Helen's use of πλεκταῖσιν (anything twisted, i.e., ropes) in line 959, thus introducing the phrase βρόχους ἀρτωμένη (fastening halters or nooses) and arriving at the vital question—why did Helen not commit suicide? She makes her point clearly and in doing so casts further light on how the Athenian audience would have regarded the method of suicide chosen:

κἄπειτα πλεκτάις σῶμα σὸν κλέπτειν λέγεις
πύργων καθιεῖσ' ὡς μένουσ' ἀκουσίως;
ποῦ δῆτ' ἐλήφθης ἢ βρόχους ἀρτωμένη
ἢ φάσγανον θήγους', ἃ γενναία γυνὴ
δράσειεν ἂν ποθοῦσα τὸν πάρος πόσιν;

And you say you let your body down with cords climbing down from the towers, as if remaining unwillingly? Where, pray, were you found fastening a noose round your neck or whetting steel, as a noble wife would have done, yearning for her former husband.'[1]

In other words a woman who conformed to the social code, a γενναία γυνὴ (a noble-hearted woman) would have hanged herself had she willingly committed and been detected in adultery, or used the sword had she been overcome by force. Hecuba then gives her reasons for Helen's behaviour. She maintains that Helen is a really bad woman, who preferred to flaunt herself through Alexander's halls in all her shamelessness (she uses the word ὑβρίζεις) rather than do her duty.

What of the case of young women who were sexually pure and thought of or actually did commit suicide? Deianira was a good woman with no thought of being disloyal to her husband, as we are told in the *Trachiniae*:

τῆς μητρὸς ἥκω τῆς ἐμῆς φράσων ἐν δις
νῦν ἐστιν ὥς θ' ἥμαρτεν ὀυχ ἑκουσία

I have come to tell you of my mother
How she fares and that she sinned unwittingly.[2]

Because she sinned unwittingly she dies by the sword:

λέγω· τέθνηκεν ἀρτίως νεοσφαγής

Hear then. She is dead, slain recently.

πρὸς τοῦ; τέρας τοι διὰ κακῶν ἐθέσπισας

By whom? I do not like this portent; it is strange.

[1] *Troades*, l. 1010. [2] *Trachiniae*, l. 1122.

αὐτὴ πρὸς αὑτῆς, οὐδενὸς πρὸς ἐκτόπου

She is dead, slain just now by her own hand
And no one else was near.[1]

Electra (whose virginity was mocked at by Helen in the *Orestes* of Euripides[2]) when she envisages suicide as an escape from defeat knows how noble it is to die by the sword and encourages Orestes with hopes of glory:

ὡς εἰ παλαισθεὶς πτῶμα θανάσιμον πεσῇ
τέθνηκα κἀγώ, μηδέ με ζῶσαν λέγε.
παίσω γὰρ ἧπαρ τοὐμὸν ἀμφήκει ξίφει.

If you are overcome by fate [worsted in the struggle] and fall a deadly fall,
I am also dead; do not speak of me as living, for
I with sharp-edged sword will smite my heart.[3]

Early in the *Orestes* the fates of brother and sister are discussed without any mention of hanging as a possible death;[4] later, on three occasions,[5] the possibility of their deaths is discussed and hanging is not mentioned at all.

The idea of hanging is introduced by a messenger for the first time in the play in line 954:

ἀλλ' εὐτρέπιζε φάσγαν' ἢ βρόχον δέρῃ.

Prepare the sword or halter for your neck.

He tells Electra that an Argive had persuaded the Assembly that Orestes and Electra should be stoned to death, and Orestes then persuaded the Assembly not to enforce death by this means. But Orestes repeats the messenger's idea in his confusion when he arrives on the scene:

τόδ' ἦμαρ ἡμῖν κύριον· δεῖ δ' ἢ βρόχους
ἅπτειν κρεμαστοὺς ἢ ξίφος θήγειν χερί

This is our day of doom. We must apply the
twisted noose or put our hands to the sword.[6]

Electra asks Orestes to kill her, but he has had enough, and says she can die in whatever way she wishes by her own hand; in her reply to this Electra, however, clearly omits any mention of hanging

[1] Ibid., ll. 1130–32.
[2] *Orestes*, l. 72.
[3] Euripides, *Electra*, l. 688.
[4] Euripides, *Orestes*, l. 50.
[5] Ibid., ll. 614, 625 and 863.
[6] Ibid, l. 1036.

ἔσται τάδ'· οὐδὲν σοῦ ξίφους λελείψομαι·

Yes, indeed; I'll not lag behind thy sword.[1]

She continues:

πῶς ἂν ξίφος νὼ ταὐτόν, ἐι θέμις κτάνοι
καὶ μνῆμα δέξαιθ' ἓν κέδρου τεχνάσματα;

Oh, might the very same sword, if this may be
Kill us, and one cedar-wrought coffin contain us.[2]

The introduction of hanging by the Chorus in line 954 may be due to their fear that Electra would have no sword available, and this, too, is a possible explanation to be offered of Antigone's suicide in the *Antigone* of Sophocles, though this may be the kind of exception referred to above (see p. 12). She has been shut up to perish by Creon's orders:

ἄφετε μόνην ἔρημον, εἴτε χρῇ θανὲιν
ἐίτ' ἐν τοιαύτῃ ʒῶσα τυμβεύειν στέγῃ

Leave her alone at liberty to die,
Or, if she wish, to live in solitude,
The tomb her dwelling.[3]

She has no other means of killing herself and in her case a quick death was desired; that she had to kill herself in this manner may have been the real reason for Haemon's attempt on his father's life and subsequent suicide. In view of the statements in the *Iliad*, the *Odyssey*, *Hippolytus*, *Helen*, *Troades*, *Trachiniae* and *Electra* it might seem obvious that not only the evilly disposed but the average citizen would consider her mode of dying indicated dishonour. Again, the Queen in the *Antigone* has a choice of deaths, and, as there is no slur on her virtue, makes use of the sword:

ἥ δ' ὀʒυθήκτῳ βωμία περὶ ξίφει
λυέι κελαίνὰ βλεφάρα

Beside the altar on a keen-edged sword
She fell and closed her eyes in night.[4]

The description is repeated in line 1315:

παίσασ' ὑφ' ἧπαρ αὐτόχειρ ἁυτήν, ὅπως
παιδὸς τόδ' ᾔσθετ' ὀξυκώκυτον πάθος

Hearing the loud lament above her son
She stabbed herself to the heart with her own hand.

[1] Euripides, *Orestes*, l. 1041. [2] Ibid., ll. 1052. [3] *Antigone*, l. 887. [4] *Antigone*, l. 1301.

III

There are two other references to suicides by women, which, on first examination, appear to contradict previous findings. These hangings concern the two Erigones. The first Erigone was apparently a very noble maiden, as Hyginus asserts in his *Fable* (180):

> Icarium autem occisum canis ululans Maera Erigonae monstravit ubi Pater sepultus iaceret; quo cum venisset, super corpus parentis in arbore suspendio se necavit ...
>
> The bitch Maera by her howling for the slain Icarius showed Erigone where her father lay buried; when she had come thither she killed herself by hanging from a tree above her parent's body.

Ovid, however, has provided us with a different story, and one which probably gives the true reason for the method of her suicide:

> Liber ut Erigonen falsa deceperit uva
> how Bacchus deceived Erigone with the false bunch of grapes[1]

The second Erigone is mentioned in Dictys Cretensis:

> Erigona, quae ex Aegistho edita erat, ubi fratrem absolutum intelligit, victa dolore immodico, lacqueo interiit ...
>
> Erigone, the daughter of Aegisthus, overcome by immoderate grief when she heard her brother was discharged, perished by the noose.[2]

but again there is a different reason for the method of her suicide which is given by Pausanias:

> Τὸν δὲ 'Ορέστου νόθον πενθίλον κιναίθων
> ἔλραψεν ἐν τοῖς ἔπεσιν 'Ηριγόνην τὴν 'Αιγίσθου τεκεῖν.
>
> Kinaethon wrote that Erigone, the daughter of Aegisthus bore a bastard son of Orestes, Penthilus.[3]

There are some later examples of hanging women in the love romances of Parthenius; these women were all guilty of dishonourable love. Byblis[4] hanged herself because of her love for her brother Caunus; Cleoboea,[5] the wife of Phobius, fell in love with Antheus,

[1] *Metamorphoses*, VI, 125.

[2] See Dictys Cretensis, *Ephemeridos Belli Troiani* (ed. Werner Eisenhut), 1958, p. 123. On p. 121 we are told she was the daughter of Clytaemnestra and Aegisthus. The reference to 'discharged' related to Orestes being tried in Athens.

[3] II.18.6. [4] *Love Romances of Parthenius*, XI, 3. [5] Ibid, XIV, 4.

found her advances repelled and killed him, but 'being also fired with an exceeding passion for the lad hanged herself'; Clite[1] ostensibly hanged herself for love of Cyzicus (but her father lay with her before she was married); Evopis,[2] who was married to her uncle Dimoetes, hanged herself 'for fear and shame' when he informed her father of her incest with her brother.

IV

The whole question of hanging women has attracted the attention of the anthropologists, and the origins of this Greek custom of suicide by hanging where sexual dishonour was involved are obviously rooted in some primitive belief. Sir James Frazer collected some of the early examples:

> In Greece the great goddess Artemis herself appears to have been annually hanged in effigy in her sacred grove of Condylea among the Arcadian hills, and there accordingly she went by the name of the hanged one (Pausanias, VIII.23.6 seq.). Indeed a trace of a similar rite may perhaps be detected even at Ephesus, the most famous of her sanctuaries, in the legend of a woman who hanged herself and was thereupon dressed by the compassionate goddess in her own divine garb and called by the name of Hecate (Eustathius on Homer *Odyssey*, XII.85, p. 1714. Bekker-*Anecdota Graeca* (Berlin 1814–1821), I.336 seq.). Similarly at Melite in Phthia [Phthiotis or Achaea Phthiotis], a story was told of a girl named Aspalis who hanged herself, but who appears to have been merely a form of Artemis. For after her death her body could not be found, but an image of her was discovered standing beside the image of Artemis, and the people bestowed on it the title of Hecaerge or Farshooter, one of the regular epithets of the goddess. Every year the virgins sacrified a young goat to the image by hanging it, because Aspalis was said to have hanged herself (Antoninus Liberalis, *Transform.* XIII). The sacrifice may have been a substitute for hanging an image or a human representative of Artemis. Again at Rhodes the fair Helen was worshipped under the title of Helen of the tree, because the Queen of the island had caused her hand-maids, disguised as Furies, to string her up to the bough. (Pausanias, III.19.9).[3]

Farnell associates the hanging goddess with a tree cult and vegetation rite:

[1] *Love Romances of Parthenius*, XXVIII, 1.
[2] Ibid., XXXI, 1.
[3] *The Golden Bough*, II, 5, 291.

> The goddess of still and running water is also naturally a goddess of trees and fish. The strange worship of Artemis Apagschomene, the 'hanging Artemis', at Kaphyae in Arcadia must have originally been consecrated to the goddess of vegetation. Pausanias (VIII.23.6) tells us a curious story concerning it which conceals the meaning of the ritual; once upon a time certain children in play attached a noose to the neck of her idol and said that they were hanging Artemis; whereupon the men of Kaphyae stoned them, but the angry divinity smote their wives with a disease, and the oracle bade them atone for the innocents' death; the Kaphyans [Kaphyaeans] obeyed its injunction, and instituted the cult of the 'hanging Artemis'.
>
> The custom of hanging the mask or image of the divinity of vegetation on a tree to secure fertility, of which other instances will be noted, sufficiently explains these and other stories; and we may illustrate the ritual of Kaphyae by a relief found at Thyrea showing the image of Artemis hanging on a garlanded tree.[1]

Farnell explains these hanging stories as aetiological, and connects them with the fertility cults:

> A fairly frequent rite is the hanging of the puppet of the vegetation-daimon on a tree, for the magical purpose of fertilization; the masks or images of Dionysos were often used thus, and a certain legend about a Xoanon of Artemis in Arcadia has this meaning. Hence arose various 'aetiological' stories about heroines who for certain reasons hanged themselves or were hanged upon trees. The peartree maiden—ὄχνα—[Ochna] hanged herself in the story of Eunostos. Erigone, the daughter of Ikarius of Ikaria, hanged herself on a tree in grief when the villagers murdered her father. Helen of Troy herself was captured by the Rhodian women and hanged in revenge for the deaths of their husbands, and was worshipped under the name Δενδρῖτις, 'Helen of the tree'. All these stories are afterthoughts to explain a simple rite of theistic or daimonistic magic. The name Ochne speaks for itself; so does Ἠριγόνη [Erigone], the 'early-born', who is no mortal maiden, but a vegetation-heroine of the prime, whose name recalls Kore's title of 'Protogeneia'. Once a year in the ritual called Αἴωρα [Aiora] the Attic maidens came to Ikaria and swung on trees for some vague purpose of fertilization or purification, but, as was afterwards explained, in memory of Erigone. Her father is Ikarios, the priest of Dionysos, who is flung into a well and buried under a tree, because this was an efficacious way of treating the decaying puppet or the decaying priest of the god of fertility. We note also that the first-fruits of the vintage were offered both to Ikarios and to Erigone. Helen having become, if she was not born, a goddess, is made to work the same tree-magic. The puppet

[1] *Cults of the Greek States*, II, 428.

that was hung up, being compacted of twigs and leaves, would wither away and decay, and might then stand for the winter-daimon, or Death or Famine, and would be then pelted at or rent to pieces. Such a ceremony would explain part of the story of Pentheus.[1]

Was Farnell correct in supposing that these hanging legends are afterthoughts to explain fertility rites of theistic or daimonistic magic? In primitive communities it was believed that the fertility of the earth was intimately bound up with the sexual relations of its inhabitants, which could affect the crops either beneficially, if regular, or adversely, if irregular. In any primitive form of community life irregular sexual union was viewed with abhorrence, and we can see the reasons which underlay the suicides of women who had been detected in adultery or incest. 'Certainly,' wrote Sir James Frazer, 'a course of conduct which was supposed to endanger or destroy the general supply of food and therefore to strike a blow at the very life of the whole people could not but present itself to the savage imagination as a crime of the blackest dye, fraught with the most fatal consequences to the public weal.'[2] Farnell did not explain how the women who committed suicide came to be worshipped as goddesses; he mentions Helen, Erigone and Ochna as aetiological explanations of fertility puppet hanging. Now, Helen was hanged by the Rhodian women because she had harmed the community; Erigone's incest with Oedipus was responsible for the blighting plague at Thebes which caused sterility of crops, cattle and women;[3] Ochna hanged herself for shame because, as Farnell put it, she wooed the virtuous Eunostos in vain (Eunostos is obviously a god-hero whose destinies are bound up with a successful season). Why should these ladies suddenly be deified when they have obviously endangered the general well-being of their communities by their misguided amours? Farnell states that 'these hanging stories, whose names or legends convey an allusion to the fertility of the trees and crops arose from the old agrarian ritual of hanging images on trees', but might not the theory be advanced that the custom of hanging up these images could follow on the previous death of the wrongdoer and offender against sexual morality? It is, of course, quite clear that there are different strata of the legends and Farnell's explanation of

[1] *Greek Hero Cults and Ideas of Immortality*, II, 31.

[2] *The Golden Bough*, II, 117.

[3] See G. Daux, 'Oedipe et le Fléau, *Oedipe roi*, l. 275', *Rev Ét. Gr.* LIII, 97–122. I owe this reference to Mr Maurice Platnauer, who gave me much help with other points in this paper.

the legend of Charila (Plutarch Q.C. 12p, 293e) seems to illustrate the difficulty. Briefly, the theory is that a begging orphan girl Charila is brutally repulsed by the Delphic king in a time of famine and hangs herself for shame. The famine increases and the oracle orders atonement to be made to the maiden's spirit. How is this done? By hanging her *effigy*. She had hanged herself and obviously since her death could be taken as a sacrifice for the benefit of the community the oracle orders that respect be paid to her spirit. (That her death was accepted as a sacrifice can be seen by the fact that the wrongdoing of the king is not important; he is not required to pay any personal penalty.) Hence her images are hung up and because they cause an alleviation of the plague they come to be worshipped regularly for their positive beneficial powers instead of being regarded, as formerly, as merely negative. So they become the emblems of a vegetation cult which grows in importance as their original specifically apotropaeic function is neglected.

Farnell, however, gives a different explanation of this legend:

> She is hung among the trees as beneficent and full of vitalizing power; she is then insulted and beaten and buried in a barren place among the hills as if she embodied the spirit of decay and famine; this is negative and apotropaic magic and explains why the ceremony is described as partly cathartic.[1]

This explanation reverses the order which he previously gives to the growth of the legend, that there are two stages: that Helen is hanged at Rhodes and *afterwards* becomes worshipped as the goddess Helen Dendritis; that Hecate is adopted by Artemis *after* she has hanged herself; that Aspalis hanged herself and *afterwards* is worshipped as Hecaerge; that Helena of Sparta was made a goddess *after* she had hanged herself. The transition to a fertilizing goddess could perhaps be regarded as coming after the individual sacrifice of the offender for the common good had been adopted as a commemorative rite, e.g. a woman hanged (whether by herself or not is immaterial) lest harm come to the community; the sacrifice is repeated afterwards in effigy and eventually becomes part of a fertility cult. The idea of alternate fertility and decay may not be part of the original hanging rite, but may come from the Dionysiac cult which was mingled with the hanging goddess legends in later periods of history. Plutarch's story does not necessarily justify Farnell in combining the two; it seems merely to

[1] *Greek Hero Cults and Ideas of Immortality*, II, 34.

tell the story of how a girl who hanged herself gradually becomes part of a fertility rite and shows how this rite is perpetuated by means of hanging puppets. The puppets are apotropaic and they are used after the deaths of the bad women.

Farnell probably incorporates the ideas of alternate fertility and decay from his knowledge of the Pentheus legend which has some features corresponding to the legends of hanging women:

> It is now recognized that Pentheus is in his original character no secular hero, a royal enemy of the god, but the god himself, or rather the priest that incarnates the god; hence he is led solemnly through the city in the same female attire that the deity himself occasionally wears, he is hung on a tree and pelted at, and we find the image of Dionysos commonly hung on trees; there follows the dismemberment, and then—we may suspect—either in reality or simulation 'the sacrificial banquet of men's flesh'. For a strong corroboration of this story we should note the important statement of Pausanias that the Pythian oracle bade the Thebans honour the tree on which Pentheus was hung 'as it were a god', and that two of the most sacred idols of Dionysos at Corinth were made out of its wood.[1]

The hanging rite and the sparagmos rite were different sacrifices, but obviously had some features in common which were probably due to the fusion of the old and new religions in Greece. Where this blending has taken place has been indicated by M. P. Nilsson:

> That Ariadne, daughter of Minos, was once something more than the heroine abandoned by Theseus is agreed. According to the ordinary story, Ariadne became the wife of Dionysos; according to a much disputed passage in the *Odyssey*, she was killed by Artemis upon the testimony of Dionysos. We have probably here a reflection of the conflict between the cult of Dionysos and the worship of the old Native goddess. Sometimes it led to a struggle, sometimes to a union between the two. The outstanding feature is the death of Ariadne .. In Crete she is said to have hanged herself in despair.[2]

J. H. Powell, when discussing Duarte Barbosa's account[3] of how an interior tribe of Malabar used to bring a maiden to the temple of an idol suspended by hooks, suggests a treatment of the development of the legend which is parallel to the views advanced in this article on the growth of the hanging women stories in Greek legend:

[1] *Cults of the Greek States*, V, 167.
[2] *A History of Greek Religion*, pp. 29–30.
[3] *A Description of the Coasts of East Africa and Malabar in the Beginning of the Sixteenth Century*, translated by the Hon. H. E. J. Stanley (Hakluyt Society, 1866), pp. 95–96.

As for the choice of this particular rite as a substitution for the sacred prostitution by which marriage was often preceded I can only suggest that, if any importance is to be attached to the words which Duarte Barbosa puts into the girl's mouth, a blood offering, probably of menstrual blood, may well have been the first substitute for the act of prostitution; then any blood sacrifice, later a prosacrificial rite. These would appear to be more or less the natural stages of development by which the actual sacrifice of a woman's virginity to a male deity became the mock sacrifice of the woman herself.[1]

V

What light do these legends of hanging women cast on the lines from the *Agememnon*? It is generally agreed that there was no moral turpitude attaching to suicide in conventional Greek morality.[2] The act was not in itself bad. But it does seem as if in certain cases suicide by hanging did carry a stigma. Why, then, did Clytaemnestra decide to commit suicide by this means? Had she been placed by Aeschylus in a strictly realistic Homeric household it might perhaps be possible to argue that the swords were kept in the men's hall and she would not have had access to them. But this argues greater knowledge than we possess of the division of the sexes and it also argues greater antiquarian knowledge than Aeschylus himself may have possessed about Homeric conditions.

Was her story true or false? If she was lying in order to convince him of her loyalty it would not seem curious that she should tell him she had often tried to commit suicide. But why should she needlessly risk perturbing him in a speech designed to assure him of her faithfulness? For he should surely have wondered why she had attempted to die by a method regarded as δυσπρεπὲς (disgraceful or shameful), and his suspicions of her past conduct should have been answered at once.

[1] J. H. Powell, 'Hook Swinging in India', *Folk Lore*, 1914, p. 155. This article, which describes a hanging custom used to promote fertility, containing a parallel to the Dionysiac adoption of the hanging puppets as part of a fertility rite in the way in which 'Hindu respectability and prestige was cast as a cloak over a rite which was probably aboriginal'.

[2] The following works (to which Dr Robert Brittain has kindly drawn my attention) contain much useful information on aspects of suicide: Antonio Fossati, *Del Suicidis nei suoi Rapporti colla Medicina legale, colla filosofia, colla storia e colla statistica*, Milan 1831, p. 136; Alfred Legoyt, *Le Suicide Ancien et Moderne*, Paris 1881, pp. viii, 468; Paul Baron, *Mechanisme de la Mort dans la pendaison* (*Étude historique et experimentale*), Paris 1893, p. 103; E. Lisle, *Du Suicide; statisque, médecine, histoire et legislation*, Paris 1856; and *Bibliografia del Suicido*, Bellinzone, *c.* Salviori, 1890, pp. 110 ff. I am also indebted to Professor Denys Page for bringing to my attention the very interesting article by Rudolf Hirzel, 'Die Strafe der Steinigung', *Abhandlungen der Akad*, Leipzig, 1909, pp. 225 ff.

Was she telling the truth, then? If she did try to hang herself why did she confess this to Agamemnon? Was she trying to arouse his sympathy for the intolerable position in which she had been left at home? She was committing suicide because of the injurious rumours[1] (ἕκατι κληδόνων παλιγκότων) of his death. But was she not planning his death at that very moment? Can there be a simpler explanation? She is confused, her nervous tension is great at the moment of this return, and she blurts out the truth. She had indeed often been terrified by rumours, but rumours of a different kind, and, thinking the secret of her affair with Aegisthus had, through these rumours, become public property, had attempted to conform to custom by hanging herself. On recovery, finding she was still secure—at least until Agamemnon's return—she continued to live with Aegisthus, grasping hold of the present and beginning to think of the disposal of Agamemnon—either, as Pindar put it, for revenge or because of her love for Aegisthus.

This argument would rest on the fact that there appears to be a clear case of ambiguity in the words ἕκατι κληδόνων παλιγκότων (because of 'injurious rumours'), and indeed Clytaemnestra's use of the words in her speech may well have sent a *frisson* through the audience. Her mixture of confused protestation—and truth—may have greeted an over-confident husband intent on his homecoming, unaware, obviously, of the 'destruction wrought by truant female sexuality', and Aeschylus may have been deepening, through his subtle wordplay in Clytaemnestra's speech, the tragic ironies inherent throughout his study of this problem.

[1] See note in Fraenkel, op cit., where he translates παλιγκότων as 'hostile, injurious, adverse', drawing on Car. Guil. Elbering, *Observ. in aliquot locos Ag. Aesch.* (Copenhagen 1828), p. 9 seq., to indicate there is no sense of *nova mala* in the phrase.

The Incomparable Lady Ranelagh

KATHLEEN M. LYNCH

KATHERINE, Viscountess Ranelagh, the most gifted of the daughters of the first Earl of Cork, was celebrated in her own time as 'the incomparable Lady Ranelagh'. In the sermon[1] which he preached at the funeral of her scientist brother, Robert Boyle, Bishop Burnet devoted as lavish praise to Lady Ranelagh as to the brother who survived her by a single week. Although some allowance must be made for elegiac hyperbole, Burnet seems to have expressed, with the eloquence which the occasion inspired, the consensus of opinion regarding this remarkable woman.

Burnet was impressed by the exceptional friendship of a sister and brother who lived together for more than forty years and in their death, 'Nature being quite spent in both', were not divided. Beyond her own family circle, Lady Ranelagh extended her friendship and generosity to an extraordinary degree and became 'the general Intercessor for all Persons of Merit or in want', regardless of their sect or party. Her influence, Burnet noted, exerted in so broad a compass, was singularly effective. 'When any Party was down, she had Credit and Zeal enough to serve them, and she imployed that so effectually, that in the next Turn she had a new stock of Credit.' Certain 'particular

[1] G. Burnet, *A Sermon Preached at the Funeral of the Honourable Robert Boyle* (London, 1692).

Opinions might shut her up in a divided Communion, yet her Soul was never of a Party'. Burnet paid due homage to Lady Ranelagh's affability, easiness of access, breadth of knowledge, wise counselling and Christian piety. He believed that 'she made the greatest Figure in all the Revolutions of these Kingdoms for above fifty Years, of any Woman of our Age'.

Lady Katherine Boyle was born at College House in the Irish seaport of Youghal on March 22nd, 1615. She was the seventh child and fifth daughter of Richard Boyle, first Earl of Cork, by his second wife, Catherine, daughter of Sir Geoffrey Fenton. The 'great Earl of Cork', as he was called, had begun life as an obscure and penniless adventurer, but before his death rose to the dignity of being the richest and most powerful subject in Ireland of King Charles I.

When Katherine was eight, she was wooed by Lord Beaumont of Cole Orton, Leicestershire, for his son, Sapcote Beaumont; and when she was ten, her father sent her to live at the home of her prospective husband. What appeared to be satisfactory financial arrangements were made for Katherine's marriage, and the Earl of Cork showered Lord Beaumont with anticipatory gifts, including one hundred pounds in gold, a saddle gelding, nine bundles of coloured Irish frieze, and a barrel of pickled scallops. Four years later, the bargain fell through, the match was broken off, and the lonely child was returned to her parents.

Lord Cork was ostensibly more successful in his second attempt to secure a husband for Katherine. At sixteen she was married to Arthur Jones, son and heir of Richard Jones, first Viscount Ranelagh, her marriage portion having been duly paid at Strongbow's tomb in Dublin. She was carried off to gloomy Athlone Castle in Co. Roscommon, and there, three years later, her first child, a daughter, was born.

In 1638, when Katherine spent a winter in London at the Savoy Palace, which Sir Thomas Stafford had loaned to the Earl of Cork, her cousin, Sir John Leeke, wrote of her: 'a more brave wench or a braver spiritt you have not mett wth all. She hath a memory that will hear a sermon and goe home and penn it after dinner verbatim. I know not how she will appeare in England, but she is most accounted of att Dublin.'[1] Leeke was saddened to observe that the young lady's face, 'the sweetest face I ever saw', was 'somewhat decayed'.[2] Was it grief or smallpox, one wonders, which had caused that alteration?

[1] *Memoirs of the Verney Family*, ed. F. P. and M. M. Verney (London and New York, 1904), I, 123.
[2] Ibid., 124.

During this London visit Katherine was a competent hostess for her father. She had her share in the royal favours by which he was flattered and for which he paid a heavy price. When the King gave a feast to celebrate the marriage of Francis Boyle to Lady Elizabeth Killigrew, one of the Queen's Maids of Honour, Katherine was one of Cork's three daughters who sat at the royal table 'amongst all the great Lords and Ladies'.[1] But the pleasures of a frivolous Court, to which some members of her family succumbed, had no attraction for Katherine.

She exerted a sympathetic and steadying influence on her 'unruly' younger sister Mary. When Mary married Charles Rich without the knowledge of her father and went to live with him at Leighs, Katherine was the only friend who went with her, 'whose great goodness', said Mary, 'made her forgive me, and stay with me some time at Lees'.[2] In Mary's subsequent illnesses Katherine was always at hand to nurse and comfort her. To 'that excellent sister of mine' Mary paid the high tribute of 'being from my youth constantly to me the most useful and best friend, for soul and body that ever any person I think had'.[3]

In England Katherine had opportunities to make and renew congenial friendships. That serious-minded young nobleman, Lucius Cary, Viscount Falkland, who kept open house for scholars and men of letters, admired Katherine more than any other member of Cork's family, and her regard for him was equally warm. When she had returned to Ireland and was a virtual prisoner in Athlone Castle, during the first years of the Irish rebellion, Falkland expressed in his letters to his sister-in-law, Lady Dungarvan, the utmost concern for Katherine's safety.

The Irish Rebellion served at least one good purpose, for it permanently freed Lady Katherine Jones from her titled but worthless husband, who, according to Leeke, was 'the foulest Churle in the world', with 'only one vertu that he seldom cometh sober to bedd'.[4] From this highly obnoxious mate, to whom otherwise she might have been chained for life, Katherine escaped with her daughters and infant son during the siege of Athlone Castle. She accepted a promise of safe conduct, faithfully carried out, from one of the rebel leaders. Many

[1] Lismore MSS. 27, f. 278.

[2] *Autobiography of Mary, Countess of Warwick*, ed. T. Crofton Croker (London, 1848), Percy Society Publications No. 76, p. 14.

[3] Ibid., 22.

[4] *Memoirs of the Verney Family*, I, 124–5.

years later, she took particular pains to befriend 'a very honest minister',[1] who had fled to Athlone Castle and had cheered her during that grim siege.

In 1643 Katherine became Lady Ranelagh, when her husband (to whom she did not return) succeeded to his father's title. She was in London to welcome with open arms her youngest brother Robert—'the dear 'squire', she affectionately called him—when he returned to England without funds after six years of travel. For more than forty years, with occasional absences from each other, Lady Ranelagh and Robert Boyle lived together in her house in Pall Mall. She entertained his scientific friends and took an active interest in his experiments and his publications.

Robert Boyle was singularly dependent upon his sister as his most intimate friend, and in her constant solicitude for him, she took the place of mother and wife. Although he found his laboratory 'a kind of Elysium', in which he could forget 'almost all things', even there he could not forget his 'unchangeable resolution'[2] to continue his sister's devoted brother until death. It was her 'importunity' which persuaded him to publish his *Occasional Reflections upon Several Subjects*, which had long remained in manuscript; and to her, as 'Sophronia', he dedicated this volume. In his dedicatory preface,[3] Robert praised Lady Ranelagh's rare qualities. She might, he asserted, 'if her Modesty did less confine her Pen to excellent Letters, both make the Wits of our Sex envy a Writer of hers; and keep our Age from envying Antiquity, for those celebrated Ladies, who, by their triumphant Eloquence, ennobled the People of Rome, and taught their Children to sway those rulers of the World'. Of the depth of Robert Boyle's personal attachment to his sister, however formally expressed, there can be no doubt. 'The Blessing of your Affection', he declared, 'is a Felicity that I know you enough to value above all the Praises I can miss of.' When Lady Ranelagh died at the age of seventy-six, her brother 'began evidently to droop apace'.[4] Unable to survive the shock of so great a loss, he lived only seven days longer. He was buried near Lady Ranelagh's grave in the chancel of St. Martin's-in-the-Fields.

Lady Ranelagh was proud of her brother's ability to help 'the considering part of mankind to a clearer prospect into this great frame

[1] Spencer MSS. [2] R. Boyle, *Works* (London, 1772), VI, 50.
[3] R. Boyle, *Occasional Reflections upon Several Subjects* (London, 1665).
[4] Evelyn, *Diary and Correspondence*, ed. William Bray (London, 1870), III, 352.

of the visible world'.[1] Once in his absence, as she informed him, she read and reread all of his books; and she confessed that her fingers would soon be 'itching' to look into a sealed roll of his papers on 'religious matters'. If he denied her permission to open the roll, she added, 'I know not what I may be tempted to'. She longed to have a share in his conjectures, to the extent of 'my capacity of understanding'.[2]

But politics was Lady Ranelagh's absorbing passion. Had she been a man, she would probably have been a statesman, like her older brothers, Lord Burlington and Lord Orrery. Capable of viewing current affairs with detachment, shrewd but tolerant, she watched anxiously, but at a safe distance, the stormy career of Lord Orrery, who was so deeply involved in political intrigues that he once had to choose between the Tower and fighting for Cromwell. She was hostess to great men of opposite convictions and was an influential behind-the-scenes figure in the political life of her times. On one occasion she offered advice (not taken) to that fatally vacillating monarch, Charles I, imploring that he make peace with Parliament before it was too late. Although a royalist at heart, Lady Ranelagh was admired by Oliver and Richard Cromwell; and she was respected by Charles II. It is probable that it was partly through her intervention that John Milton's life was spared at the Restoration.

Perhaps literature was not one of Lady Ranelagh's major interests, although she was the best letter writer among the Earl of Cork's children. She spoke severely of Edmund Waller's poetry, which she found but a 'sound of words', and wished for him 'gifts more excellent than this wit'.[3] Whether or not she cared for the poetry of Milton, she was the kindest friend and best patroness that Milton ever had. Usually rather sparing in his praise of women, Milton remarked of her: 'to me she has stood in the place of all kith and kin'.[4] Lady Ranelagh was Milton's neighbour and one of his most frequent visitors from about 1646 until her departure for Ireland, ten years later, caused him 'no ordinary regret'. It may have been on Milton's advice that she took lessons in Hebrew from a Scottish teacher in London, who dedicated to her his *Gate to the Holy Tongue*, praising her 'proficiency in so short a time' and 'amidst so many abstractions as she was surrounded with'.[5]

[1] Boyle, *Works*, VI, 525. [2] Ibid., 528. [3] Ibid., 522.
[4] Milton, *Epistolarum Familiarium Liber Unus* (London, 1674), p. 47.
[5] Masson, *The Life of John Milton* (London, 1877), V, 232.

Milton served as tutor to Lady Ranelagh's young son Richard and continued to take a cordial but necessarily critical interest in his former charge after Richard had entered Oxford. Four Latin letters which Milton wrote to the boy have been preserved.[1] One of these letters was carried by Lady Ranelagh to her son, when she visited him in Oxford on her way to Ireland. Milton urged the young man to follow the example of 'that most exemplary woman, your mother' and to give 'very different proofs' than he had thus far done of an interest in his studies. When young Jones left Oxford to make the Grand Tour of Europe, Milton admonished him to 'climb the slope of virtue'. Robert Boyle subsequently tried, with moderate success, to interest his young nephew in chemical experiments. Jones is the 'Pyrophilus' to whom Robert Boyle addressed *Certain Physiological Essays.*

As third Viscount Ranelagh, Lady Ranelagh's son became in due course Chancellor of the Exchequer in Ireland, in which capacity he yielded, as did many of his unscrupulous contemporaries, to the almost irresistible temptation to exploit the native Irish. That this unsatisfactory son, whom Swift described as 'the vainest old fool I ever saw', cherished the memory of his mother is indicated in a clause in his will in which he mentions 'my dear mother's picture hanging up in my closet in Chelsea'.

The portrait of Lady Ranelagh with her sister-in-law, the Countess of Burlington, at Bolton Abbey is misleading. Both ladies are placidly fingering a garland; and the portrait gives no hint of the strenuous living which was their daily routine. But Lady Ranelagh's face shows character and dignity.

There is a small amount of agreeably feminine gossip in Lady Ranelagh's letters,[2] as when she observes that 'Lady Ann Knolles about midnight Wed. night got over Newport House garden wall with her maid and ran away with Mr Fry of the life guard'. Lady Chesterfield, she writes, has died, 'leaving a greater stock of plate and fine goods ... than has been owned by any private person. She carried none of it with her, and those who possess it are more pleased with her room than with her company'. The Duchess of Newcastle, she concludes, 'scapes Bedlam onely by being too rich to be sent theather. but she is madd enough to convay y^{t} title to ye place of her Residence'.

In the main, Lady Ranelagh was rather grave. Her distaste for social frivolity is reflected in her complaint that 'the entertainment of lords,

[1] See *Epistolarum Familiarium Liber Unus*, pp. 46–7, 51–2, 57–8, 64.
[2] Spencer MSS.

ladies, and reasonable creatures, are yet several things'.[1] When the little Duke of Cambridge, only surviving son of the Duke of York, lay dying, she was almost constantly at his bedside, 'my lookes & dress being fittest for such Seasons'.[2] Like her brother, Lady Ranelagh was a too fluent, though sensible, moralist. The revolutions in government which she witnessed convinced her that 'people seldome remember y^{t} power is but for a season w^{hn} its in their own hands though they can dicerne soe much w^{hn} its in ye hand of other y^{t} they would gladly see it out off'.[3]

After the Restoration, Lady Ranelagh withdrew herself as much as she civilly could from Court society. In a letter written in August 1667 she comments disapprovingly: 'Porter is runn away & soe is Harry Killigrew. if they had binn attended wth their whole tribe of Hectors, ye nation would have been blessed by their absence, to whose presence & practises it owes noe smale share of ye Myseries it has suffered or ye ruin y^{t} seems to be aproaching'.[4] Only after receiving from the Queen repeated invitations to wait on her, Lady Ranelagh reluctantly did so 'to fence my selfe from great rudeness towards her to whom I owe soe much defference'.[5]

Lord Burlington and Lord Orrery helped Lady Ranelagh to secure a grudging separate maintenance from her husband. In most respects, the members of her family leaned heavily on her and rarely made any important decisions without consulting her. Their health was one of her major concerns; and she prescribed for their physical ailments with hopeful confidence in the efficacy of spirit of wormwood, plaster of carvene, Sir Walter Raleigh's cordial, Jesuit's powder and other popular remedies of her day. When the news of Lord Orrery's death in Ireland reached England prematurely the day before he died, his grieving sister despatched cordials to him that same night, 'as not beleeving him dead'.[6]

For the remainder of Lady Orrery's life, Lady Ranelagh exerted herself in behalf of her brother's widow and grandchildren. She undertook the education of Jamey O'Brien and found a tutor to travel with Lionel Boyle and another to train him for military service. She reminded her sister-in-law, whose equable temper was tested by many trials, that 'most people will be taught by nothing but their owne experience and some not by y^{t}'. She gave Lady Orrery the comforting assurance: 'As long as I live I must affectionately be yours.'[7]

[1] Boyle, *Works*, VI, 523. [2] Spencer MSS. [3] Lismore MSS. 31, f. 11.
[4] Spencer MSS. [5] Leconfield MSS. [6] Ormonde MSS. 92, f. 341. [7] Leconfield MSS.

Sixteen of Lady Ranelagh's letters have been printed: fourteen in the *Works* of Robert Boyle, one in the *State Papers* of Thurloe, and one in the *State Papers* of Clarendon. In a variety of places, sixty-seven unpublished letters have been preserved,[1] making a total of eighty-three letters. This may not seem a very impressive number, but it must be remembered that the letters of seventeenth-century ladies, even to devoted husbands, are scarce. No doubt it was Lady Ranelagh's flair for politics, the immediacy of her reflections on important events, that caused so many of her letters to be saved. It is possible, of course, that other letters by her lie neglected in the cupboards of English or Irish country houses.

The earliest in date of Lady Ranelagh's surviving letters[2] is the one in which she relates her escape in 1642 from 'a most miserable captivity' after enduring a siege of twenty-two months in Athlone Castle. This letter found a casual resting place on a dusty shelf in the Public Record Office in Dublin, in a heap of unsorted, loosely strewn papers from the cupboards of Lismore Castle. It is one of a small number of family letters, scattered on that shelf, which must have reached the ageing Earl of Cork too late to be included in the precious red box of writings which he hurriedly shipped to England at the outbreak of the Irish Rebellion. The old earl undoubtedly valued this last letter from 'my Kate', the most beloved of his daughters. The sufferings which she had witnessed had made Katherine decide to leave 'this bleeding & well neare ruined Commonwealth'. A report that her father was dangerously ill had troubled her greatly. The recent death of her brother, Lord Kinalmeaky, in the Battle of Liscarrol, she must not lament, 'encountered in soe just a cause, & so noble a way'.

In the collection of Clarendon MSS. in the Bodleian Library there is a letter from Katherine to Sir Edward Hyde, later Earl of Clarendon, written after the death of Lord Falkland in the Battle of Newbury.[3] Katherine took the occasion of Falkland's death to plead very sensibly with Hyde for renewed efforts to secure the peace between King and Parliament of which that 'gallant man', dying, had despaired. It must be a parliament, she affirmed, where its houses are, 'whereof you call yourselves members'.

Lady Ranelagh was always eloquent in the service of the distressed.

[1] These collections were consulted at Chatsworth, Althorp, and Petworth by kind permission of the Duke of Devonshire, Earl Spencer and Mr John Wyndham.

[2] Lismore MSS. at the Public Record Office, Dublin.

[3] Clarendon MSS. 23, f. 114. Printed in *State Papers Collected by Edward, Earl of Clarendon* (Oxford, 1767–73), II, 166–8.

After Cromwell's conquest of Ireland, Sir Percy Smith, former governor of Youghal, was on trial for his life. Lady Ranelagh appealed to her brother Broghill, afterwards Earl of Orrery, to obtain a pardon for his former friend.[1] She acknowledged that this man was guilty, that he deserved nothing from Broghill and was not likely to be grateful to him; but his wife and children would suffer from his death, nor was he prepared for it. It was her judgment that as many lives should be saved 'as may bee both because they cannot be restor'd when once taken away and I see very few that deserve death fitt for it'. Since we all live by mercy 'every moment', we should show mercy to one another.

Several of Lady Ranelagh's letters are among the Lismore MSS. at Chatsworth. On February 18th, 1659, she wrote a graphic account to Lord Cork, afterwards Lord Burlington, of a more than usually dangerous voyage from Ireland to Bristol which she made with two of her daughters and Lord Broghill. After passing Minehead, the ship violently struck a shoal and 'scattered' the small party in the cabin. They commended themselves to God, expecting that at any moment the waves would come in and sweep them away. But Broghill's never-failing courage and presence of mind saved their lives. He hastened on deck, just managing to avoid having his brains beaten out by the beam of the detached rudder, calmed the terrified crew, and forced them to take down the sails and mend the rudder. The ship struck no more, and with 'a good stiff gale' the travellers safely completed their journey.[2]

That spring Lady Ranelagh reported to Lord Cork her concern over Broghill's depressed state of mind. Richard Cromwell, whose brief Protectorate was already threatened, was 'very obligeing' to Broghill, visiting him at his lodgings, telling him his thoughts 'wth great freedome', sending for him when in need of advice, and offering to make him a member of his council; but Broghill 'seemes fastened in his resolutions of liveing privatly'.[3] It may be surmised that Lady Ranelagh was also referring to Richard Cromwell in her mention of 'ggg', by whom Broghill was 'much courted' and who manifested 'a passionate affection' for him. This attachment disturbed her, for she feared that Broghill was building upon 'a sinking interest'.[4]

A few months later, Richard Cromwell's interest was indeed sunk, he had been forced to abdicate, and 'an evil eye'[5] was against Broghill. Ten years before, Lady Ranelagh had been partly responsible, it has been assumed, for saving her brother from the Tower, for the service

[1] Add. MSS. 46,932, f. 12. [2] Lismore MSS. 30, f. 95. [3] Ibid., f. 99.
[4] Ibid., 31, f. 2 and f. 4. [5] Boyle, *Works*, VI, 122.

of Oliver Cromwell. Just in time for him to escape arrest and imprisonment, she now sped Broghill on his way to Ireland, where he was to open a back door for Charles Stuart. She summed up Lord Broghill's turbulent career with the comment: 'As he has had some Cares and troubles soe he has had very great mercyes & deliverances, as he often striking upon ye sands & yet geting off safe being proofe enough of y^{t}.'[1]

Thirty-one of Lady Ranelagh's letters are in the possession of Earl Spencer at Althorp. The most interesting is a detailed account, written four days after the event—a 'playne & sad relation' Lady Ranelagh calls it—of an episode in the First Dutch War of the Restoration, when the Dutch fleet sailed unopposed up the Medway to Chatham, burning six vessels and taking possession of the *Royal Charles*. All London was stunned and humiliated by the incredible carelessness which had made the Dutch triumph possible. 'We are in miserable confusion', wrote Lady Ranelagh. The enemy's ships now ride 'in our very Ports upon those seas y^{t} we soe long injoyed ye Lordship of y^{t} we were not able to endure any other should pretend to share wth us therein'.[2]

Lady Ranelagh's letters are rewarding in many ways, most of all in her references to the leading men of her time. She apprehended the doom of Charles I, when she pled in vain for the King to come to terms with his Parliament and 'stop their mouths'. She appraised the overthrow of the Commonwealth with the collapse 'of y^{t} famelly interest wch is now vanishing from $among^{st}$ us' and expressed astonishment that by a sudden and bloodless revolution a free and full Parliament had been dissolved and a chief magistrate laid aside 'whose father has such an interest in y^{e} very Army by whose motion this was donn'.[3]

This clear-sighted royalist lady seems also to have foreseen the decline of England's prestige under Charles II. On being informed of Oliver Cromwell's death, she reflected sombrely:

> I must owne not to have received the news of his highness's death unmovedly ... He ... who a few days before shooke all Europe by his fame and forces was not able to keep an ague from shaking him ... If the common charety allowed to dead men be exercised towards him, in burying his faults in his grave with himselfe, and keepeing alive the memory of his vertues and great aymes and actions, he will be allowed to have his

[1] Lismore MSS. 31, f. 15. [2] Spencer MSS. [3] Lismore MSS. 31, f. 15.

place amongst the worthyest of men ... I doubt his loss will be a growing affliction upon these nations, and that we shall learne to value him more by missing him, than we did when we injoyed him ... I confes his performances reached not the makeing good of his professions; but I doubt his performances may goe beyond the professions of those, who may come after him.[1]

It must be regretted that Lady Ranelagh herself is a half-obscured figure. Most of her life record remains in shadow; and only bright fragments of it can be recovered and held to the light to be admired. It is her imaginative perception of the implications of great events which brings her closest to us. Briefly, in vivid phrases, she illuminates one of the most dramatic epochs of English history.

[1] *A Collection of the State Papers of John Thurloe* ... (London, 1742), VII, 395 6.

Prologues, Epilogues and Audience in the Restoration Theatre

JAMES SUTHERLAND

I

WHATEVER value we may place on the drama of the Restoration period, there can be no question that this was the golden age of the prologue and epilogue. Both forms took on a new importance, and developed along lines which sometimes carried them very far from the prologues and epilogues of classical times, or from those written by the English dramatists of 'the last age'. Traditionally the prologue briefly expounded the theme of the coming play, and made a bid for the goodwill of the audience; the epilogue, more briefly, begged for their kind applause. With such limited aims in view neither prologue nor epilogue was much more than a polite gesture, comparable to the action of a self-effacing chairman introducing a lecturer, or moving a vote of thanks in some well-worn phrases. Yet even in the Elizabethan-Jacobean period, in the hands on Ben Jonson, the prologue had occasionally developed into something much more arresting, and even pugnacious. In the prologue to *Every Man Out of his Humour* Jonson had launched a downright attack on his audience, and elsewhere he is often critical of the low standard of intelligence in the public theatres. In this he even had some imitators, but not many; and the main function of the pre-Restoration prologue was still to introduce the play with proper deference to the audience, and of the epilogue to solicit its approval. So long as nothing more than this was attempted they necessarily remained conventional and relatively uninteresting.

But in the theatre of Charles II, because conditions had changed, both prologue and epilogue became prominent parts of the entertainment. What chiefly had changed was the composition of the audience. The patrons of the Restoration theatre formed a comparatively homogeneous class of playgoers, who did not just visit the theatre occasionally, but who could be counted upon to see every new play, and who attended one or other of the two theatres on most days of the week. When the actor who was to speak the prologue walked on to the stage, he looked out on, and could actually see, the ladies and gentlemen in the boxes, socially and economically much the most important part of the audience. Above the boxes was a gallery, seating for the most part such citizens as chose to attend the theatre; and below the boxes was the pit, traditionally the noisiest and worst-behaved section of the house, and therefore the target for many of the satirical shafts that became common form at this period. In the pit were to be found 'gentlemen and others', often in a state of intoxication, sparks, bullies and fops, the ladies of the town, and that characteristic group in the Restoration theatre, the critics. The critics had their own traditional corner in the pit, and did not hesitate to express their opinion of a new play with audible brutality.

From the point of view of the author and the players, the centre of gravity in a Restoration audience was undoubtedly the ladies and gentlemen in the boxes, whose wit and good sense and informed judgment were invariably commended, and whose good manners and fine taste were contrasted with the rude behaviour of those in the bear-garden below them. The citizens above were objects not so much for satirical comment as for easy ridicule. The audience, then, was not homogeneous in the sense that it was all of a kind; but in each of its different layers it was homogeneous, and the expected compliments and thrusts and jibes could be counted upon to recur with each new prologue to each new play. The significant point is that as Betterton or Hart or Lacy or Nokes spoke his lines, he would address himself in turn to different parts of the house, until, in one fashion or another—respectfully, or satirically, or jocularly—every section of the audience had received its greeting. The speaker of a prologue, in fact, was acting as a sort of host to the theatre's guests. The theatre was not merely a place of entertainment; it was also, and perhaps most of all, a place of rendezvous. Most of the audience seated in the boxes were known to each other already, for they met frequently at Court, at balls and assemblies; and the gentlemen in the pit were so regular in their attendance at the theatre that most of them had probably a nodding acquaintance at least. The prologue and the epilogue were therefore a kind of acknowledgment of a social occasion: before the play began, and immediately it had ended, London society became part of the show.

In this new and intimate relationship between author and player on the one side and the public on the other, the critics formed an isolated group who received special treatment. Judging from the frequency with which they are referred to in prologue and epilogue, they must have had some power to damn or save a new play, but their influence can be exaggerated. Indeed, if we are to judge from the way in which they were manhandled by Dryden and other dramatists, they probably antagonized a large part of the audience. For one thing their qualifications for their self-appointed task were often questionable or non-existent. In Durfey's *The Fool turn'd Critick* (1676) Old Winelove, who wishes his booby son to learn fashionable London behaviour, wants the boy to grow familiar with the theatre:

> And when the Play's begun, I'de have him sit
> In the Wit's Corner, play the Critick, hiss
> At anything he do's not understand:
> Be the Scene ne're so witty—That's no matter,
> 'Tis Modish and Gentile.[1]

Real or pretended fear of the critics begins to appear surprisingly early in Restoration prologues. It forms, for example, the sole topic of the well-turned prologue that Cowley wrote for *Cutter of Coleman-Street* (1661). When the pirates of Tunis or Argier (Cowley writes) are coasting about the Mediterranean, the merchant ships are afraid to put out to sea, and 'trade decays and scarcity ensues'. Just so, the critics have of late been so terrorizing the playwrights that they refuse to venture any new plays on the stage.

> But yet, Gentlemen Critiques of *Argier*,
> For your own int'rest I'de advise ye here
> To let this little Forlorn Hope goe by
> Safe and untoucht; That must not be (you'l cry)—
> If ye be wise, it must; Ile tell yee why.

[1] Op. cit., Act I, Sc. ii.

There are Seven, Eight, Nine, ... stay ... there are behind
Ten Playes at least, which wait but for a Wind ...
All these, if we miscarry here to-day,
Will rather till they Rot in th'Harbour stay,
Nay, they will back again, though they were come,
Ev'n to their last safe Rode, the Tyring room.
Therefore again I say, if you be wise,
Let this for once pass free; let it suffise
That we your Soveraign power here to avow,
Thus humbly ere we pass, strike sail to You.

On two separate counts, both important in this kind of writing, this is an admirable prologue: it is built upon a sustained and beautifully appropriate image, which carries satirical overtones without being overtly abusive, and it preserves throughout a tone of polite address to the critics without ever truckling to them. ('I hope you will give my little comedy a polite hearing,' Cowley is saying, 'for if you go on blasting each new play that appears upon the stage, it is you yourselves who will ultimately be the ones to suffer most.') The final couplet in which Cowley refers to the 'soveraign power' of the critics is not actually a sneer, but in combination with the words 'strike sail to You' (at which point, no doubt, the speaker sweeps his hat from his head) it suggests rather a mock humility than any sort of anxiety to placate.

In the years that follow, the attitude to the critics varies a good deal from one author to the other, and even with the same author from one play to another. Sir Robert Howard was one of those who favoured the tactful approach; he may have been a Sir Positive At-All in real life, but in addressing an audience he was noticeably complaisant. In the prologue to *The Vestal Virgin* (1664?) he even takes the audience into his confidence about the whole problem:

Wou'd you wou'd tell him which of all the ways
You like in Prologues us'd to help out Plays.

He considers some of the existing modes—the prologue written by the author who apparently believes

you'l do as you are bid,
And that you paid your money to be chid;

or the prologue in which the author abuses his fellow dramatists. His own preference is for a different kind of approach:

Some Prologues are more modestly address'd,
Just like Petitions, those he thinks are best.

But this was far from being the view of his brother-in-law, Dryden. Almost from the first Dryden carried the war into the critics' camp, and so far from trying to placate them, he seems to have felt that they were fair game for the amusement of the rest of the audience. In the prologue to *The Rival Ladies* (1664) and in the epilogue to *The Indian Emperour* (1665) he had shown how little he cared for them; in the Second Prologue to *Secret-Love*; or, *The Maiden-Queen* (1667) he went out of his way to ridicule them and to declare their incompetence. He was ready, he said, to bow to 'every great and noble wit' (seated, no doubt, in the boxes)—

> But to the little Hectors of the Pit
> Our Poet's sturdy, and will not submit.
> He'll be before-hand with 'em, and not stay
> To see each peevish Critick stab his Play:
> Each Puny Censor, who his skill to boast,
> Is cheaply witty on the Poets cost.
> No Criticks verdict should, of right, stand good,
> They are excepted all as men of blood:
> And the same Law should shield him from their fury
> Which has exclud'd Butchers from a Jury.

Dryden knew that *Secret-Love* was a good play; it was to turn out, in fact, to be one of his most successful. It may be thought, therefore, that when he wrote this prologue he was filled with the sort of confidence that once prompted Ben Jonson to tell his audience:

> By God, 'tis good, and if you lik't you may.

If there is something of that in Dryden's attitude, his attack on 'the little Hectors of the Pit' also enables us to get them into their proper perspective. In many prologues and epilogues he indicates what sort of people composed this noisy and opiniative claque:

> They who write Ill, and they who ne'r durst write,
> Turn Critiques, out of meer Revenge and Spight ... [1]

Some of them were, perhaps, the

> little Infants of the Time
> Who Write new Songs, and trust in Tune and Rhyme,[2]

or they were writers of burlesques or lampoons. In refusing, therefore, to submit to the loud-mouthed gentry in Wit's Corner, Dryden had

[1] Prologue to the second part of *The Conquest of Granada*.
[2] Epilogue to *The Indian Emperour*.

probably the greater part of the house with him; for although the critics could make themselves a nuisance, and even spoil the first night of a play, Dryden could almost certainly count on that dislike of 'egg-heads' which is common to every age, and he could also rely on the shattering effect of his wit when a Hart or a Nell Gwyn scored off them in a prologue. Dryden's thrusts at the critics may even be looked upon as an exercise in that most popular of all forms of Restoration wit—repartee. It is true that this was repartee in monologue, but what the speaker of the prologue was, so to speak, replying to could easily be supplied by the imagination. That even the critics themselves came to expect this sort of treatment, and would have felt that something was missing if they had not been given it, is indicated by some further lines in the prologue to *Secret-Love*. Still taunting the critics, Dryden tells them that they would all be wits if they could:

> But writing's tedious, and that way may fail;
> The most compendious method is to rail:
> Which you so like, you think your selves ill us'd
> When in smart Prologues you are not abus'd.

And then, with the sort of simile that we are likely to meet with only on the Restoration stage:

> A civil Prologue is approv'd by no man;
> You hate it as you do a Civil woman:
> Your Fancy's pall'd, and liberally you pay
> To have it quicken'd, er'e you see a Play.
> Just as old Sinners worn from their delight,
> Give money to be whip'd to appetite.

II

How early in the history of the Restoration theatre the audience began to expect wit and satirical comment in prologues and epilogues, and how soon the dramatists came to realize and exploit the new freedom that this gave them, it is hardly possible to say precisely. For one thing, when the two new companies formed by Davenant and Killigrew began to act, they were forced for some time to fall back on old plays by Beaumont and Fletcher, Jonson, Shakespeare and other dramatists who had written before the closing of the theatres. It seems reasonable to suppose that those may have been furnished with new prologues and epilogues written for the occasion, but almost nothing of this sort has survived; and it is perhaps fair to assume that if the old plays were introduced by prologues as witty and provocative as those written a few years later they would have been preserved in print. We must turn, therefore, to those Restoration dramatists who supplied the two theatres with the earliest new plays of the new reign. Here we meet with a fresh difficulty: not all of those plays have prologues and epilogues, or if, as seems probable, one was actually spoken, it has not survived. We have neither prologue nor epilogue for Orrery's *Henry the Fifth* (1664) or his *Mustapha* (1665), for John Wilson's *The Cheats* (1663), or for any of Thomas Killigrew's plays. What is more surprising is that although we have a prologue and epilogue for Etherege's *Love in a Tub* (1664), we have none for *She Wou'd if she Cou'd* (1668), and it is hardly credible that by 1668 a new comedy would have been tolerated without them. However those facts are to be explained, there are enough prologues and epilogues in the first years of the new reign to give us a good idea of how they were developing.

An old-fashioned dramatist like Sir Robert Stapleton writes for *The Slighted Maid* (1663) an old-fashioned prologue; the tone is that of old Capulet welcoming his guests, decent and courteous. Similarly, the epilogue, spoken by the Slighted Maid herself, makes the traditional appeal for applause, although Stapleton manages to give it a poetical turn:

> Behold, your Candidate before you stands:
> Your *Semele* sees Thunder in your hands,
> Let's hear it: Claps that would make some afraid,
> Will make the *Slighted* the *Exalted Maid.*

So far was Stapleton from subscribing to the bawdiness that was rapidly spreading through the Restoration theatre that one hesitates to credit him with the *double entendre* on 'Claps', although it is hard to believe that he could have been unconscious of it. Again, the prologue to Tuke's *The Adventures of Five Hours* (1663) is, like the play itself, entirely decent, and the author adopts a tone of modest self-denigration. But in an epilogue written at some later date, and first published in the 'third impression' of 1671, he shows his awareness of the growing taste for obscenity by ironically assuring the audience that they can now turn all that he has written to raillery:

> A Fopp! in this brave Licentious Age,
> To bring his musty Morals on the Stage!
> .... Why, Vertue now is Impudence;

And such another modest Play would blast
Our new Stage, and put your Palates out of Tast.

In *The Surprisal* (1662) and again in *The Committee* (1662) Sir Robert Howard is scrupulously polite to his audience, modestly depreciating his dramatic wares; and in the epilogue to *The Committee* he shows a pleasant turn of wit when he tells the audience that it is itself a committee which the author has to compound with:

For, till your equal censures shall be known,
The Poet's under Sequestration:
He has not Title to his small Estate
Of Wit, unless you please to set the Rate.

Although there is considerable variety of treatment in those early prologues and epilogues, nearly all of them tend to deal with the play or the author or both. But this cramping relevance was not to last for long. In the epilogue to John Lacy's *The Old Troop* (1663?) the change is already noted:

Prologues and epilogues should something say,
In order to the excusing of a play;
But things to the purpose being laid aside,
We shoot at random at least six bows wide—
Speaking of this or that, of sea or land,
Of any matter but the thing in hand.

By the end of the first decade, and even earlier, the emancipation was complete: a prologue could be about anything that might interest the audience, but it had to be witty; and though it did not have to be bawdy, it frequently was. If it had no connection whatsoever with the play, nobody cared—nobody even noticed. As early as 1664 Dryden had remarked on the new value set on prologues. In former days

Good Prologues were as scarce, as now good Plays.

Now we have excellent prologues, but the poets have exhausted 'their poetique rage' on those before they reach the play:

Expect no more when once the Prologue's done;
The Wit is ended e'r the Play's begun.[1]

Four years later the Earl of Orrery, who had perhaps less wit to spare than Dryden, was complaining that the prologue had become 'a needless tax' on wit, which 'Poets now are grown too poor to pay':

[1] Prologue to *The Rival Ladies.*

Would you decree (what I for them implore)
Poets with Prologues ne're should meddle more.
'Tis the best thing you for your selves could do,
For Prologues first tire Poets and then you.[1]

III

With the expectations of the audience keeping time with their growing sophistication, it became more and more necessary to avoid repetition, and the search for novelty had begun. The search for novelty took many forms. The ironical vein was nicely worked by John Lacy in his prologue to *The Old Troop*, where the wits were humorously warned that this was not a play for them, but for the upper gallery. Why, in fact, were they in the theatre at all?

What made you wits so spitefully to come? ...
Order there was, and that most strictly gi'n,
To keep out all that look'd like gentlemen.

In his first play, *The Wild Gallant*, Dryden had the notion of introducing two astrologers to forecast the fortune of his comedy. Even allowing for his interest in astrology, this was a heavy-handed attempt at novelty and one that he would not have used a few years later when he had learnt how to arouse and hold the attention of an audience. How easily that could be done may be seen from his well-known epilogue to *Tyrannick Love*, 'spoken by Mrs Ellen [Gwyn], when she was to be carried off dead by the bearers':

Hold, are you mad? you dam'd confounded Dog,
I am to rise, and speak the Epilogue ...

Here we have Dryden, the experienced man of the theatre, who knows his actress and his audience, and who knows that the two know each other, and that this outrageous opening will 'pit, box and gallery it'.

Prologues in dialogue between two speakers, and even between three or four, were fairly common, and were often, because of their dramatic form, very effective. The Hon. Edward Howard, whom it is usually difficult to praise, has a surprisingly lively one to *The Women's*

[1] Prologue to *Tryphon*, and cf. Orrery's epilogue to *Mr Anthony:*
Our next new Play, if this mode hold in vogue,
Shall be half Prologue, and half Epilogue.

Conquest (1671). It opens with a conversation between two of the leading actors of the day, Angel and Underhill, the first delighting in the fact that they are going 'to act a Farce that hath sixteen Mimicks in it, several Jack-Puddings, and Punchinellos, never presented before, with two and thirty Dances and Jiggs *a-la-mode* besides', and the other deploring the wretched taste of the public, who no longer want wit, good plays, or genuine comedy. At this point Nokes enters to announce that he is going to speak a prologue entirely by looks and grimaces, and proceeds to do so. In due course he is succeeded by a dancer who proceeds to dance a prologue and who is still capering about when, in a burst of thunder and flash of lightning, the indignant ghost of Ben Jonson appears. Howard would have done even better if he had known when to leave off; but he now brings on a Second Prologue in which Jonson praises true comedy and attacks farce; and this is followed by a rather flat Third Prologue of a more conventional kind. No doubt it was a good joke in 1671 just to have three prologues; nobody had thought of that before. Again, in Durfey's *The Virtuous Wife* (1680) Mrs Barrer, who played the title rôle, comes on the stage and complains that she has been given an impossible part, and decides to throw it up. At this point 'Lee peeps out of a little window over the stage', and argues with her:

> Hold, hold,—'death are you mad, shall we lye down,
> Lose all our shares, nay, and affront the Town?

This must all be a plot, he says, between Nokes and her: whereupon 'Nokes peeps out of a little window the other side of the stage' and argues with Lee. Finally, after more bickering, Mrs Barrer agrees to carry on. Although prologues and epilogues of this dramatic sort were not uncommon, they were uncharacteristic to the extent that they were not directly addressed to the audience. The audience was always there, waiting to be amused, shocked, flattered, propitiated—even insulted, so long as it was noticed.

With the constant struggle to interest and amuse a jaded audience, it was inevitable that the dramatists should have recourse to the bawdy joke, the *double entendre*, the obscene allusion. Obscenity stimulates the appetite it feeds on; and, to use a metaphor that Restoration writers were fond of using themselves, the palate that had grown accustomed to highly seasoned dishes found decency insipid. In the prologue to Ravenscroft's *Dame Dobson: or, The Cunning Woman* (1683) Mrs Currer complains that she has not 'one smutty jest' in all her part:

A Bawdy Play was never counted Dull,
Nor modest Comedy e'er pleas'd you much,
'Tis relish'd like good Manners 'mongst the *Dutch.*

Dryden, who once confessed that his chief endeavour was 'to delight the age I live in', was one of the chief offenders. The prologue to *An Evening's Love*, for example, is one long, sustained, sexual metaphor:

When first our Poet set himself to write,
Like a young Bridegroom on his Wedding-night
He layd about him, and did so bestir him,
His Muse could never lye in quiet for him;
But now his Honey-moon is gone and past,
Yet the ungrateful drudgery must last ...

If this is indecent enough, it is no worse than many of the other prologues and epilogues that he was to write: Dryden's bays were certainly not unspotted. The conscious, calculated obscenity of such writing is its worst feature; the jest that might pass in a momentary sally becomes less tolerable when it is deliberately produced. The final refinement came when those smutty prologues and epilogues were given to children to recite. The search for novelty along this particular path had then reached its utmost limit; and by 1683 Shadwell summed up the situation fairly enough in 'A Lenten Prologue Refus'd by the Players':

Our Prologue-Wit grows flat: the Nap's worn off;
And howsoe're we turn, and trim the Stuff,
The Gloss is gone, that look'd at first so gaudy,
'Tis now no Jest to hear young Girls talk Baudy.

IV

The art of writing successful prologues and epilogues lay to a large extent in adopting the tone suitable for the occasion. Most of the dramatists of the period, and those of their friends who from time to time obliged them with a prologue, had learnt the knack of addressing an audience in the theatre and of being easily colloquial in the modish idiom of polite society. But here, as in other ways, Dryden stands out from his contemporaries. Between 1663 and 1700, when he wrote his last prologue and epilogue for a performance of Fletcher's *The Pilgrim* which was being given for his own benefit, he produced more than one hundred of these pieces; and though he was necessarily driven to ringing the changes on the traditional themes and the stock jokes, he showed a remarkable variety in subject-matter, in his approach to the audience, and in his mode of addressing them.

A prologue or epilogue written by Dryden was almost always tailor-made. For one thing, it might be written for either an actor or an actress; and those that were to be spoken by women, if often no less indecent than those spoken by men, were always adapted to their sex. In addition, they were usually intended for one particular actor or actress; and the personality (and, indeed, the private life) of an actress such as Nell Gwyn were well-known to the audience, and could be expressed and exploited in the words that the poet gave her to speak. Again, some of Dryden's prologues were written for other dramatists, and if he were introducing a work by a female author or by a young beginner, his approach to the audience would be influenced by those circumstances. Even with his own work the circumstances might differ from one play to another. The series of prologues and epilogues that he wrote for the players when they visited Oxford are quite distinct from those he wrote for the London theatre. The Oxford prologues are comparatively decent in tone, and the academic audience is duly flattered, and contrasted favourably with the ignorant playgoers in London. No words are too good for those 'Athenian judges', who alone are fit to pronounce upon poetry, which in Oxford is an art, and in London no better than a trade. The dramatists whose works the Oxford audience are now to see were once (they are told) university men:

> But as Embassadours, when long from home,
> For new Instructions to their Princes come;
> So Poets who your Precepts have forgot,
> Return, and beg they may be better taught ... [1]

The tone is heightened throughout by elaborate similes and classical allusions, and the verse is measured and formal. This sort of thing evidently came easily to Dryden, and perhaps he had just enough belief in what he was saying to allow him to write with an air of conviction. But if he was willing to praise Oxford to its face so long as he was actually in Oxford, he had no wish to offend the men of wit and taste in London. Writing to the Earl of Rochester in 1673 (probably with reference to the prologue just cited, and to an epilogue he had written for the same occasion) he remarks:

[1] 'Prologue, To the University of Oxon, Spoken by Mr Hart, at the Acting of *The Silent Woman*, 1673'.

> I heare since they have succeeded; And by the event your Lordship will judge how easy 'tis to passe any thing upon an University; and how grosse flattery the learned will endure.[1]

Still more dignified than the Oxford prologues are those that Dryden wrote to be spoken in the presence of the King or other members of the royal family. When Charles II and his Queen came to the Theatre-Royal to see a performance of John Banks's *The Unhappy Favourite*, they were greeted with a prologue 'written on purpose by Mr Dryden'. There is no mistaking the elevation of the tone, which is immediately obtained by the biblical reference of the opening lines:

> When first the Ark was Landed on the Shore,
> And Heaven had vow'd to curse the Ground no more,
> When Tops of Hills the Longing Patriark saw,
> And the new Scene of Earth began to draw;
> The Dove was sent to View the Waves Decrease,
> And first brought back to Man the Pledge of Peace ...

The same lofty note is heard in the prologue that Dryden wrote in the spring of 1682 for the first appearance of the Duke of York at the theatre after his return from virtual banishment in Scotland, and in the prologue with which he similarly greeted the Duchess some weeks later. Dryden's awareness of an occasion, and his ability to respond to it appropriately, distinguish his prologues and epilogues from the more rigid work of lesser men.

What almost invariably distinguished them, too, was his sense of form, his ability to develop a theme or to elaborate upon an idea. Too many of the prologues of the period (and not merely those amateur productions 'Written by a Person of Quality' or 'Sent by an Unknown Hand') were shapeless exercises in laboured wit, a casual accumulation of disjointed couplets which stopped when the writers' hard-bound brains could do no more. Not all of Dryden's prologues are satisfactorily constructed, but most of them have the sort of shape that results from developing a coherent and progressive argument. He was not, then, one of those writers who 'fagotted his notions as they fell'; and yet in those addresses to an audience he always succeeded in giving the impression of casual and extempore speech.

A good example of a prologue that holds the attention of the audience in one continuous and developing argument from beginning to

[1] *The Letters of John Dryden*, ed. Charles E. Ward (1942), p. 10.

end is the one that he wrote for *Don Sebastian* in 1689. It is also another fine example of his ability to adapt himself to special circumstances. When this play came upon the stage, Dryden's fortunes were at a low ebb. He had thrown in his lot with James II and the Tories, and now his royal master had abdicated, a Protestant King and Queen were on the throne, and the Whigs were in power. Dryden had lost his two offices of poet-laureate and historiographer-royal, and consequently the pension that went with them. He was now a Catholic in a country that had become more anti-Catholic than ever; and both in and out of the theatre he had identified himself so completely with the anti-Whig Court party that he could count on finding numerous enemies in any public assembly ready to triumph over his downfall. For some time he had simply lain low and waited for the storm of hostility to blow over; but his necessities drove him at last to write again for the stage, and now, in December 1689, he had come before the public with the first play he had written since the Revolution. The prologue to *Don Sebastian* is a reasoned plea for fair play; the poet does not cringe, he chooses rather to throw himself on the generosity of an English audience. We do not know who was given this prologue to speak, but we know that it was spoken by a woman, and this, in his precarious circumstances, is a further example of Dryden's tact in appealing to an audience.

> The Judge remov'd, tho he's no more My Lord,
> May plead at Bar, or at the Council-Board:
> So may cast Poets write; there's no Pretension,
> To argue loss of Wit from loss of Pension.
> Your looks are cheerful; and in all this place
> I see not one, that wears a damning face.
> The *British* Nation, is too brave to show,
> Ignoble vengeance, on a vanquish'd foe.
> At least be civil to the Wretch imploring;
> And lay your Paws upon him, without roaring:
> Suppose our Poet was your foe before;
> Yet now, the bus'ness of the Field is o'er;
> 'Tis time to let your Civil Wars alone,
> When Troops are into Winter-quarters gone.
> *Jove* was alike to *Latian* and to *Phrygian*;
> And you well know, a Play's of no Religion ...

The unknown actress continues to plead the poet's cause, drops in her one little bawdy joke (the occasion is too serious for more) when she tells the men in the audience what she could bribe them with, and then concludes by offering a bargain on behalf of the author:

> I heard him make advances of good Nature;
> That he for once, wou'd sheath his cutting Satyr:
> Sign but his Peace, he vows he'll ne'er again
> The sacred Names of Fops and Beau's profane.
> Strike up the Bargain quickly; for I swear,
> As Times go now, he offers very fair.
> Be not too hard on him, with Statutes neither,
> Be kind; and do not set your Teeth together,
> To stretch the Laws, as Coblers do their Leather.
> Horses, by Papists, are not to be ridden;
> But sure the Muses Horse was ne'er forbidden.
> For in no Rate-Book, it was ever found
> That *Pegasus* was valued at Five-pound:
> Fine him to daily Drudging and Inditing;
> And let him pay his Taxes out, in Writing.

This is surely the manly Dryden, pleading his cause at the bar of public opinion, and building up his case in a reasoned argument.

When, a little more than four years later, he announced his retirement from the stage in the prologue to *Love Triumphant* (1694), his constructive sense was as firm as ever, and he cast this valedictory prologue in the form of his last will and testament. To each section of the audience he bequeathed a legacy—to the beaux, to the 'roaring boys'

> Who come in Drunk, and fill the House with noise,

to the critics (and especially 'Shakespeare's critic', Thomas Rymer), and lastly to the ladies—

> Tho' he pretends no Legacy to leave you,
> An Old Man may at least good wishes give you.

(It is characteristic of the unrepentant poet that the word 'legacy' should contain a *double entendre.*) That even Dryden could repeat himself may be seen from the sprightly and salacious epilogue to *Cleomenes* (1692) which he wrote for Mrs Bracegirdle, who had 'died' in the play, and who proceeded to distribute *her* various legacies to the audience. When the two companies were united in 1682 Dryden wrote both the prologue and the epilogue for the opening night. In the epilogue he seized the occasion to propose some rules for the behaviour of the audience:

> New Ministers, when first they get in place
> Must have a care to Please; and that's our Case:
> Some Laws for publick Welfare we design,
> If You, the Power supreme, will please to joyn.

He proceeds therefore to reprehend in turn the 'Pratlers in the Pit', the 'Vizard-Masque' and the fluttering sparks who crowd noisily around her, the loud footmen keeping seats for 'their unpaying Masters' who have failed to appear, and the gallants who are too ready to draw their swords in quarrel or to force themselves upon the actresses behind the scenes. It is a comprehensive indictment, effective in each detail, but gaining in force (as so often with Dryden) from the cumulative effect of its ordered presentation.

There is one final aspect of Dryden's excellence in this form which must be at least briefly discussed: he had, to an unusual degree, the art of communicating his ideas easily by means of witty allusion and lively metaphor. So far as allusion is concerned, his prologues and epilogues require far more annotation today than they have ever been given; and they abound in contemporary references that must have made his points brilliantly for a Restoration audience. To look no further than the prologue to *Don Sebastian* already quoted, 'The Judge remov'd' of the opening line offers a nice parallel to the poet's own loss of the laureateship for political reasons: there had been numerous instances in recent years of judges being removed from the bench for failing to secure convictions that the King and his ministers desired. (In the famous trial of the Seven Bishops in 1688, two of the judges, Powell and Holloway, who summed up for the Bishops against the King had been summarily dismissed.) In the third line 'cast Poets' plays obviously but wittily on the phrase 'cast mistress', one of the recurring characters in Restoration comedy. The 'Winter-quarters' of line 14 refers, of course, to the cessation of political hostility now that the nation has, almost unanimously, accepted the Revolution settlement; but it may allude, too, to the winter that has descended on the poet's fortunes, and may perhaps carry a further allusion to the fact that *Don Sebastian* was first performed in the cold month of December 1689. The later references to 'Statutes', 'Horses, by Papists ... not to be ridden', and 'valued at Five-pound' are to an 'Act for the better securing the Government by disarming Papists and reputed Papists', which made it illegal for any Roman Catholic 'to have or keep in his own possession ... any Horse or Horses which shall be above the value of five pounds'. The easy transition to the Muses' horse, and so to ill-paid poets, could not be neater.

Dryden's command of metaphor is rarely seen to better advantage than in his prologues and epilogues. In the prologue to *Don Sebastian*, 'And lay your Paws upon him, without roaring' follows naturally upon 'The British Nation' three lines earlier, symbolized by the King of the Beasts. But Dryden can do better than this. In the prologue that he wrote for the first part of *The Conquest of Granada* he attacks those dull dramatists who repeat the same old jokes and situations, and plagiarize their betters:

> They bring old Ir'n, and glass upon the Stage,
> To barter with the Indians of our Age.
> Still they write on; and like great Authors show:
> But 'tis as Rowlers in wet gardens grow;
> Heavy with dirt, and gath'ring as they goe.

The unusual image of the garden roller suggests perfectly the heavy and laborious writers that Dryden has in mind, and the foreign matter that they are continually picking up from other authors; while that of 'old Ir'n, and glass' again conveys the idea of worn-out theatrical material, but, in conjunction with 'Indians' has the more specific suggestion of plagiarism from such successful plays as *The Indian Queen* and *The Indian Emperour*. The application of 'the Indians of our Age' to the less intelligent members of the audience is characteristic of Dryden's attitude to 'the many-headed monster of the pit'. Nowhere is his metaphor more effective than when he is satirizing the taste of the age. In the prologue to *Albion and Albanius* it is barbed:

> Give you strong Sense, the Liquor is too heady;
> You're come to farce, that's Asses milk, already;

and in his epilogue for the opening of the theatre in 1682 he finds a fine contemptuous simile for the excited sparks clamouring about the vizard-mask who has invitingly shown them her face:

> Now growling, sputtring, wauling, such a clutter,
> 'Tis just like Puss defendant in a Gutter.

Dryden's metaphors and similes in those packed and witty addresses to the audience are distinguished by their relevance, their variety, their topicality, their power to evoke the desired reaction, and often by a surprising unconventionality.

'I do believe', wrote the anonymous author of *Remarques on the Humours and Conversations of the Town* (1673), 'that never in any Age was there such a violent and universal thirst after the Fame of being Wits.' This thirst was most frequently satisfied by the writing of prologues and epilogues. It could fairly be claimed that, both by reason of their number and their excellence, those constitute the most considerable body of Restoration verse, exercising the skill of writers great and small, and in turn influencing the way they wrote on other occasions. If this is so, we may see one good reason why the witty colloquial mode became so firmly established in the verse-writing of the period. The familiar, conversational manner of prologue and epilogue spread outwards from the theatre into much of the satire, the narrative poetry, the ratiocinative poems like *The Hind and the Panther*, and various other kinds. It is by no means the only manner, but beyond all question it is the one that came most easily to the average poet of the later seventeenth century.

In Defence of *Moll Flanders*

ARNOLD KETTLE

I

PROFESSOR IAN WATT'S *The Rise of the Novel* is one of the works of literary criticism of the last decade that have added substantially and rewardingly to our ability to read eighteenth-century literature better. If this paper revolves around some disagreements with Mr Watt that is to be taken as a mark of gratitude rather than an attempt to denigrate. It is because *The Rise of the Novel* has a deservedly wide currency that it is worth examining what seems to be fundamentally wrong in Mr Watt's approach to Defoe.[1]

It is with *Moll Flanders* that I am concerned and I agree with Mr Watt that it is the key work in any estimate of Defoe's significance as a novelist. In *The Rise of the Novel* forty-two pages are spent on *Moll* and constitute the fullest discussion of the book I know. Towards the end of the discussion the conclusions are summarized:

> Defoe's forte was the brilliant episode. Once his imagination seized on a situation he could report it with a comprehensive fidelity which was

[1] I should add, in fairness, that I am also concerned to correct what I now regard as inadequacies in my own approach to Defoe in my *Introduction to the English Novel*, vol. I (London, 1951). For a realization of these inadequacies I am indebted not only to time, with its gift of second chances, but, in particular, to Mr Watt, to Mr Alick West and to Professor Bonamy Dobrée who was the first person I heard talk of Defoe with the right kind of enthusiasm.

> much in advance of any previous fiction, and which, indeed, has never been surpassed ...
>
> How far we should allow Defoe's gift for the perfect episode to outweigh his patent shortcomings—weaknesses of construction, inattention to detail, lack of moral or formal pattern—is a very difficult critical problem.[1]

It is a problem, however, about which Mr Watt has left us in little doubt as to where he stands. The passage I have quoted is followed by a couple of pages of generous and perceptive appreciation of Defoe's genius, happily described as 'confident and indestructible'. But these pages cannot eclipse the thirty-five that have preceded them in which scepticism—peppered, it is true, with valuable observations and insights—has reigned. Mr Watt praises Defoe highly for verisimilitude and not for much else. The conclusion is clearly stated:

> His blind and almost purposeless concentration on the actions of his heroes and heroines, and his unconscious and unreflective mingling of their thoughts and his about the inglorious world in which they both exist, made possible the expression of many motives and themes which could not, perhaps, have come into the tradition of the novel without Defoe's shock tactics ... [2]

Blind, purposeless, unconscious, unreflective: the adjectives are damaging and lead us—for all Mr Watt's scrupulous reservations—in the same direction as Dr Leavis's 'brush-off' footnote in *The Great Tradition*:

> Characteristic of the confusion I am contending against is the fashion (for which the responsibility seems to go back to Virginia Woolf and Mr E. M. Forster) of talking of *Moll Flanders* as a 'great novel'. Defoe was a remarkable writer, but all that need be said about him as a novelist was said by Leslie Stephen in *Hours in a Library* (First Series). He made no pretension to practising the novelist's art, and matters little as an influence. In fact, the only influence that need be noted is that represented by the use made of him in the nineteen-twenties by the practitioners of the fantastic *conte* (or pseudo-moral fable) with its empty pretence of significance.[3]

It is worth recalling that this footnote—which has, incidentally, along with a couple of others in the same work, had more influence in

[1] *The Rise of the Novel* (London, 1957), p. 130. [2] Ibid, p. 134.

[3] *The Great Tradition* (London, 1948), p. 2.

keeping students of English literature away from the eighteenth-century novel than any other pronouncement—is attached to a sentence which distinguishes as major novelists those who 'not only change the possibilities of the art for practitioners and readers, but ... are significant in terms of the human awareness they promote: awareness of the possibilities of life'.

It is precisely on such grounds that I would claim that *Moll Flanders* is indeed a great novel.

II

Mr Watt uses, to pinpoint his doubts about Defoe's literary status the famous passage in *Moll Flanders* in which Moll doesn't steal the watch in the meeting-house.

> The next thing of moment was an attempt at a gentlewoman's gold watch. It happened in a crowd, at a meeting house, where I was in very great danger of being taken. I had full hold of her watch, but giving a great jostle as if somebody had thrust me against her, and in the juncture giving the watch a fair pull, I found it would not come, so I let it go that moment, and cried as if I had been killed, that somebody had trod upon my foot, and that there was certainly pickpockets there, for somebody or other had given a pull at my watch; for you are to observe that on these adventures we always went very well dressed, and I had very good clothes on, and a gold watch by my side, as like a lady as other folks.
>
> I had no sooner said so but the other gentlewoman cried out, 'A Pickpocket' too, for somebody, she said, had tried to pull her watch away.
>
> When I touched her watch I was close to her, but when I cried out I stopped as it were short, and the crowd bearing her forward a little, she made a noise too, but it was at some distance from me, so that she did not in the least suspect me; but when she cried out, 'A Pickpocket', somebody cried out, 'Ay, and here has been another; this gentlewoman has been attempted too.'
>
> At that very instant, a little farther in the crowd, and very luckily too, they cried out, 'A Pickpocket', again, and really seized a young fellow in the very act. This, though unhappy for the wretch, was very opportunely for my case, though I had carried it handsomely enough before; but now it was out of doubt, and all the loose part of the crowd ran that way, and the poor boy was delivered up to the rage of the street, which is a cruelty I need not describe, and which, however, they are always glad of, rather than be sent to Newgate, where they lie often a long time and sometimes they are hanged, and the best they can look for, if they are convicted, is to be transported.

Mr Watt's comments on this scene may be summarized as follows. It is very convincing: full marks for verisimilitude and prose. But (*a*) the tone is too laconic, the scene is not planned as a coherent whole; (*b*) the point of view of the narrator is not consistent; (*c*) the relationship of the passage to the rest of the book is suspect; (*d*) the passage suffers from a general fault of the book—repeated falls in tension between episodes. Let us examine these criticisms.

(*a*) Mr Watt complains that

> Defoe gets into the middle of the action, with 'I had full hold of her watch', and then suddenly changes from laconic reminiscent summary to a more detailed and immediate presentation, as though only to back up the truth of his initial statement. Nor has the scene been planned as a coherent whole: we are soon interrupted in the middle of the scene by an aside explaining something that might have been explained before, the important fact that Moll Flanders was dressed like a gentlewoman herself: this transition adds to our trust that no ghost-writer has been imposing order on Moll Flanders's somewhat rambling reminiscences, but if we had seen Moll dressed 'as like a lady as other folks' from the beginning, the action would have run more strongly, because uninterruptedly, into the next incident of the scene, the raising of the alarm.[1]

Surely the point Mr Watt objects to is an important part of Defoe's intended effect. Moll isn't a novelist, planning ahead. She lives from moment to moment; she suddenly remembers things she ought to have said before; and she remembers them haphazardly, partly because that is the way people do remember things, but also because she is such an incurable self-deceiver, yet doesn't want to deceive herself or other people. Moll wants to be honest—with herself, with us, even with the woman she steals from—but of course she can't be. And the confusion is expressed in the organization and disorganization of her prose. If Moll's consciousness is a disorganized and impromptu business, so is her life.

> (*b*) Defoe goes on to stress the practical moral, which is that the gentlewoman should have 'seized the next body that was behind her', instead of crying out. In so doing, Defoe lives up to the didactic purpose professed in the 'Author's Preface', but at the same time he directs our attention to the important problem of what the point of view of the narrator is supposed to be. We presume that it is a repentant Moll, speaking towards the end of her life: it is therefore surprising that in the next paragraph she should gaily describe her 'governess's' procuring

[1] Op. cit., p. 97.

activities as 'pranks'. Then a further confusion about the point of view becomes apparent: we notice that to Moll Flanders other pickpockets, and the criminal fraternity in general, are a 'they', not a 'we'. She speaks as though she were not implicated in the common lot of criminals; or is it, perhaps, Defoe who has unconsciously dropped into the 'they' he himself would naturally use for them? And earlier, when we are told that 'the other gentlewoman' cried out, we wonder why the word 'other'? Is Moll Flanders being ironical about the fact that she too was dressed like a gentlewoman, or has Defoe forgotten that, actually, she is not?[1]

This carries the same point further. Of course, there are inconsistencies here. They are the very life's blood of the book. It is true that Moll speaks as though she were not implicated in the common lot of criminals. She doesn't think of herself as a criminal. When she learns what the other criminals in Newgate think of her she is morally outraged. Occasionally, for a moment, like Joyce Cary's Sara, she catches sight of herself in some mirror and sees herself, surprised. And she *does* think of herself, in the episode under discussion, as a gentlewoman. What Mr Watt sees as Defoe's carelessness I see as his imaginative absorption in his subject, a penetration into the layers of self-deception of which a human being, even a relatively honest one, is capable. Sir Leslie Stephen's reproach, in the essay Dr Leavis admires so much, that Defoe's novels lack 'all that goes by the name of psychological analysis in modern fiction' makes sense only if one is concerned to blame Defoe for not being Proust. There is no need for formal analysis of Moll's psychological processes in the meeting-house. They are revealed in all their complex, awful, funny, human contradictoriness in the very texture of the scene. This is a triumph of art.

(*c*) The connection between the meeting-house scene and the narrative as a whole confirms the impression that Defoe paid little attention to the internal consistence of his story. When she is transported to Virginia Moll Flanders gives her son a gold watch as a memento of their reunion; she relates how she 'desired that he would now and then kiss it for my sake', and then adds sardonically that she did not tell him 'that I stole it from a gentlewoman's side, at a meeting house in London'. Since there is no other episode in *Moll Flanders* dealing with watches, gentlewomen and meeting-houses, we must surely infer that Defoe had a faint recollection of what he had written a hundred pages earlier ...

These discontinuities strongly suggest that Defoe did not plan his novel as a coherent whole, but worked piecemeal, very rapidly, and without any subsequent revision.[2]

[1] Ibid., p. 98. [2] Ibid, pp. 98–9.

There is a confusion of critical method here. It may well be (and, as Mr Watt says, external as well as internal evidence suggests it) that Defoe worked piecemeal and that his novels therefore lack a certain planned coherence. But this is a general critical statement about the kind of book we are dealing with, relevant no doubt, but not to be confused with our judgment of artistic success. The passage Mr Watt refers to can be read equally well as a further example of Moll's difficulty of separating the false from the true and of the curious tricks of the extended conscience. She happens to connect watch-stealing with the meeting-house episode because that gave her a shock and imprinted itself deep in her memory; she may even have found it necessary, for her peace of mind, to transform her failure—with its uncomfortable accompaniment of the taking of the boy pickpocket—into a comfortable success. Certainly time has dealt interestingly with the episode. This may not have been Defoe's intention. But certainly the main *point* in the Virginia scene from which Mr Watt quotes is to illuminate the wry twinge of half-conscience, half-triumph that Moll by now feels. She has become complacent in a way which in former days, for all her conscience-blocking, she dared not be. Whether she is referring to the same watch doesn't matter. To suggest that it does would seem to reveal an attitude towards the novel and novel-writing not quite relevant to the sort of book Defoe offers us. I will return to this point.

(*d*) The question of fall of tension between episodes is a valid point of criticism. That opening sentence, 'The next thing of moment was etc.' does indeed betray a weakness, a technical problem unsolved. There is, it is true, the sense in which Moll does indeed see her life as a kind of inventory of episodes, with nothing much of note between them. There is also the sense in which the book proceeds from one moral warning to the next on the old beggar-book level, and there is no doubt that this aspect of his book tends all the time to conflict with Defoe's major concern—to show us what Moll Flanders is like (in the way that the remnants of the old *Hamlet* revenge-drama tend to conflict with Shakespeare's major concern in his play).

In his analysis of the meeting-house scene Mr Watt omits to discuss what is surely its greatest, most moving moment; the taking of the boy pickpocket. The effect here is not at all due to verisimilitude or any of the qualities habitually, and rightly, granted to Defoe; it is almost entirely moral and psychological. The phrase 'and very luckily too' leads us into it. What is lucky for Moll is the lynching of the boy for whom she can afford no more fellow-feeling than a single use of the adjective 'poor' and the dubious consolation that lynching is better than hanging or transportation.

The effect that Defoe achieves here is one that is central to the nature of *Moll Flanders* as a work of art. Moll's reactions to the episode, humanly speaking, are quite inadequate. It is easy, therefore, to underestimate Defoe's art, which can look, at first glance, to be inadequate in the same way. The paragraph is a flat one, a disclaimer, a refusal to see what has happened. But the phrase 'a cruelty I need not describe' is an indication of cowardice not on Defoe's part but Moll's. Of course, she can't bear to dwell on the scene: it is too near the bone. But that last sentence of the paragraph is, objectively considered, all compassion. The phrase 'and sometimes they are hanged', the whole rhythm of the sentence, the toneless forcing out of facet after facet of horror, all these contribute to a marvellous effect. Moll is playing it all down; she can't do anything else, she who has put herself beyond the possibility of looking at such a scene objectively. But Defoe allows *us* to see all round the situation even if Moll can't. And a far more important link between this whole episode and the later reaches of the novel than the link represented by the watch which turns up in Virginia is the connection between this last sentence and the whole Newgate episode of the book. It is only then that we get the full force of the word 'luckily'.

I stress the power of this paragraph because it illustrates very well the nature of the moral organization of *Moll Flanders*, a feature of the book that Mr Watt, and almost everyone else, plays down.

III

The underlying tension which gives *Moll Flanders* its vitality as a work of art can be expressed by a contradiction which is at once simple and complicated. Moll is immoral, shallow, hypocritical, heartless, a bad woman: yet Moll is marvellous. Defoe might almost (though he wouldn't have dreamed of it) have subtitled his book 'A Pure Woman'.

Moll's splendour—her resilience and courage and generosity—is inseparable from her badness. The fair and the foul are not isolable qualities to be abstracted and totted up in a reckoning, balancing one against the other. The relationship is far more interesting. One is reminded, perhaps, of Yeats's Crazy Jane:

'Fair and foul are near of kin
And fair needs foul', I cried.
'My friends are gone, but that's a truth
Nor grave nor bed denied,
Learned in bodily lowliness
And in the heart's pride.'

That is too metaphysical for Moll; she wouldn't say that fair needs foul. But the contradiction Yeats is expressing and, in expressing, resolving, is essentially the contradiction Defoe's book expresses. And the phrase 'the heart's pride' is not inappropriate to Moll.

The episode in *Moll Flanders* which tells us most about the underlying pattern of the book is the one very near the beginning in which Moll as a little girl talks of her fear of going into service and her desire to be a gentlewoman. Mr Watt picks out this passage as one of the few examples in the book of an irony that we can be quite sure is fully conscious, and his fastening on the scene tells us that he is a good literary critic. But he lets go much too quickly. This is an absolutely essential episode, as Mr Alick West, in the best analysis of *Moll Flanders*, I know, has well pointed out:

> The life the child wants—working for herself in freedom—is the contrasting background to the life the woman gets in a world where a gentlewoman does not live on the threepences or fourpences she earns by her own labour, but on riches of unexplained origin.[1]

This sentence not only shows what *Moll Flanders* is about but illuminates the specific artistic pattern of the book. It leads us straight to what makes Moll at the same time splendid and contemptible. What makes her splendid—a great heroine—is that she wants her independence, to work for herself in freedom. She is a woman who is determined to be a human being, not a servant, and the feeling of what it means to be a servant is what generates the impulses which carry her through most of the book, until she too has become a gentlewoman with servants, living on riches whose origin she likes to forget about or to confuse but which Defoe has only too clearly explained.

Unless we see Moll in history we cannot grasp her moral stature as a heroine. Instead, we will bring to her the flat and static sort of moral judgment which she herself (and one side of Defoe himself) brings when she is forced to enter the sphere she calls morality or religion. And here Virginia Woolf's feminist preoccupations offer a more central

[1] *Mountain in the Sunlight* (London, 1958), p. 90.

and artistically relevant approach to the book than any other. The examination of Defoe's social and economic attitudes that Mr Novak[1] has offered us is not, of course, irrelevant; nor are Mr Watt's observations on the significance of the criminal class at this period; but neither emphasis goes to the heart of the matter. Moll becomes a criminal because she is a woman, and it is not at all by a chance in the book's structure that she comes to her second career (that of a thief) by way of her first (that of a wife). Too little is known about the position of women in the eighteenth century, but the general outlines are clear enough and Mr Watt himself in the chapters on Richardson in *The Rise of the Novel* has notably contributed to our appreciation of many of the problems involved. So have recent emphases on the importance of arranged marriages and contemporary feelings about them in Restoration and eighteenth-century literature.[2] Such extra-literary confirmation is not irrelevant to a critical approach to *Moll Flanders* because only on the basis of a just assessment of the facts can we form an opinion as to whether Moll's childish fears about the consequences of not being a gentlewoman are justified—whether in fact they represent an amiable delusion or a naive but genuine moral insight. All the evidence points to the conclusion that Moll is right, that to become a maidservant in that period meant the end of any possibility that could conceivably be subsumed under the words freedom or independence, any possibility therefore of individual human development or flowering. The choice Moll makes is therefore one which, with whatever reservations, deserves our positive sympathy, and the moral tensions about which Defoe's novel is constructed are not trivial or arbitrary.

Not to stress this point is to prejudice artistic judgments. It is only within the social context that we can begin, for instance, to assess Defoe's treatment (or lack of it) of Moll's role as mother. Mr Watt writes:

> Here the conclusion about her character must surely be that, although there are extenuating circumstances, she is often a heartless mother. It is difficult to see how this can be reconciled either with her kissing the ground that Humphrey has trodden, or with the fact that she herself loudly condemns unnatural mothers, but never makes any such accusation against herself even in her deepest moments of penitent self-reprobation.[3]

[1] Maximilian E. Novak, *Economics and the Fiction of Danie. Defoe* (California, 1962).

[2] Especially C. Hill, 'Clarissa Harlowe and her Times' (*Essays in Criticism*, V (1955), 315–40) and P. F. Vernon, 'Marriage of Convenience and the Moral Code of Restoration Comedy' (*Essays in Criticism*, XII (1962), 370–87).

[3] Op. cit., p. 110.

This puts the cart before the horse. Surely the very point that Defoe has been making us understand is that Moll is *at the same time* unusually honest and extraordinarily dishonest, and that the significance of her situation (whether it be horror or irony) is that she dare not be any more compassionate than she is. What Mr Watt sees as inconsistency I see as profundity. Moll is genuinely sorry that she has been a heartless mother; but that is part of the price she pays *and has to pay* for her independence. The really dreadful aspect of the book lies in Moll's ultimate absorption, via her 'repentance', into the very way of life against which she has so vigorously rebelled.

The Newgate section of the book is an extraordinary achievement and not primarily on the level of verisimilitude. If Newgate is hell to Moll it is above all because it is a place where her habitual habits of self-deception cannot do their job, a real eighteenth-century *huis clos*. Newgate is reality, the eighteenth-century world with the lid off, the world from which Moll set out and to which she comes back, defeated, to emerge as a conformist.

IV

It is worth looking at *Moll Flanders* in its historical context in a rather different sense from the one I have so far emphasized. Moll is perhaps the first major plebeian heroine in English literature. The Doll Tearsheets and Doll Commons of the Elizabethan drama are her literary ancestors, but they are never right at the centre of the plays they appear in, any more than the sensible peasant-bred servants in Molière. Moll is unique. And throughout the eighteenth century she remains so. For Pamela, precisely because she makes the opposite choice to Moll's, is not a heroine. She bears on her shoulders none of the weight of human aspiration which heroism—including the fictional kind—involves. Polly Peachum is nearer to being a heroine; but the Polly of *The Beggar's Opera* need Lucy Lockit to complete her and together they do—also within the walls of Newgate—throw a great deal of light on the problems and emotions of eighteenth-century plebeian women. Strictly speaking, however, it is impossible to speak of a plebeian heroine after Moll until Jeannie Deans, who is different because she is a peasant, not a townswoman. If one looks further afield the important figure among Moll's successors is another peasant girl, Susannah (Mozart's even more than Beaumarchais'), who is an anti-Pamela and a great advance on the Molière servants.

V

We must see the place of *Moll Flanders* in total history if we are to see it in literary history. The book is not to be judged as though it were an imperfect forerunner of *Pride and Prejudice* or *What Maisie Knew*. Behind almost all the unsatisfactory criticism of Defoe today is a predisposition to judge his books in terms relevant to the novel as it developed in the nineteenth century and to praise in Defoe primarily those aspects of his art which point, so to speak, in that direction. 'Dramatization' (or what Percy Lubbock calls 'scenic' presentation), a conscious manipulation of 'point of view' and a moral preoccupation of the sort one associates with, say, George Eliot: these are assumed to be the elements of maturity in a novelist's development. 'Personal relationships' in the more analytical and isolable sense of the term are seen as the proper, even the ultimate, subject of the novel. And, of course, in an important sense, this is true. Novels will always be about men and women in their living, and therefore personal, relationships.

The trouble with Moll Flanders, however, is that by her very mode of existence she is precluded from having personal relationships of the sort modern critics most value. Mr Watt seems to recognize this when he writes:

> .. it is certain that, at the end of the long tradition of the European novel, and of the society whose individualism, leisure and unexampled security allowed it to make personal relations the major theme of its literature, Defoe is a welcome and portentous figure. Welcome because he seems long ago to have called the great bluff of the novel—its suggestion that personal relations really are the be-all and end-all of life; portentous because he, and only he, among the great writers of the past, has presented the struggle for survival in the bleak perspectives which recent history has brought back to a commanding position on the human stage.[1]

But he is arguing here that Defoe's positive quality is his concentration on isolated individuals. I think this is a mistaken argument. Moll's life is not an isolated life; she has as many personal relationships as anyone else. That she is unable to have full and satisfactory personal relationships is due not to her individualism but to the actual problems she is faced with. Moll is forced to be an individualist by her decision to try to be free in the man's world of eighteenth-century England; but her impulse to be free is due not to individualism but to a desire for better relationships with other people than life as a servant will permit.

[1] Op cit., p. 133.

The whole nature of Defoe's book—its construction, its texture, its detail, its vitality, its power to move us—is determined by his awareness of the contradiction between Moll's human aspiration and the facts of the human world she lives in. Because so much of the contradiction was, in the year 1722, insoluble and yet had to be resolved, much of the resolution takes the form of ambiguous or ironical statement.

It is interesting to compare Defoe's methods with those of a contemporary artist facing a comparable problem, the Italian novelist Pier Paolo Pasolini in his impressive film *Accattone*. Accattone, Pasolini's 'hero', is in many respects very like a twentieth-century Moll Flanders. He is a feckless young man who lives as a ponce in Rome, and the film treats his life episodically. There is one scene in particular reminiscent of Defoe's novel. Accattone, needing money to buy a present for his girl, steals a chain from the neck of his young son, telling himself all the time what a swine he is. The moral impact of the film is in one sense much the same as that of *Moll Flanders*: we feel a deep sympathy for Accattone without approving of him, and we are shocked at the human inadequacies of the total situation that is revealed. Yet the similarities are scarcely less striking than the differences, of which perhaps the most important is that we know precisely where Pasolini stands: there is no moral ambiguity in *his* attitude. Accattone is presented to us clearly, objectively, as a product of contemporary society, and although he is not sentimentalized or excused, the social situation of which he is a part, and at least to some extent a victim, is implicitly condemned.

This is not a matter of chance. Pasolini knows very well that Accattone is unable to resolve his problems; but he also knows that, in the middle of the twentieth century, Accattone's problems are not insoluble. Whereas, to Defoe, at the beginning of the eighteenth century, Moll's problem is indeed insoluble and this inevitably affects the whole nature of his artistic handling of it.

The question 'How far is Defoe's irony intentional?' is not really a fruitful question. For one thing, it is impossible to know the answer for sure; for another, it oversimplifies the nature of artistic consciousness and indeed of all consciousness. Defoe's writing was presumably not *un*intentional, not *un*conscious. He knew what he was doing. But, of course, he will not have been aware of all the implications of what he was doing; no one ever is. It is true that Defoe's own comprehension of some of the most important implications of Moll Flanders' story must seem to us to be incomplete. He underwrites her own ultimate complacency, obviously taking her salvation much too much at its face value. But this limitation is far less important than that 'negative capability' which allowed him to reveal the humanity of Moll. What is important is that he tackled the big, central human problems of his time and went deep, revealing the contradictions as well as the surface qualities, and revealing them in a form which in itself illuminates their nature because it springs from them.

Pope: The Man and the Poet

JOHN BUTT

POPE'S career was exceptional in many respects. His ability was recognized by the best judges of poetry before he was twenty years old; and before he was thirty he was famous. Already at the age of twenty-nine he was showing his concern for his text and for the canon of his writings by publishing *The Works of Mr Alexander Pope* in sumptuous quarto and folio editions, adorned with a portrait of the author by Kneller and with head- and tail-pieces to the poems by Gribelin, and recommended by the verse addresses of Wycherley, Parnell, the Countess of Winchilsea, the Duke of Buckingham and others. This collection of poems, containing the *Essay on Criticism*, *Windsor Forest*, and *The Rape of the Lock*, besides many others, he was inclined to look back upon in later life with some measure of affectionate condescension; yet it was a volume which both in poetical merit and in physical appearance could rival what other poets had achieved at the end of a life-time's endeavour. Thus Prior's poems were to be published in an equally handsome format, but at the end of his career, and at the expense of friends; and Congreve's early work had been almost equally well received a few years before, but Congreve did not live up to his youthful promise. It is remarkable, however, that each of Pope's subsequent publications added both to his fame and to his fortunes. At a time when a writer needed the support or patronage of a political party to make a living—and very good livings were to be had that way, as the careers of Addison and Prior bear witness—Pope was excluded from such patronage because he was a Roman Catholic. Yet in spite of this disability he could claim that he was the first poet to live at ease by his pen. And if he was not the last poet who could make such a claim, I suppose he has had few rivals since in that respect. Though he was quite right in admitting that it was

> Thanks to Homer that I live and thrive
> Indebted to no Prince or Peer alive,

we now know that he was also very skilful in marketing the pretty little collected editions of his works in octavo, which he published during the last nine years of his life.

His career was exceptional, too, in that his success was not confined to this country. Milton had been known abroad during his lifetime, but he was known as a prose controversialist; Pope seems to have been the first English poet to achieve contemporary fame by his poetry in France, in Italy, and in Switzerland. And far away in the American colonies he also had admirers and correspondents.

Such an exceptional reputation doubtless derived some support from extraneous circumstances and from qualities in Pope's work that are not essentially poetic. Thus he wrote at a time when there seems to have been a considerable growth in literacy and an unusually large market for poetry, a market to be matched in size only by the first twenty years of the nineteenth century, when Scott, Byron, and Crabbe made fortunes for themselves and their publishers. Then, too, it must be allowed that much of his later poetry had a contemporary appeal to the inquisitiveness of those who think they can detect a smell of scandal. But when such allowances have been made, it must be admitted that Pope's reputation rested, and still rests, upon sheer merit—the charm of one who can handle common things with propriety (as in the *Moral Essays*), the skill (shown both in the *Essay on Criticism* and the *Essay on Man*) of one who can reconcile conflicting opinions and achieve a new synthesis, the imaginative power (shown in *The Rape of the Lock* and *The Dunciad*) of investing the social scene in a new light, of presenting a new criticism of society; and, what perhaps appealed most to the readers of his generation, the conviction he gave them in the *Imitations of Horace*, the translation of Homer, and the *Essay on Criticism* that 'Still green with Bays each ancient Altar stands'; in those and other poems he was able to convince his generation that the spirit of the ancients was still a living force in that latter age, that Homer and Horace had still their relevance to eighteenth-century life, that there was indeed such a concept as

> Unerring Nature, still divinely bright,
> One clear, unchang'd, and Universal Light.

And besides these qualities he was endowed with peculiar charms of diction and versification; of diction, in that he practised so skilfully the doctrine of decorum, whether it be in judging the exact degree of diminution required in *The Rape of the Lock*, or the precise placing of a colloquialism in the elegant yet easy verse of the *Moral Essays* and *Imitations of Horace*; of versification, in that he learned how to produce an incredible number of rhythmical variants in the tiny space of the couplet. The charge of monotony is levelled against Pope's couplet only by those who have not learned to hear it and to read it.

Pope's achievement was substantial and widely recognized. It brought him in his lifetime not only literary fame but social fame. As a boy he had been courted by the wits who survived from Dryden's day, Wycherley, Congreve, Walsh and Granville, and by the statesmen, too. William III's Secretary of State, Sir William Trumbull, took him out riding in Windsor Forest, and in a charming passage of the *Epistle to Dr Arbuthnot* Pope tells us how

> The Courtly Talbot, Somers, Sheffield read,
> Ev'n mitred Rochester would nod the head,
> And St. John's self (great Dryden's friends before)
> With open arms received one Poet more.

It is not surprising that he should have taken his natural place amongst his intellectual equals like Swift and Berkeley, or with painters like Kneller and Jervas, or with architects like Kent: this is to be expected of a great writer in any age. What is more remarkable is the ease with which this Roman Catholic son of a wholesale linen-draper entered the society of statesmen, and counted amongst his closest friends lords temporal and spiritual, generals, diplomats and maids of honour. He could even conquer that formidable old dowager, Sarah Duchess of Marlborough:

> Had you sent away Sir Timothy, to re-call another [he writes to her in her still active 82nd year], it had been but a natural Change in a Lady who knows her Power over her Slaves; and that how long soever she has rejected or banish'd any one, she is sure always to recover him. But to

> use me thus—to have won me with some difficulty, to have bow'd down all my Pride, and reduced me to take That at your hands which I never took at any other; and as soon as you had done this, to slight your Conquest, and cast me away with the common Lumber of Friends in this Town—what a Girl you are![1]

The range of his noble acquaintances and his adaptability in meeting them is best conveyed in two extracts from his poems, the first a few verses from a poem he never acknowledged, 'The Court Ballad: to the tune of *To all you Ladies now at Land*'. In it he shows his whimsical habit of referring slightingly to his diminutive appearance (especially compared with the bulk of his friend Gay), which he permitted also to the affection of his intimates, as when he reminds Atterbury of Atterbury's likening him sitting in a little chariot to Homer in a nutshell,[2] or when in the January before his death he writes to Bolingbroke: 'If your charity would take up a small Bird that is half dead of the frost, and set it a chirping for half an hour, I'll jump into my Cage, and put myself into your hands tomorrow, at any hour you send':[3]

To one fair Lady out of court
    And two fair Ladies in
Who think the Turk and Pope a sport
    And Wit and Love no Sin,
Come these soft lines, with nothing Stiff in
To Bellenden, Lepell, and Griffin
                    With a fa.

In truth by what I can discern,
    Of Courtiers from you Three,
Some Wit you have and more may learn,
    From Court than Gay or me,
Perhaps in time you'll leave High Diet,
And Sup with us on Mirth or Quiet.

In Leister fields, in house full nigh,
    With door all painted green,
Where Ribbans wave upon the tye,
    (A Milliner's I ween)
There may you meet us, three to three,
For Gay can well make two of me.

[1] *Correspondence*, ed. Sherburn, IV, 381. [2] Ibid., IV, 490. [3] Ibid., II, 110.

But shou'd you catch the Prudish itch,
And each become a coward,
Bring sometimes with you Lady Rich
And sometimes Mistress Howard,
For Virgins, to keep chaste, must go
Abroad with such as are not so.

These verses are as well adjusted to three mettlesome young maids of honour as are the following lines to the noblemen for whose eyes they were intended:

But does the Court a worthy Man remove?
That instant, I declare, he has my Love:
I shun his Zenith, court his mild Decline;
Thus Sommers once, and Halifax were mine.
Oft in the clear, still Mirrour of Retreat,
I study'd Shrewsbury, the wise and great:
Carleton's calm Sense, and Stanhope's noble Flame,
Compar'd, and knew their gen'rous End the same;
How pleasing Atterbury's softer hour!
How shin'd the Soul, unconquer'd in the Tow'r!
How can I Pult'ney, Chesterfield forget,
While *Roman* Spirit charms, and *Attic* Wit:
Argyle, the State's whole Thunder born to wield,
And shake alike the Senate and the Field:
Or Wyndham, just to Freedom and the Throne,
The Master of our Passions, and his own.
Names, which I long have lov'd, nor lov'd in vain,
Rank'd with their Friends, not number'd with their Train;
And if yet higher the proud List should end,
Still let me say! No Follower, but a Friend.[1]

If today we recognize that proud list ending in no one more eminent than 'Poor Fred', who proved so ineffectual a Prince of Wales, we should recall that when Pope wrote those lines Prince Frederick was regarded as the nation's best hope and in Bolingbroke's eyes was the very image of a Patriot King. The Prince, who lived at Kew Palace, was a neighbour of Pope's, and their friendship was cemented by the gift from Pope of one of the puppies of Bounce, his great Dane. The puppy was accompanied by a collar on which Pope had had engraved a motto that seemed to epitomize the contemporary political situation under Sir Robert Walpole:

[1] *Epilogue to the Satires*, II, 74–93.

I am his Highness' Dog at Kew;
Pray tell me Sir, whose Dog are you?

Intellectual and social success of such an order might well be enough to turn a man's head, and it is not surprising that Pope should exhibit some measure of self-esteem. In him self-esteem did not take its ugliest forms. He was never addicted to ostentation; on the contrary, his manner of life seems to have been studiously modest: Lord Orrery, who frequently visited him, reports that he 'treated his friends with a politeness that charmed, and a generosity that was much to his honour. Every guest was made happy within his doors. Pleasure dwelt under his roof and elegance presided at his table'.[1] It was never reported of him that he cut an old but humble friend, or behaved with an air of offensive patronage towards modest worth, and he never forsook a friend in disgrace: his behaviour to Oxford and Atterbury when imprisoned in the Tower shows him as the sort of friend that any man in distress would wish to have. No, his self-esteem took more innocent forms. Thus he was quite convinced that his poetry had achieved a classical status, and he behaved towards it in a way that I cannot recall any other poet behaving. Other poets, like Hopkins and Mr Eliot, have written notes to their poetry, and others, like Spenser, have engaged a friend to write a commentary; but perhaps no other poet but Pope has printed a selection of discarded readings from manuscript and printed editions of poems no more than two years old. Furthermore, a few years before his death he had surrendered himself to an editor, secure (it would seem) of his matriculation amongst the Ancients: and he caused the following announcement to be printed in the revised version of *The Dunciad*:

Speedily will be publish'd,
In the same Paper, and Character, to be bound up with this,
The ESSAY ON MAN, the ESSAY ON CRITICISM,
And the rest of the Author's Original Poems,
With the commentaries and notes of
W. Warburton, A.M.

'You must be the vainest man alive', said Lord Marchmont to Pope on this occasion; 'you must want to show posterity what a quantity of dullness you can carry down on your back without sinking under the load.'

Yet in spite of this evidence, Pope affected to slight his poetical achievements. He wrote to Aaron Hill in 1731:

[1] *Remarks on the Life and Writings of Dr Jonathan Swift*, fifth edition, 1752, p. 158.

> I only wish you knew, as well as I do, how much I prefer Qualities of the Heart to those of the Head: I vow to God, I never thought any great Matters of my poetical Capacity; I only thought it a little better, comparatively, than that of some very mean Writers, who are too proud.[1]

To this Hill replied:

> I am sorry to hear you say, you never thought any great Matters of your *Poetry*.—It is, in my Opinion, the Characteristic you are to hope your *Distinction* from: To be *Honest* is the Duty of every *plain Man*! Nor, since the *Soul* of Poetry is Sentiment, can a *Great Poet* want *Morality*. But your *Honesty* you possess with a *Million*, who will never be *remembered*; whereas your *Poetry* is a Peculiar, that will make it impossible, you should be forgotten.[2]

Pope deserved the rebuke; but it was a rebuke that was difficult to take amiss, and he was content to reply that though his poetical talent was all that might make him remembered, it was his morality only that would make him beloved and happy. This was the idea of himself into which he had grown over the years. His earlier notion of his own character had baffled him. In 1713 he told Caryll that every hour of his life his mind was strangely diverted, one moment above the stars, with a thousand systems round about him, looking forward into the vast abyss of eternity, the next below all trifles, 'even grovelling with Tidcombe in the very center of nonsense':

> Good God! [he reflects] what an Incongruous Animal is Man? how unsettled in his best part, his soul; and how changing and variable in his frame of body? The constancy of the one, shook by every notion, the temperament of the other, affected by every blast of wind. What an April weather in the mind! In a word, what is Man altogether, but one mighty inconsistency.[3]

The kaleidoscopic nature of his personality in these early years is delightfully illustrated from a passage in a letter to his friend, Patty Blount:

> Every one values Mr Pope, but every one for a different reason. One for his firm adherence to the Catholic Faith, another for his Neglect of Popish Superstition, one for his grave behavior, another for his Whymsicalness. Mr Tydcomb for his pretty Atheistical Jests, Mr Caryll for his moral and christian Sentences, Mrs Teresa for his Reflections on Mrs Patty, and Mrs Patty for his Reflections on Mrs Teresa.[4]

[1] *Correspondence*, III, 166. [2] Ibid., III, 168. [3] Ibid., I, 185–6. [4] Ibid., I, 269.

But sobriety was to win the day. In so far as anyone can resolve what character he will choose to exhibit to the world, Pope had resolved upon the character of the Good Man. He cannot be shown in the act of trying on this character, as we can see Boswell in his London Journal deciding to adopt 'Mr Addison's character in sentiment, mixed with a little of the gaiety of Sir Richard Steele and the manners of Mr Digges'; but there can be little doubt that Pope designed the publication of his letters to exhibit this view of the dutiful son, the kind-thoughted friend, the well-bred host, the disinterested critic of society, yet warm in wishes for his country's good and patient under attack: in short, the man of plain living, high thinking and unimpeachable integrity. This is the view of himself that he discovered in his letters as he reread them, rather than the view that he designedly wrote into them. Not every critic of Pope in his own day or since has been able to see him in this light; and when allowance has been made for contemporary malice and subsequent prejudice, it must be admitted that his moral character was not perfect. He can be convicted of equivocation and of devious dealing; and though he was slow in replying to attacks, and not infrequently forgave the injuries done him, he hit harder than perhaps his profession as a Christian permitted; he hit hard, but deftly, in an age of hard hitting.

But though I think that his moral character has been unduly impugned, it is not my present purpose to defend it. Of greater interest is his employment of the character he had chosen. He had decided that goodness should be the profession of his mature years just as he had decided that wit was to be the profession of his youth. Doubtless he was aware from time to time that he did not always succeed in living up to his profession, just as a Christian is aware of committing sin; but either he had lived so long with his *persona* that he failed to recognize the mask he carried, or he was unable to abandon what had become the inspiration of his poetry.

He was as much accustomed as his friend Swift to the use of a *persona* in his writings. He had taught himself to write by imitating the styles of different masters, and most of his earliest surviving verses bear witness to this habit: 'Of a Lady singing to her lute; in imitation of Waller', for example, or 'To the author of a Poem intitled Successio, in imitation of the Earl of Dorset'; and though the famous 'Ode on Solitude' bears no similar subtitle, it is clearly intended as an exercise in the manner of Cowley on the popular theme of 'The Happy Man'. No one is misled by these straightforward adoptions of a poetic *persona*, and of others equally straightforward in such poems as 'Eloisa to Abelard' and 'The Dying Christian to his Soul'. But beginning with the 'Epistle to Miss Blount with the Works of Voiture', which probably belongs to the year 1710, and continuing in some later verse epistles, that 'to Miss Blount, on her leaving the Town, after the Coronation' (1714), 'to Mr Jervas, with Dryden's Translations of Fresnoy's Art of Painting' (1715), 'to Mr Gay' (1720), the noble epistle to the Earl of Oxford, with the poems of Parnell (1722) and the affectionate verses 'To Mrs M. B. on her Birthday' (1723)—in all these poems there is evident a *persona* that is clearly intended to resemble the features of the historical Alexander Pope. Accustomed as he was to model himself upon verse precedent, it is not unlikely that Pope had his models here, too; and they are not far to seek. There were the urbane verse epistles of Dryden to Sir Godfrey Kneller and to his 'dear friend Mr Congreve'; and behind Dryden was the urbanity of Horace. In learning to adjust his features to the mask of Horace, Pope discovered a set of countenance and a manner of behaviour that he felt suited him best of all; the April weather of his mind was allowed to settle at last into an Horatian midsummer. Early eighteenth-century society dictated its own modifications of the Horatian pattern. The predominant masculinity of Dryden's and Horace's epistles were not altogether suited to a society where women had begun to take a more prominent place. But *The Tatler* and the letters of Voiture served to teach Pope how to 'fair sex' it, to add that touch of gallantry required. And how successfully the lesson was learned!

But, Madam, if the Fates withstand, and you
Are destined *Hymen*'s willing Victim too;
Trust not too much your now resistless Charms,
Those, Age or Sickness, soon or late, disarms;
Good Humour only teaches Charms to last,
Still makes new Conquests, and maintains the past:
Love, rais'd on Beauty, will like That decay,
Our Hearts may bear its slender Chain a Day,
As flowry Bands in Wantonness are worn;
A Morning's Pleasure, and at Evening torn:
This binds in Ties more easie, yet more strong,
The willing Heart, and only holds it long.
Thus *Voiture*'s early Care still shone the same,
And *Monthausier* was only chang'd in Name:
By this, ev'n now they live, ev'n now they charm,
Their Wit still sparkling, and their Flames still warm.

Now crown'd with Myrtle, on th' *Elysian* Coast,
Amid those Lovers, joys his gentle Ghost,
Pleas'd while with Smiles his happy Lines you view,
And finds a fairer *Ramboüillet* in you.
The brightest Eyes of *France* inspir'd his Muse,
The brightest Eyes of *Britain* now peruse,
And dead as living, 'tis our Author's Pride,
Still to charm those who charm the World beside.[1]

That is the tone he had already learned to use in 1710, at the age of twenty-three, learned it, before *The Spectator* could have taught it him, to apply two years later in the greatest poem of his juvenilia, *The Rape of the Lock*.

We may watch the features settling both in Pope's letters and in his poems. The reason why the process can be watched in his poetry is that as time went on he conducted an ever-deepening exploration of his personality. His first massively personal intrusion into his own poetry is in 'The Farewell to London' (1715), where 'the gayest valetudinaire, most thinking rake alive' sees himself against the background of a gay society frequenting theatres and coffee-houses; and from 1730 onwards there are few of his poems in which the poet himself does not take up a prominent position. The *Moral Essays* are one and all conceived as verse epistles, and the same is true of the *Imitations of Horace*, while the presence of an interlocutor in the epistles to Bathurst and Arbuthnot and in the *Epilogue to the Satires*, with their snatches of dialogue, emphasize even more strongly the poet's presence. The *Essay on Man*, too, is framed within the addresses to Bolingbroke that open and close the poem. These addresses pay Bolingbroke the highest of compliments, but they are so arranged that we should see his associate also. That attractive picture of the two friends setting out on their shooting expedition:

Together let us beat this ample field,
Try what the open, what the covert yield!
The latent tracts, the giddy heights explore
Of all who blindly creep, or sightless soar;
Eye Nature's walks, shoot Folly as it flies,
And catch the Manners living as they rise:
Laugh where we must, be candid where we can;
But vindicate the ways of God to Man—

[1] *Epistle to Miss Blount, With the Works of Voiture*, ll. 57–80.

What purpose does the picture serve but to define the elegant yet easy spirit of debate in which the discussion will be conducted? It will be found on examination that every other personal intrusion of the poet into these later poems, whether he be conversing with friends in his grotto in the first *Imitation of Horace* or offering them hospitality at Twickenham in the second, or the scene of domestic irritation with which the *Epistle of Arbuthnot* opens or the deliberately contrasting scene of domestic calm at his mother's death-bed with which it closes—each is designed to control the mood of the poem, and to win the reader to the poet's point of view.

A wide assortment of factors have combined to produce this very personal poetry of Pope's maturity. Since 1711 he had been the victim of unremitting attacks that libelled both his moral character and his personal appearance. 'If I am not like that,' he seems to have asked himself, 'what am I like?' And he set himself to correct the libels, encouraged by that sense of self-esteem which fed upon his early success and helped to determine what character he would choose to exhibit to the world, not only in verse, but on the canvasses of numerous portrait-painters and in the busts of Roubiliac and other sculptors, whose work he seems to have directed with attentive care. Then, too, he had the example of Horace before him, and a lifetime's practice in poetical imitation which makes it second nature to adopt a *persona*, as well as the inheritance of a hundred years of experiment in the Theophrastan character sketch; and finally, perhaps, at some level of consciousness there was the recognition that the personality that charmed such a wide circle of friends could be harnessed to his verse to charm an even wider circle of readers.

And where in all this is the real man? Professor Maynard Mack, in an essay called 'The Muse of Sature',[1] has shown how closely modelled the poet's *persona* is upon the traditional figure of the satirist. Yet at the same time it is possible to annotate each incident from the satires and show its derivation from the poet's own biography. We are presented with a peculiar blending of the artifact and the real, one of the strangest confusions of life and letters. So accustomed had he become to this blend that Pope himself may not have known how precisely to distinguish the historical portrait from the literary one. That is the enigma that a study of his life and writings offers.

[1] *The Yale Review*, XLI (1951), 80–92.

Speculations on Three Eighteenth-Century Prose Writers

D. W. JEFFERSON

THE question that forms the topic of this essay is whether some eighteenth-century prose writers may have been so saturated with the Augustan style that it became the instrument not only of conscious artistic purpose but also of more or less unconscious idiosyncrasy. In some of the passages to be considered here style seems almost to be having a game of its own. The game, of course, is the author's but it is uncertain how he would have accounted for it. Where a gap of two centuries lies between the author's intention, whatever it was, and the reader's impression, speculations of this kind need to be rather tentative, and the following examples are offered in this spirit.

The works chosen for illustration are by Smollett, Goldsmith and Johnson. They belong to the 1750s and 1760s, a period of ripeness in prose when certain Augustan features had become thoroughly established and the accepted idiom was being used with an habitual facility that might well offer scope for personality to betray itself. It is impossible, of course, to distinguish absolutely between deliberate and unconscious uses of convention. Smollett's habit of applying an Augustan surface to all kinds of situation, impartially maintaining his urbanity through scenes of horseplay and of serious sentiment, could be viewed simply as an example of conscious fidelity to the civilized code. The measured distance from actuality imposed by the style is the expression of a fastidious sense of order which contrasts effectively with his taste for so much that is rank and pungent in the subject-matter. This is Augustanism *par excellence*, but do we not sense an element of temperamental idiosyncrasy, something obsessive, in the unflagging consistency with which it is sustained? The more the style can include and subdue, the more agreeable is our impression of an all-presiding decorum; but, paradoxically, the sense of congruity may, by a change of stress, be one also of incongruity. Our entertainment may lie in the variety and juxtaposition of effects encompassed within the imperturbable unity of the treatment.

Ferdinand Count Fathom provides a curious example. In most important respects this is an unsatisfactory novel, its near-tragic themes of wickedness, suffering and repentance being quite beyond Smollett's range. The plot is tediously complicated and the characters uninteresting. Precisely because of these faults the relative success of the style is worth examining. As a narrative, conducted with his characteristic briskness and steadiness of pace, and moulded to an Augustan shapeliness in the details, *Fathom* achieves surprising readability. It is by the sheer verbal life of the book that, in spite of everything, we are beguiled. When we read of Melvil that 'he repaired to the house of the generous Jew, whose rheum distilled very plentifully at his approach',[1] or that Monimia's 'sustenance was scarcely such as exempted her from the guilt of being accessory to her own death; her drink was the simple element',[2] we are pleased with the diction for its own sake, or, rather, as an expression of something in Smollett's temperament. The passage which illustrates most strikingly his inveterate augustanizing is the 'Gothic' episode of Melvil's vigil at the tomb of Monimia, during which he is confronted with what seems to be the apparition of Monimia but is actually her living presence. At the moment of her appearance, Melvil 'gazed with a look, through which his soul seemed eager to escape', and, at the sight of her features, 'seemingly improved with new celestial graces, the youth became a statue, expressing amazement, love, and awful adoration'.[3] The encounter, in fact, is handled with a proper solemnity; but, without a change of idiom, Smollett can step down from this to the level of the scene that follows, where Melvil profusely kisses Monimia, and Madam Clement, seeing her blushes, interposes with her pleasantries:

[1] Ch. LXII. All quotations are from first editions.
[2] Ch. LXIX. [3] Ch. LXIII.

> In the midst of these ejaculations, he ravished a banquet from her glowing lips, that kindled in his heart a flame, which rushed thro' every vein, and glided to his marrow: this was a privilege he had never claimed before, and now permitted as a recompense for all the penance he had suffered; nevertheless, the cheeks of Monimia, who was altogether unaccustomed to such familiarities, underwent a total suffusion; and Madame Clement discreetly relieved her from the anxiety of her situation, by interfering in the discourse, and rallying the count upon his endeavours to monopolize such a branch of happiness.[1]

The good faith and indeed fervour with which the elevated diction is applied give a kind of purity and distinction to the extravagance. The reader can have it both ways, treasuring the style while enjoying the absurdity. Even more felicitously absurd is the sequel in which the reverend gentleman who has assisted in the benevolent subterfuge resulting in Monimia's restoration now lays on light refreshments:

> The letter having so effectually answered their warmest hopes, in bringing back Renaldo such a pattern of constancy and love; the confederates, in consequence of his enthusiastic sorrow, had planned this meeting, as the most interesting way of restoring two virtuous lovers to the arms of each other; for which purpose the good clergyman had pitched upon his own church, and indulged them with the use of the vestry, in which they now were presented with a small but elegant collation.[2]

The whole episode is a monument to the Augustan sense of accommodation. Melancholy meditations in a church, a mysterious apparition, a rapturous reunion of lovers, are the main ingredients in a composition which requires also politeness, good humour and food. With Smollett's language all this is negotiated with perfect ease and aplomb.

Goldsmith has much in common with Smollett. A master of the Augustan style, he is so completely at home with its forms and amenities that, while he is deliberately making use of them, he also expresses himself through them in a manner that can hardly have been calculated. In the following passage from *An Inquiry into the Present State of Polite Learning* the diction is alive with witty and elegant antitheses:

> The French nobility have certainly a most pleasing way of satisfying the vanity of an author, without indulging his avarice. A man of literary merit, is sure of being caressed by the Great, though seldom enriched. His pension from the crown just supplies half a competence, and the sale

[1] Ch. LXIII. [2] Ch. LXIV.

> of his labours makes some small addition to his circumstances; thus the author leads a life of splendid poverty, and seldom becomes wealthy or indolent enough, to discontinue an exertion of those abilities, by which he rose. With the English, it is different; our writers of rising merit are generally neglected; while the few of an established reputation, are overpaid by luxurious affluence. The first encounter every hardship which generally attends upon aspiring indigence; the latter enjoy the vulgar, and, perhaps the more prudent satisfaction, of putting riches in competition with fame. Those are often seen to spend their youth in want and obscurity; these are sometimes found to lead an old age of indolence and avarice.[1]

But what was probably not foreseen by Goldsmith is the slightly puppet-like effect, produced by the bright little phrases—'splendid poverty', 'luxurious affluence', 'aspiring indigence', 'indolence and avarice'—which define so engagingly the ways of life open to authors. Goldsmith had an idiosyncratic liking for neatness and small-scale effects. In another place[2] I have tried to show that the art of *The Vicar of Wakefield* consists in a reduction of scale of the conventional components, including even feelings and values, and that this is partly the effect of neatness and precision in the handling of the diction.

The Vicar's sermon preached to his fellow prisoners raises a question of artistic intention in one or two places. The fact that it is generally Augustan in style, and that many of his hearers were ignorant felons, need not occupy us: a sermon in a novel was a set piece, governed by non-realistic conventions. But certain phrases are peculiarly Augustan:

> The Author of our religion everywhere professes himself the wretch's friend ...
>
> No vain efforts of a refined imagination can soothe the wants of nature, can give elastic sweetness to the dank vapour of a dungeon ...
>
> ... those shackles that tyranny has imposed, or crime made necessary[3] ...

Was the smooth urbanity intended as an amiable limitation in the Vicar? This is unlikely. The sermon as a whole is a perfectly serious discourse on faith in adversity. To have tampered in this way with the idiom would have been in poor taste, and the result does not give the impression of tampering. It seems more probable that Goldsmith, though he intends the Vicar to be comic and lightweight in some respects, expresses unconsciously a good deal of his own temperament through

[1] Ch. VII.

[2] 'Observations on the *Vicar of Wakefield*,' *Cambridge Journal*, July 1950.

[3] Ch. XXIX.

him, and that these turns of phrase reflect the almost too easy poise of his Augustanism.

Johnson is a much more interesting case than Smollett and Goldsmith and very different. To follow the play of temperament, in its relation to what one takes to be conscious intention, over his work as a whole would be a large task. *Rasselas* will provide us with examples in sufficient abundance for our present purpose.

Johnson, though one of the greatest and most entertaining of English prose writers, habitually gives the impression—it is part of his charm, when one comes to know him—of having embarked on some literary task for which he is not naturally fitted, and of being obliged to apply his somewhat heavy equipment to materials calling for a lighter and more varied prose. What business, many readers may have asked, has a writer like Johnson with prose narrative? In *Rasselas* his style is more than usually generalized, partly because he chose as the scene of the story a remote world, the social customs of which are largely left unspecified. Portrayal of manners in any local and particular sense is out of the question. A vaguely exotic note is conveyed by rhetorical phrasing and by a use of amplification which keeps the pace of both speech and narrative remarkably slow and distends the generalized effect. The reader who has not come to terms with Johnson may be rather dismayed by sentences like the following:

> In the morning they found some shepherds in the field, who set milk and fruits before them.[1]
>
> As they advanced, they heard the sound of musick, and saw youths and virgins dancing in the grove .. [2]
>
> ... revelry and merriment was the business of every hour from the dawn of morning to the close of even.[3]

The rhetorical insistence, in the last sentence, on the stretch of time so employed only calls attention to the vagueness of the pleasures. Earlier in the chapter we were told that in the happy valley 'the sons and daughters of Abissinia ... [were] gratified with whatever the senses can enjoy'; but it seems to be a convention of *Rasselas* that we accept such expressions as mere words. It seems clear, from Chapter XVII and elsewhere, that Rasselas, during his sojourn in the happy valley, had not been a sensualist, but we are given no idea of where he drew the line. If the sentences quoted above were taken literally we should have to imagine a state of limitless opportunity for every kind of indulgence;

[1] Ch. XV. [2] Ch. XX. [3] Ch. II.

but we need not analyse the implications of this situation. What we are asked to accept here is simply a rhetorical formulation which, on scrutiny, would not render a meaning. It is when we have schooled ourselves to accept *Rasselas* on this level that the pleasant surprises come. In the account of the special entertainments provided for the Emperor's annual visit we read:

> Every desire was immediately granted. All the artificers of pleasure were called to gladden the festivity; the musicians exerted the power of harmony, and the dancers showed their activity before the princes, in hope that they should pass their lives in this blisful captivity, to which these only were admitted whose performance was thought able to add novelty to luxury. Such was the appearance of security and delight which this retirement afforded, that they to whom it was new always desired that it might be perpetual; and as those, on whom the ivory gate had once closed, were never suffered to return, the effect of longer experience could not be known.[1]

The first sentence is a gesture in the style already noted. But with the Augustan blandness of 'blisful captivity' a change occurs, and the rest of the sentence is a good example of Johnson's habit of withholding expressiveness from a statement which, if the reader himself applies a little pressure, is rewarding enough. Without departing from the ceremonious idiom, which seems so well adapted to the cushioning of realities, he can convey an ominous sense of what goes on beneath the cushioning way of life in the happy valley. The intensity of the competition to get in reflects the intensity of the need of those already there to add something new to lives long wearied with having everything. Details would spoil such a conception. The following description (in Chapter XVII) of Rasselas' brief experiment with gay companions has a touch of the virtuoso. Johnson can afford a rather jejune opening and a conventional, generalized moral vocabulary:

> 'Youth, cried he, is the time of gladness: I will join myself to the young men, whose only business is to gratify their desires, and whose time is all spent in a succession of enjoyments.' [It is here that one might ask, were the convention of the book other than it is, what Rasselas has been doing, or avoiding, during his years in the happy valley!] To such societies he was readily admitted, but a few days brought him back weary and disgusted. Their mirth was without images, their laughter without motive; their pleasures were gross and sensual, in which the mind had no part; their conduct was at once wild and mean; they laughed at order

[1] Ch. I.

and at law, but the frown of power dejected, and the eye of wisdom abashed them.[1]

The devastating phrase, 'at once wild and mean', suffices to give distinction to the simple, unexciting integrity of the rest. Every now and again, the wit of a Rochefoucauld is present to flavour Johnson's observations:

> We are long before we are convinced that happiness is never to be found, and each believes it possessed by others, to keep alive the hope of obtaining it for himself.[2]

But he never forces his wit, and one learns to value the passages where it does not occur. There is an air of solemn good faith in every passage of Johnson: the truth, presented with dignity and decency, is his concern, and entertainment is seldom an object in itself. Not every statement lends itself to a sharpening of edge or a hint of deeper implications. Even at his most frugal Johnson can please; he can offer simple fare with propriety. As we have seen, there are places where he shows indifference to, or unawareness of, the common craving for a touch of detail or colour or novelty; but if we are to regard this as a pardonable (almost acceptable) ineptness, there are places where a bald general statement has the unexpected charm of a fine stroke of style. Imlac's wording of the most obvious fact about the Pyramids—that they are 'one of the most bulky works of manual industry'[3]—is memorable.

How far was Johnson aware of the comic element in *Rasselas*? The episode of the projector who experiments with flying is certainly intended to be amusing at one level at least. He is deluded and overconfident, and his attempts end in sorry failure; there are many such examples in the story of the general inability of human beings to live up to their pretensions. But his speeches, apart from the errors they contain and their note of ill-founded confidence, are surely not intended to be comic, since he expresses himself in the same idiom as the other characters. Yet the effect is entertaining, as if Johnson, like a Ben Jonson, had specially designed the diction as a vehicle for eccentricity and obsession:

> I have long been of opinion, that instead of the tardy conveyance of ships and chariots, man might use the swifter migration of wings; that the fields of air are open to knowledge and that only ignorance and idleness need crawl upon the ground.

[1] Ch. XVII. [2] Ch. XVI. [3] Ch. XXIX.

> He that can swim needs not despair to fly: to swim is to fly in a grosser fluid, and to fly is to swim in a subtler.
>
> I have considered the structure of all volant animals, and find the folding continuity of the bat's wings most easily accommodated to the human form. [1]

If Johnson had actually intended it to be entertaining, he would have differentiated the idiom more sharply from that of Rasselas, who converses with the projector:

> ... I have been told, that respiration is difficult upon lofty mountains, yet from these precipices, though so high as to produce great tenuity of air, it is very easy to fall ...

In making all his characters talk the same Johnsonian language he does, in fact, provide the ideal vehicle for learned folly as for wisdom, but he can hardly have known that the erudite vocabulary and fastidious phrasing would so enhance the comic effect: the flavour is too near to that of passages that have no absurd element. The point perhaps is that, though a great difference exists between Johnsonian wisdom and the crazy reasoning of such characters, both have a sublime earnestness. By endowing the projector with his own meticulous and stately habits of speech, Johnson lends a touch of distinction to his aberration, and this provides a gratuitous element of entertainment.

The same effect occurs more strikingly in the episode of the astronomer who declares his conviction that he has been entrusted with the organization of the weather. He expresses this hallucination in language that has both grandeur and elegance to a remarkable degree:

> ... I have possessed for five years the regulation of the weather, and the distribution of the seasons: the sun has listened to my dictates, and passed from tropick to tropick by my direction; the clouds, at my call, have poured their waters, and the Nile has overflowed at my command; *I have restrained the rage of the dog-star, and mitigated the fervours of the crab* ... [2] [Italics mine].

The italicized sentence is for me one of the most exquisitely amusing in English literature. Another kind of appropriateness may be seen in the use of this dignified diction in the astronomer's speeches. Johnson presents him as an entirely worthy person, capable of being cured of his delusion. With the help of Pekuah and others, who approach him with solemn and delicate respect, he gradually returns to a sound

[1] Ch. VI. [2] Ch. XL.

state of mind. It is characteristic that the Johnsonian language, which gives a quintessential flavour to the poor man's eccentricity, should also give nobility to the episode as a whole.

The idiosyncratic quality of Johnson's prose is partly due to the mixed character of his aims, to the unexpected way in which different sides of his personality are stylistically fused or juxtaposed. He is very much the polite Augustan: no one can be more polished or urbane than Johnson, when he so chooses; but as the lexicographer, he can be a fanatic in his dealings with words. He is the most austere of moralists, but also a wit and a pillar of good sense. Severity with charm, heaviness with ease, quaint erudition with elegance: these are the mixed effects that continually confront us in his work. Whatever Johnson thought of the various ingredients in his character and literary equipment, and of the ways in which they might come together, we can perhaps take it that the particular combination that gives us pleasure is unstudied. Great care goes into the refinement of each of the components; the blend of the components gives the unconscious style of the personality. It is a personality in which contrasting elements sometimes seem to be having a game with each other, a game which may go on at moments when Johnson would appear to be concerned with something quite straightforward.

One of the contradictions in Johnson to which his style gives expression is between moral sobriety and a taste for the more formidable and portentous possibilities of moral situations. Passages of reflection are liable to move surprisingly from the moderate to the extreme. For example, in the passage where Imlac confesses that he is 'less unhappy' than others because he has a mind 'replete with images', which he can 'vary and combine with pleasure' (could anything be more coolly Lockean?), he concludes with a disconcerting description of the less fortunately equipped inhabitants of the valley:

> The rest, whose minds have no impression but of the present moment, are either corroded by malignant passions, or sit stupid in the gloom of perpetual vacancy.[1]

Monks, having their time 'regularly distributed', are not 'left open to the distraction of unguided choice, nor lost in the shades of listless inactivity'.[2] In the princess's speech about the perils of a single life, insight into real evils is mingled with a Johnsonian rage for extremes:

[1] Ch. XII. [2] Ch. XLVII.

... They are peevish at home, and malevolent abroad; and, as the out-laws of human nature, make it their business and their pleasure to disturb that society which debars them from its privileges.[1]

The reader of *Rasselas* reconciles himself readily to what would be deprivation, were the compensatory virtues of the work not so considerable. He does not look for effective narrative as such; but occasionally he is pulled up by some passage in which this very style, apparently so inappropriate for story-telling, is actually instrumental in producing an effect unexpectedly relevant to narrative art. The little episode where Rasselas is seized with a compulsive need to exert himself violently owes its success to the unruffled stateliness of the language. The incident is unnerving in what it reveals of the stagnation and desperation of Rasselas's existence, but the narrator conveys no sense of shock in his meticulously worded account. It seems to be a case of artistic contrast between the event and the style of the telling;

> One day, as he was sitting on a bank, he feigned to himself an orphan virgin robbed of her little portion by a treacherous lover, and crying after him for restitution and redress. So strongly was the image impressed upon his mind, that he started up in the maid's defence, and ran forward to seize the plunderer with all the eagerness of real persuit. Fear naturally quickens the flight of guilt. Rasselas could not catch the fugitive with his utmost efforts; but, resolving to weary, by perseverance, him whom he could not surpass in speed, he pressed on till the foot of the mountain stopped his course.
>
> Here he recollected himself, and smiled at his own useless impetuosity ... [2]

This is one way of reading the passage, but perhaps there are others. *Rasselas* is a romance; extreme ignorance of the world and of life is one of the central characteristics of its hero; and his being carried away to such an extent by his delusion could be regarded as the sign of an imagination too fresh to have begun to suspect its own operations. His complete submission to the spell could be regarded then as engaging and mildly amusing. Or again the passage could be regarded as, among other things, an example of Johnson's literary courtesy. He handles the imaginary adventure almost as if it were a real act of romantic intervention. The prince, though a prey to vain imaginings, has the thoughts of a hero, and acts with real ardour, and when he comes to himself he is not ridiculous. The passage is good from a

[1] Ch. xxvi. [2] Ch. iv.

number of possible viewpoints which do not altogether exclude one another, but which involve differences of stress. I do not know, as one always knows with Fielding and Gibbon, in what way it was intended to succeed. It is difficult to say what Johnson thought of his style, as a vehicle for narrative, or whether he was aware of its having a distinctive function in this case.

Similar ambiguities arise in the charming scene where Imlac, *à propos* of the deluded astronomer, dwells upon the common human tendency to be a victim of imagination; and his hearers solemnly confess their own private fantasies and renounce them. It is possible to regard this as morally impressive. How admirable that they should recognize themselves as sharing, if only superficially, in the weakness of the man to whom they are to extend their friendship, and who is to recover his grasp of reality through their help! The Johnsonian manner serves to give a civilized quality to their disclosures, and a fine effect of surprise is achieved by the dignified precision with which Pekuah begins to formulate hers, as soon as Imlac's discourse is over:

> 'I will no more', said the favourite, 'imagine myself the queen of Abissinia ... '[1]

The queen's description of day-dreams in which she plays the role of a shepherdess is more openly amusing: a good opportunity for Johnson to indulge in a refined mixture of prettiness and silliness that suited his humour. The question is whether these speeches were all primarily designed to be taken more lightly than I have suggested. It may be that, by the mere operation of the Johnsonian manner, as a force in itself, a vehicle of rectitude and candour, the speakers sound a finer note than their creator realized. There is no doubt that the scene as a whole was intended to contain both humour and moral seriousness, but the blend that Johnson achieved is especially attractive and has the appearance of being unstudied.

[1] Ch. XLIII.

Sterne and Painting

R. F. BRISSENDEN

'While Images reflect from Art to Art.'
ALEXANDER POPE: *To Mr. Jervas, with Fresnoy's Art of Painting, translated by Mr. Dryden*

I

'BOOKS, painting, fiddling, and shooting were my amusements', declared Sterne in the memoir of his life and family which he prepared for his daughter Lydia. Since the first volumes of *Tristram Shandy* made their appearance the books with which their author amused himself have aroused the curiosity and attention of his readers. The other pursuits he mentions have, not surprisingly, attracted less notice. There exists, however, a significant relationship between Sterne's interest in painting and his peculiar qualities as a writer; and it is rewarding to bear this in mind when examining his work. It becomes apparent, for instance, that his technique as a novelist benefited from his experience as an amateur artist; and at the same time an investigation of his treatment of various theoretical studies of painting, well known in the eighteenth century, illuminates the philosophical bases of his satire: it reveals, in particular, a remarkable similarity between some of his own ideas and methods and those of William Hogarth.

Even if biographical evidence were not available a reading of

Sterne's published works–including the *Sermons*–would be enough to demonstrate that he was unusually well acquainted with both the theory and the practice of painting. He often uses the language of the artist, speaking of strokes, tints, outlines, attitudes, lights, keeping, colouring and design with the fluency and assurance of one who knows exactly what such terms mean. This is most obvious, perhaps, in his treatment of character. He does not, in general, give detailed physical descriptions of people, but when he speaks of 'drawing' a character he uses the phrase with deliberate precision. His statement of the method he has employed in presenting Uncle Toby is typical:

> I was just going ... to have given you the great out-lines of my uncle *Toby*'s most whimsical character;—when my aunt *Dinah* and the coachman came a-cross us ... Notwithstanding all this, you perceive the drawing of my uncle *Toby*'s character went on gently all the time; —not the great contours of it ... —but some familiar strokes and faint designations of it, were here and there touch'd in, as we went along ... (I, XXII).

Here, as in his account of his dedication—'it is far from being a gross piece of daubing ... the design, your Lordship sees, is good, the colouring transparent,—the drawing not amiss' (I, IX)—Sterne's main concern is not to create a visual effect but to play with a fashionable jargon. Yet he is capable of achieving such effects, of making the reader 'see' what he is describing; and in *Tristram Shandy* these effects can sometimes be rather extraordinary. There are a number of episodes—Trim reading the sermon, Slop falling off his horse, Walter struggling for his handkerchief or lying grief-stricken on his bed—in which figures are presented in formally posed and minutely described attitudes. Although the primary purpose of these scenes is satiric, they have a strange, hallucinatory vividness and clarity. There is something almost cinematic about the slow-motion with which Slop meets Obadiah and tumbles in the mud, or the exaggerated close-up in which we are shown Walter's recumbent figure or, more alarmingly, Mrs Shandy's eye, that 'thin, blue, chill, pellucid chrystal with all its humours so at rest, that the least mote or speck of desire might have been seen at the bottom of it, had it existed' (IX, I). And in the account of the delivery of the sermon it is as if Sterne has stopped his film completely for a moment in order to describe Trim's attitude. It is all very deliberately done: Trim stands

> with his body swayed, and bent forwards just so far, as to make an angle of 85 degrees and a half upon the plain of the horizon ... his right-leg

> firm under him, sustaining seven-eighths of his whole weight,—the foot of his left-leg ... advanced a little ... his right arm falling negligently by his side, as nature and the laws of gravity order'd it ... (II, XVII).

The effect on the reader of such descriptions is to make him suddenly and almost uncomfortably conscious of Trim, Walter, or Dr Slop as physical objects merely, rather than as people. Painters and sculptors must sometimes contemplate their subjects in this way—so must anatomists and engineers. In such scenes Sterne is clearly interested both in the formal pictorial values of his 'composition' and in the physical relationships whch govern the disposition of the objects that come within its boundaries. When, for example, Walter throws himself 'prostrate across his bed' he is, like a statue or a figure in a painting, in 'the most lamentable attitude of a man borne down with sorrows'. But the explanation of the attitude is severely anatomical:

> The palm of his right hand ... receiving his forehead, and covering the greatest part of both his eyes, gently sunk down with his head (his elbow giving way backwards) till his nose touch'd the quilt ... —his right leg (his left being drawn up towards his body) hung half over the side of the bed ... (III, XXIX).

There is an air of premeditated comic exaggeration to such scenes which is quite absent from the episodes in *A Sentimental Journey*. A major reason for this is that in *Tristram Shandy* Sterne, though obviously making some attempt to achieve through the medium of language something analogous to what the artist attains through the use of paint, is mainly interested in satirizing and parodying some of the conventional aesthetic theories of the day. In *A Sentimental Journey*, however, this particular satiric motive does not operate: as a result the work has a visual coherence, a consistent, though muted, pictorial quality which is one of its unique charms.

One has only to examine a typical scene, such as the encounter with the monk at Calais, to realize how much Sterne's mode of rendering what he sees has been conditioned by his experience both of painting pictures and of looking at them. Much of the delicate power of the description comes from the painterly precision with which the Franciscan is observed:

> It was one of those heads, which Guido has often painted—mild, pale —penetrating, free from all common-place ideas of fat contented ignorance looking downwards upon the earth—it look'd forwards; but look'd, as if it look'd at something beyond this world ...

> The rest of his outline may be given in a few strokes; one might put it into the hands of any one to design; for 'twas neither elegant or otherwise, but as character and expression made it so: it was a thin, spare form, something above the common size, if it lost not the distinction by a bend forwards in the figure—but it was the attitude of Intreaty ... [1]

This is excellently done—and Sterne's touch here, as it is in general throughout *A Sentimental Journey*, is lighter than in *Tristram Shandy*. The scenes in *A Sentimental Journey* have the fresh and limpid quality of water-colour sketches: the details are few but beautifully placed, and one remembers the clear ambience in which each small tableau is bathed, and the soft, bright touches of colour: the purse 'of green taffeta, lined with a little bit of white quilted satin', which the *fille de chambre* makes to hold the crown Yorick has given her; the gold cross, the red ribbon and the crisp white damask napkins of the Chevalier de St. Louis, selling the *patés*; the late afternoon sun shining through the crimson window curtains in Yorick's room and reflecting 'so warm a tint into the fair *fille de chambre*'s face' that she seems to blush.

II

In *Tristram Shandy* the connoisseurs and theorists of painting are among the first targets of Sterne's satire. The flattering description which Tristram gives of his dedication comes in Chapter IX of Volume I: it is a lively burlesque of the fashionable patter with which an art dealer, or the painter himself, might attempt to sell a portrait. After the opening sentences, from which I have already quoted, the passage continues:

> to speak more like a man of science,—and measure my piece in the painter's scale, divided into 20,—I believe, my Lord, the out-lines will turn out as 12,—the composition as 9,—the colouring as 6,—the expression 13 and a half,—and the design,—if I may be allowed, my Lord, to understand my own *design*, and supposing absolute perfection in designing, to be as 20,—I think it cannot well fall short of 19. Besides all this,

[1] *A Sentimental Journey* (London, 1768), pp. 11–12. Edward Mangin, in *A View of the Pleasures arising from a Love of Books* (London, 1814), singles out this passage for special comment, stating that 'the idea of a *painting* was in Sterne's mind when he undertook to give his admirable likeness of Father Lorenzo' (p. 95). He remarks of *A Sentimental Journey* that 'it abounds ... in fine specimens of ... the art of painting with his *pen*, in which the author was a very great master: he exhibits on paper the talents of Carlo Dolce, Vandyke, Teniers and Hogarth, and is often not inferior in composition, colouring and truth to any of them' (p. 92).

> —there is keeping in it, and the dark strokes in the HOBBY-HORSE, (which is a secondary figure, and a kind of back-ground to the whole) give great force to the principal lights in your own figure, and make it come off wonderfully ... (I, IX).

The painter's scale so expertly flourished here would have been instantly recognized by any of Sterne's readers with pretentions to taste. It was the invention of one of the best known authorities on painting in the seventeenth and eighteenth centuries, Roger de Piles, who had offered it to the world in 1708 in his *Cours de Peinture par Principes*. Jonathan Richardson, in his *Argument on behalf of the Science of a Connoisseur* (1719), had recommended the use of M. de Piles's scale to all gentlemen eager to learn how to judge paintings (Tristram speaks here 'more like a man of science'); and in 1752 Joseph Spence in his *Crito: or, a Dialogue on Beauty* suggested, rather less solemnly, that a similar scale might be used to determine the 'proportionall Excellence' of female beauty. An English translation of de Piles, *The Principles of Painting*, was published in 1743; but he was also known for several other treatises on art, and in particular for his translation into French of the *De Arte Graphica* of du Fresnoy. It was this inaccurate translation, and not the original Latin, which Dryden rendered into English in 1695; and for nearly a century it remained the standard version. It was reissued more than once, and was always accompanied by, amongst other things, de Piles' Preface and his voluminous and often pedantically unnecessary notes.[1]

De Piles is a natural Scriblerian victim for Sterne's wit. He is an unadventurous and dogmatic Platonist who tells the reader in his Preface to *The Principles of Painting* that 'the surest way to know infallibly the *true idea* of things is, to derive it from the very *basis* of their *essence and definition*.'[2] Like Walter Shandy he is a 'systematick reasoner': and the system he constructs is notable for the crude

[1] *The Principles of Painting* and du Fresnoy's *Art of Painting* (second edition, 1716) are listed in *A Catalogue of a ... Collection of Books, Among which are included The Entire Library of the late Reverend and Learned Laurence Sterne, A.M.*, issued in 1768 by J. Todd and H. Sotheran, booksellers in York (a facsimile of this, with a preface by Charles Whibley, was published in 1930). Other studies of painting included in the catalogue are: *Ars Pictoria: or an Academy treating of Drawing, Painting, Limning and Etching*, by [Alexander] Browne (London, 1669); *Principles of Drawing*, by Gérard de Lairesse (London?, 1739); *An Account of Some of the Statues, Bas-reliefs, Drawings and Pictures in Italy*, by Jonathan Richardson (Senior and Junior) (London, 1722); *Anecdotes of Painting*, by Horace Walpole (Strawberry Hill, 1762); and a '*Compleat Drawing Book, engraved on* 113 *Copperplates ... 1757*'. There are also several works on architecture and gardening.

[2] Du Piles [Roger de Piles], *The Principles of Painting* (London, 1743), p. 2.

generality of its idealistic assumptions, the rigid lack of imagination with which they are developed, and the trivial pedantry of the end product: a set of ruled columns like an examination record sheet in which various painters are awarded so many marks for their proficiency in 'the most essential parts' of their art. Design, 'the *intire thought* of a work' as de Piles calls it, was generally admitted to be the area in which it was most important for the painter to excel. Among the fifty or so artists listed in *The Principles of Painting* only Raphael scores eighteen out of twenty for design—the highest mark awarded by de Piles for anything. Tristram confidently allows himself nineteen for design, and a precise thirteen and a half for expression.

Sterne's general satiric purpose here is to suggest that the conventional dedication is as hypocritically flattering as the conventional portrait; and in the concluding sentence Tristram's argument depends on the compositional principle that the most important person in a history painting or a portrait should occupy the most prominent position. The rule has been enunciated by many writers; but the immediate if not the only source of Sterne's expression of it here seems to have been a passage in *The Art of Painting* by Gérard de Lairesse. According to de Lairesse,

> you must place your *principal Figures* conspicuous and elevated upon the fore Ground; give them the *main Light, and the greatest Force of Colouring, in one Mass, or Group*; the *less Objects* must be somewhat lower, and their Force of Light and Colour more spread. The second Ground ought to be in *Shade*, or filled with *shady Objects*.[1]

Such a principle has more than formal implications. Dryden, in the Preface to his translation of du Fresnoy, points out that the central figure in a painting is like the main character in a tragedy or an epic: 'the *Hero* of the *Piece* must be advanc'd foremost to the View of the *Reader* or *Spectator*: He must out-shine the rest of all the *Characters*; He must appear the *Prince* of them, like the Sun in the *Copernican System*, encompass'd with the less noble *Planets*'.[2] And de Piles, in his note on the relevant passage in du Fresnoy, makes the unwittingly prophetic remark that those painters who neglect the rule 'do just like those who in the relation of a story ingage themselves so foolishly in long digressions, that they are forc'd to conclude quite another way than they began'.[3]

[1] Gérard de Lairesse, *The Art of Painting* (London, 1738), p. 35.
[2] C. A. Du Fresnoy, *De Arte Graphica. The Art of Painting* (London, 1695), p. xli.
[3] Ibid., p. 130.

Sterne's ridicule of de Piles springs not merely from a distaste for him as a critic who measured the works of genius by rule, but also from a profoundly sceptical dissatisfaction with all hierarchical systems of value. *Tristram Shandy* is one of the most thoroughly anti-heroic works of fiction ever written; and it is not surprising that its author should have found himself out of sympathy with the uncompromisingly neo-classical orthodoxies then prevailing in the theory of painting. There is a sense, of course, in which the nominal hero is never absent from *Tristram Shandy*; but in another and equally important sense he can hardly be said to be present at all: in the composite portrait of the Shandy family Tristram is certainly not 'advanc'd foremost to the View of the *Reader or Spectator*'.

This inversion of conventional values may be as readily observed in particular episodes as in the novel as a whole. A good example is the scene in which Trim reads the sermon—a scene which Sterne has obviously amused himself by composing as if it were a painting. Trim, the most important figure, is placed in the centre: in 'the middle of the room, where he could best see, and best be seen by, his audience'(II, xv). But Trim's importance is accidental and comical: he is socially the 'lowest' person in the company, he is not the author of the sermon, and he understands it only in a superficial way—he continually steps out of his oratorical role, and is far more distressed by what he is reading than are his auditors. The illustration of this scene which, at Sterne's request, was drawn by Hogarth, is completely in keeping with this spirit of comic inversion: Trim is shown standing in the classic pose of the orator, but with his back to the viewer of the picture, and not his front or his profile, as the conventions of history painting would demand.

A striking feature of this scene is the detail with which Trim's attitude is analysed. 'Attitude', in the sense of a meaningful, expressive pose is, in the field of painting, a thoroughly technical term. 'The *Attitude* of a Figure', wrote Leonardo da Vinci in his *Treatise of Painting*, 'must be so conducted in all its parts, as that the intention of the Mind, may be seen in every Member.'[1] In the eighteenth century conventional attitude expressing such things as eloquence, grief, intreaty, terror, etc., derived from renaissance and classical models, formed an important part of the artist's stock in trade. It is one of these conventional attitudes that Trim unconsciously assumes as he prepares to deliver the sermon.

[1] Leonardo da Vinci, *A Treatise of Painting* (London, 1721), p. 117.

In his description of Trim, Sterne seems to have drawn mainly on Leonardo's *Treatise*, though he obviously had Hogarth's *Analysis of Beauty*, which had appeared in 1753, very much in mind also. He was probably directed to the *Treatise* by one of de Piles's notes to du Fresnoy. De Piles draws attention to the way in which the weight of the human body tends to distribute itself equally about a centre of gravity; and with unusual candour suggests that the reader interested in the subject consult Lomazzo's *Trattato dell arte della pittura, scultura et architettura*, and Leonardo's *Treatise*, from which, in fact, everything he has to say in this particular passage has been taken.[1]

Leonardo's *Treatise* was not published during the author's lifetime, but was assembled from various unorganized manuscripts left behind after his death. As a result, his arguments often seem rambling and repetitive; and Sterne is perhaps parodying this, and pointing also to the perils of stating the obvious, in the excessively detailed account he gives of Trim's oratorical stance. But he is clearly in agreement with Leonardo's general thesis—namely that the painter and the sculptor must pay attention to the facts of anatomy and the law of gravity. 'A Man in bearing a Burthen', Leonardo remarks, 'has always the loaden Shoulder higher than the empty one ... did not the Weight of the Body, and of the Burthen ... thus make an *Equilibrium*, the Man of necessity must tumble to the Ground.'[2] Echoing the idea if not the example Sterne recommends Trim's attitude not only to painters but also to orators, 'for, unless they practise it, —they must fall upon their noses' (II, XVII). In other words, if an attitude is beautiful it will also be natural; the physical forces which condition the form it takes will be scientifically demonstrable. Thus Trim's left foot is advanced and his knee bent

> so as to fall within the limits of the line of beauty;—and ... of the line of science too;—for consider, it had one eighth part of his body to bear up; —so that in this case the position of the leg is determined,—because the foot could be no further advanced, or the knee more bent, than what would allow him, mechanically, to receive an eighth part of his whole weight under it ... (II, XVII).

'The line of beauty' is a term which, though not invented by William Hogarth, may fairly be regarded as his, for he makes it the foundation

[1] *De Arts Graphica. The Art of Painting* (London, 1695), p. 120.

[2] *A Treatise of Painting* (London, 1721), p. 112. For a brief account of the manuscripts and their publication see Anthony Blunt, *Artistic Theory in Italy, 1450–1600* (Oxford, 1940), pp. 23–4.

of the aesthetic theory which he develops in *The Analysis of Beauty*. According to Hogarth it is an undulating S-shaped curve which is beautiful in itself and to which all beautiful forms approximate. The absolute value which he places on his line of beauty is something which may be questioned; but apart from rather uncritical assertion of this initial assumption his theory is vigorously empirical. Sterne had already, in his description of Dr Slop, recommended *The Analysis* to his readers; and his employment of 'the line of beauty' in this description of Trim is quite in accordance with the common-sense realism of Hogarth's treatise.

The painter would also have thoroughly approved of the other and more orthodox idea which this passage is meant to demonstrate—the notion that the line of beauty may be discerned as easily in the attitudes of living individual people as in the attitudes of figures created by the artist. Thus, Walter Shandy, reasoning on names and noses, falls naturally (and unconsciously) into the attitude

> in which *Socrates* is so finely painted by *Raffael* in his school of *Athens*; which your connoisseurship knows is so exquisitely imagined, that even the particular manner of the reasoning of *Socrates* is expressed by it—for he holds the fore-finger of his left-hand between the fore-finger and the thumb of his right, and seems as if he was saying ... '*You grant me* this—and this: and this, and this, I don't ask of you—they follow of themselves in course' (IV, VII)[1].

And Trim stands with 'such an oratorical sweep throughout the whole figure,—statuary might have modell'd from it' (II, XVII). But the sculptor or the painter who found his primary inspiration in the parlour of Shandy Hall, and who gave a faithful rendering of Walter or Trim, would be in orthodox eyes an inferior and defective artist—just as Hogarth and the masters of the Dutch and Flemish schools of genre-painting were considered inferior and defective. As Sir Joshua Reynolds was to pronounce, 'there is an absolute necessity for the Painter to generalize his notions; to paint particulars is not to paint nature, it is only to paint circumstances'.[2] The idea was not new: one of the earliest

[1] His 'connoisseurship' is almost certainly Jonathan Richardson the younger, from whose *Account of Some of the Statues, Bas-reliefs, Drawings and Pictures in Italy* (London, 1722) Sterne has taken practically verbatim this account of Socrates. The parallel passage in Richardson runs: 'Even the Manner of the Reasoning of *Socrates* is Express'd; he holds the Fore-finger of his Left-hand between that, and the Thumb of his Right, and seems as if he was saying, You grant me This, and This ... ' (p. 212). Cf. also *A Treatise of Painting*, by Leonardo da Vinci, p. 131.

[2] *The Art of Painting of Charles Alphonse du Fresnoy. Translated into English Verse by William Mason, M.A. With Annotations by Sir Joshua Reynolds* ... (York, 1783) p. 68.

renaissance theorists, Leon Battista Alberti, had stated in 1436 in his *Della Pittura* that the artist 'must take from all the beautiful bodies those parts which are particularly praised ... which will be difficult because perfect beauty is never to be found in any one body but is scattered and dispersed in many different bodies'.[1] It follows from this, as many succeeding Italian and French writers were to insist, that perfect beauty will be more fully (though still not completely) embodied in works of art than in nature. It is to such works, therefore, rather than to the world they represent, that the aspiring artist must first direct his eyes. 'These are the materials on which Genius is to work ... By studying these authentick models, that idea of excellence which is the result of the accumulated experience of past ages, may be at once acquired.'[2]

The *Discourses* of Sir Joshua Reynolds, from the first of which this last sentence is taken, constitute the final authoritative statement of neo-classical theory; and in his hands the orthodox dogmas receive an exposition which is flexible, profound and the antithesis of all that is petty or narrowly intolerant. But the first Discourse was not to be given until 1769, by which time Sterne and Hogarth were both dead. Reynolds had as little respect as they for shallow pedantry; and in the first of three papers on painting (numbers 76, 79, and 82) which he contributed in 1759 to *The Idler* he assailed the connoisseurs vigorously. His essay is extremely interesting for two reasons: first, because he cleverly uses his sally against the connoisseurs, who were Hogarth's avowed enemies, as cover for an attack on Hogarth's own theory of the line of beauty;[3] and second, because it is the source of one of Sterne's most thoroughly Shandean flights of rhetoric. Reynolds gives a sketch of the connoisseur

> just returned from *Italy* ... his mouth full of nothing but the Grace of *Raffaelle*, the Purity of *Domenichino*, the Learning of *Poussin*, the Air of *Guido*, the Greatness of Taste of the *Charaches*, and the Sublimity and grand Contorno of *Michael Angelo*; with all the rest of the cant of Criticism ... [4]

In Sterne's hands this undergoes an enlivening transformation, but the source remains obvious:

[1] Quoted in *Artistic Theory in Italy, 1450–1600*, by Anthony Blunt (Oxford, 1940), p. 17.

[2] Sir Joshua Reynolds, *Discourses on Art*, ed. R. R. Wark (San Marino, 1959), p. 15 [from *Discourse I*].

[3] See Joseph Burke, Intro. to *The Analysis of Beauty* (Oxford, 1955), p. xxvi.

[4] *The Idler* (London, 1761), II, No. 76, 132.

> 'Tis a melancholy daub! my Lord ... for there is nothing of the colouring of *Titian*,—the expression of *Rubens*,—the grace of *Raphael*,—the purity of *Dominichino*,—the *corregiescity* of *Corregio*,—the learning of *Poussin*,—the airs of *Guido*,—the taste of the *Carrachi*'s—or the grand contour of *Angelo*. —Grant me patience, just heaven! —Of all the cants which are canted in this canting world ... the cant of criticism is the most tormenting! (III, XII)[1]

Sterne became a friend of Reynolds, but he remained fundamentally unsympathetic to the 'grand style'; and he was too much of a natural heretic, and too interested in the variety and unpredictability of human behaviour, to subscribe to the neo-classical credo. Thus Tristram is patently delighted to announce that

> as many pictures as have been given of my father, how like him soever in different airs and attitudes,—not one, or all of them, can ever help the reader to any kind of preconception of how my father would think, speak, or act, upon any untried occasion or occurrence of life (V, XXIV).

As one might expect, he finds Janatone, the flesh-and-blood daughter of the innkeeper at Montreuil, more lovely than any statue; and he rejoices in the notion that her beauty is individual, unself-conscious and transitory. Just as Trim's body naturally falls within the limits of the line of beauty as he delivers the sermon, so Janatone needs no academic instruction in order to be beautiful: 'That Nature should have told this creature a word about a *statue's thumb*!— ... this sample is worth all their thumbs' (VII, IX). Hogarth would have agreed: 'Who but a bigot', he asks in *The Analysis*, ' ... will say that he has not seen faces and necks, hands and arms in living woman, that even the Grecian Venus doth but coarsely imitate?'[2]

The parallel is more revealing than the almost literal copying of the paragraph from Reynolds. Sterne found more in Hogarth's radically heterodox and highly individual theory of art than a few quotable phrases. It is no accident that, of all the treatises on painting which are echoed or parodied in *Tristram Shandy*, Hogarth's *Analysis* is the only one to be named; nor was Sterne's desire to have Hogarth illustrate his novel a mere fashionable whim. There is a natural affinity between the philosophical attitudes which animate and are exemplified in Sterne's

[1] Cf. the confused rhapsodies of Pallet the Painter in Ch. XLVI of *Peregrine Pickle* (1751). The ignorant connoisseur was evidently something of a stock comic figure at this time.

[2] *The Analysis of Beauty* (London, 1753), p. 68.

fiction and the ideas which Hogarth explicitly develops and illustrates in *The Analysis of Beauty*. The friendly and mutually stimulating relationship which existed between Hogarth and Fielding is well known. The sympathy and approval felt by Sterne for the artist and his attitude both to art and to life are equally interesting; and, so far as the theory of painting and fiction is concerned, perhaps in some ways more significant.

III

The relationship between Sterne and Hogarth has not passed altogether unnoticed. Some attention is paid to it by Henri Fluchère in his recent study of the novelist;[1] and Frederick Antal in *Hogarth and his Place in European Art* (1962) and, more fully, in an article, 'The Moral Purpose of Hogarth's Art', has made some extremely perceptive observations on the sympathy felt by the artist for the novelist and his ideas, and particularly on the way in which this is revealed in the sketch of Trim.

> Sterne was obviously influenced by Hogarth in conceiving the scene and the figures; and Hogarth, in his turn an admirer of Sterne, at once found motifs [from 'Beer Street' and 'The Country Dance'] agreeing with both of them. Both were equally interested in the correspondence between the mental process and the movement of the body. And ... Hogarth's art ... was congenial to Sterne's conception, ironical, fanciful, vivid, and at the same time, very visual.[2]

When he published the first two volumes of *Tristram Shandy* Sterne had apparently not met Hogarth, for he made his request for an illustration for the next edition through the offices of a friend, Richard Berenger. In his letter to Berenger Sterne remarks that he would be happy with 'the loosest Sketch in Nature, of Trim's reading the Sermon to my Father', from Hogarth, and adds that such a sketch 'w^{d} mutually illustrate his System & mine'.[3]

Sterne's knowledge of Hogarth's system was based on a close reading of *The Analysis of Beauty*. Just how close is revealed in a passage in *Tristram Shandy* concerned primarily with language, a

[1] *Laurence Sterne, de l'homme à l'œuvre* (Paris, 1961). The chapter, 'Le peintre et l'écrivain', is devoted partly to the possible effects of Sterne's knowledge of painting on his presentation of character.

[2] 'The Moral Purpose of Hogarth's Art', *Journal of the Warburg and Courtauld Institutes*, XV (1952), p. 193.

[3] *Letters of Laurence Sterne*, ed. L. P. Curtis (Oxford, 1935), p. 99.

passage which, for all its satiric overtones, may be taken as a statement of the style Sterne himself admired and sought to achieve.

> Just heaven! how does the *Poco piu* and the *Poco meno* of the *Italian* artists;—the insensible, more or less, determine the precise line of beauty in the sentence, as well as in the statue! How do the slight touches of the chisel, the pencil, the pen, the fiddlestick, *et cœtera*,—give the true swell, which gives the true pleasure! —O my countrymen! —be nice; —be cautious of your language ... (II, VI).

In addition to using Hogarth's 'precise line of beauty', Sterne seems to be recalling here two distinct though related passages in *The Analysis*:

> And if the reader will follow in his imagination the most exquisite turns of the chisel in the hands of a master, when he is putting the finishing touches to a statue; he will soon ... understand what it is the real judges expect from the hands of such a master, which the Italians call, the little more, Il poco piu ... [1]
>
> Now whoever can conceive lines thus constantly flowing, and delicately varying over every part of the body even to the fingers ends, and will call to his remembrance what led us to this last description of what the Italians call, Il poco piu (*the little more* that is expected from the hand of a master) will ... want very little more than what his own observation on the works of art and nature will lead him to, to acquire a true idea of the word *Taste*, when applied to form.[2]

The possibility of drawing formal analogies between writing and painting (at a more immediate level than the conventional parallel between painting and poetry) obviously interested Sterne; and it is clear that he had also considered the further analogies that may be drawn with music. It is extremely probable that he was familiar with Charles Avison's *Essay on Musical Expression* (1752), which contains a rather laboured section 'On the Analogies between MUSIC and PAINTING'.[3] 'The true swell, which gives the true pleasure' is attained, Sterne suggests, with similar means by those who wield the chisel, the paint-brush, the pen and the fiddlestick. And he clearly feels that Hogarth's theory, at least by implication, gives support to this idea.

Analogies must not be pushed too far. But it is possible, without straining, to discern certain parallels between Sterne's aims and achieve-

[1] Op. cit., pp. 61–2. [2] Ibid., p. 66.

[3] 'Avison [*sic*] Scarlatti', presumably an edition (1744) of twelve harpsichord pieces by Domenico Scarlatti arranged for strings by Avison, is mentioned in *Tristram Shandy*, III, V; and two copies of *An Essay on Musical Expression* are listed in the Todd and Sotheran sale catalogue.

ment in fiction, and the theory and even to some extent the practice of Hogarth in the graphic arts. Each exhibits an unusual combination of attitudes: a desire to be as realistic as possible, coupled with a delight in formal subtlety and complexity for its own sake. Hogarth's purpose in *The Analysis of Beauty* is twofold: to develop a theory of the beautiful, and to clear our minds of preconceptions about the nature of art so that we can see the world as it 'really' is, and discover the beautiful for ourselves. His aim is to 'teach us *to see with our own eyes*'; he wants to set forth

> the surprising alterations objects seemingly undergo through prepossessions and prejudices contracted by the mind. —Fallacies strongly to be guarded against by such as would learn to see truly![1]

Like Sterne, who turns to the two knobs on his arm-chair to illustrate his discussion of wit and judgment, Hogarth chooses homely objects—onions, candlesticks, turnspits, corsets, the legs of chairs—to illustrate his arguments. And this fascination with the humble details of ordinary experience is accompanied by a conscious and sophisticated appreciation of formal values.

According to Hogarth, intricacy and variety are the two most important principles of beauty: 'the art of composing well is the art of varying well',[2] and the most beautiful objects are those possessing 'intricacy in form'. This he defines as 'that peculiarity in the lines, which compose it, that *leads the eye a wanton kind of chace*'.[3] One of the most distinctive qualities of *Tristram Shandy* is the way in which, through all its apparently chaotic digressions, it still leads the mind, if not the eye, just such a wanton and delightful 'chace'. As Sterne admitted in some doggerel he wrote at Crazy Castle, he found direct simplicity impossible:

> For to this day, when with much pain,
> I try to think strait on, and clever,
> I sidle out again, and strike
> Into the beautiful oblique.
>
> Therefore, I have no one notion,
> That is not form'd, like the designing
> Of the peristaltick motion;
> Vermicular; twisting and twining;
> Going to work
> Just like a bottle-skrew upon a cork.[4]

[1] Op. cit., p. 5. [2] Ibid., p. 40. [3] Ibid., p. 25.
[4] *Crazy Tales*, ed. by A. S. [John Hall-Stevenson] (London, 1762), pp. 17–18.

In their enthusiasm for the intricate and various Hogarth and Sterne were not unusual. It was William Kent, Hogarth's old enemy, who earlier in the century had adopted as his principle that 'nature abhored a strait line'; and the 'fifties, the decade in which *The Analysis of Beauty* was published and the writing of *Tristram Shandy* begun, was the period in which the rococo established itself in England as the dominant style in the decorative arts. According to Ralph Edwards, who has described *The Analysis* as 'an essay upon a theme essentially Rococo',[1] this style 'owes its distinctive character to the cult of asymmetry'.[2] The value of extending to literary forms a term normally applied only to other arts is perhaps questionable. It is tempting, however, to describe Sterne's work as rococo. His style has the rococo qualities of lightness, elegance, surprise and wit; his formal arrangements are asymmetrical (striking into 'the beautiful oblique') but none the less fundamentally unified. He achieves his general effects by a concentration on a multitude of precisely observed and sensitively rendered minute particulars. And, like all works of rococo art, his novels are animated by the spirit of movement. Joseph Burke has pronounced Hogarth 'the supreme master of the satiric rococo':[3] the title in the art of painting is certainly his—but in literature there is no one to whom it could be applied more aptly than Sterne.

That the title, when applied to Sterne, can be even partially illuminating is an indication of the intimate relationship which existed in the eighteenth century between painting and literature. It suggests also that the question of the specific connection between painting and fiction may repay further investigation. The influence which Hogarth and Fielding exerted upon each other has, of course, long been recognized; but it has, for the most part, been treated as a special case—just as Hogarth, himself, until recently, has been treated as a special case among painters. Yet it is surely not completely fortuitous that both Sterne and Fielding, writers with very different temperaments, should find so much valuable stimulation in the work and ideas of Hogarth; nor that a painter with Hogarth's peculiarly fictive qualities should flourish at a time when the novel was so rapidly gaining in popularity and respect. It is also significant, perhaps, that when Smollett, in his Dedication to *Ferdinand, Count Fathom* (1753), attempted to define a novel he should

[1] Introduction to *English Taste in the Eighteenth Century*, Catalogue of the Winter Exhibition of the Royal Academy of Arts, London, 1955–56, p. xii.

[2] Ibid., p. ix.

[3] Introd. to *The Analysis of Beauty* (Oxford, 1955), p. xliv.

turn first to painting for his terminology: 'A Novel', he stated, 'is a large diffused picture, comprehending the characters of life, disposed in different groupes, and exhibited in various attitudes, for the purposes of an uniform plan, and general occurrence, to which every individual figure is subservient.'

What general conclusions, if any, are to be drawn about the relationship between painting and the novel in the eighteenth century must wait on further inquiry. It is clear, however, that for Laurence Sterne at least the relationship was one of special importance.

Notes on a Poem of Burns

W. L. RENWICK

BURNS never published his 'Epistle to Major Logan'. It first appeared in the *Works* edited by Allan Cunningham in 1834, with the note 'To David Auld of Ayr, I am indebted for a copy of this poem from the original in his possession'. In the same year Hogg and Motherwell also printed it, explaining that 'To the kindness of Mr Auld of Bridge of Doon, we are indebted for its appearance in the present edition, as well as for the following note from Mrs McKenzie (late Miss Logan)'. This note reads: 'Mrs McKenzie feels pleasure in having it in her power to present Mr Auld with the enclosed. It is the handwriting of Burns, and was addressed to her brother the late Major Logan. Mrs McKenzie has reason to believe it has never been published as she found it in a Drawer of an old Cabinet after her brother's death, and where, it is probable, it may have laid for the last forty years. Ayr 26 August, 1828.' A manuscript copy in the Laing Collection, Edinburgh University Library, also derives from Auld, and also includes Mrs McKenzie's note. On this copy Henley and Henderson based their text in the Centenary Edition, 1896–7.

Disregarding Henley and Henderson in favour of the MS. which they cite as their authority, we have thus three witnesses to the text which Burns sent to Logan. The two printed versions disagree in five or six readings, but with perhaps two exceptions their variations may well be editorial. Where they agree between themselves but vary from the Laing MS. we may assume coincidence between the transcripts sent by Auld, the simplest explanation being that the transcripts were made by the same man at or about the same time. The Laing MS. contains some careless errors, such as *elbrick* for *elbuck* and *Mosgul* for *Mossgiel*. Auld would never have made errors like these; the hand looks like that of a clerk; so that—even if they had followed copy exactly, which they did not—Henley and Henderson were scarcely justified in claiming, as against the first editors, that 'their inaccuracies, repeated by later Editors, are corrected in this copy'. Yet the errors are so very obvious that we may invoke the principle that a stupid copyist is a safer witness than a clever editor, and the MS. is a valuable check on the others.

To these we can now add a better authority than any of them, a copy in Burns's own hand, among the Dugald Stewart papers in the same library. It is an earlier version, but written on the same day, since it bears the same date, October 30th, 1786. It is not a rough draft. It is well written, with clear signs of care, on good foolscap paper; but Burns made some alteration in it, and had to copy it again, making some further alterations in so doing. It is these alterations that give the manuscript its interest, and are the main occasion of these notes.

The poetic epistle has always a dual reference: a personal address to an individual, and a piece of self-expression cast for convenience in a convention. The weight of the two elements varies according to circumstances and intention; and the tone of Burns's epistles varies noticeably. The 'Epistle to Logan' is definitely a real letter, written on a specific occasion. The occasion is clear enough: Burns had met Logan, with his mother and sister, and had enjoyed an evening of fun and music. The two men had hit it off, Logan invited Burns to visit him at his home, Park House, Ayr, and this is his reply.

The poem was written in haste. It has long been noticed that the lines in the third stanza

> Hale be your hert! Hale be your fiddle!
> Lang may your elbuck jink an' diddle,
> To cheer you through the weary widdle ...

are duplicated in the second stanza of the 'Second Epistle to Davie', and since that poem was first published it has been assumed that it was written first. This does not follow. The 'Second Epistle of Davie' was prefixed to David Sillar's *Poems*, 1789; if it had been written in time, it would surely have appeared in the Kilmarnock edition of July,

1786. It may have been written at any time between that date and 1789; and this exhortation to his brother poet not to neglect the Muse may have been written when the notion of publishing his verses was in Sillar's mind, and even to help his sales, since Burns was by now a man of some celebrity. Even without this, however, the seventh stanza of the 'Epistle to Logan' is proof enough of haste—

> My hand-wal'd Curse keep hard in chase
> The harpy, hoodock, purse-proud Race,
> Wha count of Poortith as Disgrace!
> Their tuneless hearts,
> May fireside Discords jar a Base
> To a' their parts.

(This is quoted from the Stewart holograph.) Editors have tried to tidy it up by desperate adjustments of the punctuation, but it is hopelessly disjointed. Though we gather what Burns was getting at, the loose grammar is quite unlike a poet whose precision of phrase is one of his most notable characteristics.

This haste adds to the interest of the poem, which is not that of brooding thought or creative imagination, but that of unpremeditated revelation of the poet's feelings at a crucial turn in his fortunes when he was deep in trouble over Jean Armour and contemplating flight to Jamaica. The Dugald Stewart MS. does not change our notion of those feelings, but its variants do emphasize the turmoil in his mind.

The poem opens with a lighthearted salutation to 'thairm-inspirin, rattling Willie', 'my careless brither', a kindred spirit in

> the cheary gang
> Wha dearly like a jig or sang;
> An' never balance Right and Wrang
> By square & rule,
> But as the Clegs o' Feeling stang,
> Are wise or fool!

In fair-copying he strengthened this character by changing the third line to

> An' never think o' right an' wrang.

In the tenth stanza he made a more significant alteration. He first wrote

> Ochon! for poor Castalian Drinkers,
> When they fa' foul o' earthly jinkers!

The witching, curst, delicious blinkers
Aft pit us hyte;
An' gar us weet our waukrife winkers,
Wi' girnan spite.

Then, crossing out and interlining, he made it

Hae put me hyte;
An' gart me weet my waukrife winkers . .

It was not a question of us jolly dogs in general, but of Robert Burns, sitting there with the pen in his hand; but he was in no contrite mood as he changed

By some sweet Elf I may be dinted

into the more defiant

By some sweet Elf I'll yet be dinted.

The other variant in the Stewart MS. is less significant, but may be noted here. He first wrote

Faites mes Baisemains, or I'll abuse ye,
To sentimental Sister Susie,

then struck out the last four words of the first line and substituted *respectueuse*. Some editors have lightlied Burns's French, which he was rather proud of—and indeed he might lose a mark here for setting a singular adjective to a plural noun—but it was not so bad as it has appeared. The printed texts all read *Baissemains*; but it is clearly written correctly, not only in the Stewart holograph, but also (as Henley and Henderson should have seen) in the Laing transcript. The error may have been in the transcripts, made about the same time, for Cunningham and Motherwell; they both read *lazie* for *saerie*; but Auld's clerks were not always wrong. In any case Burns had some notion of the value of mute final *e* in French versification.

One other discrepancy may affect our notion of the poem as a whole. All versions emanating from Auld are headed 'To Major Logan', with the date and place at the foot; the Stewart MS. is headed 'Epistle to Captn. Willm. Logan at Park—Oct: 30th, 1786'. Logan's rank was in fact that which he subscribed to the Edinburgh edition of Burns's poems, 1787, 'Lieut., late 80th Regiment'. He was commissioned in the 80th Regiment of Foot (Royal Edinburgh Volunteers, America) on January 25th, 1778, and appears thus in the Army Lists, 1779–83, when the regiment was disbanded at the end of the American war and he went on half pay. In 1794 he was commissioned in the newly raised 3rd or West Lowland Fencible Infantry with the rank of major; it was disbanded in 1799, and he reverted to lieutenant (half-pay), and so appears in the list up to March 1st, 1819, but not in that of February 28th, 1820. His promotion from captain to major in the West Lowland Fencibles is noted in the *Scots Magazine* for October 1794, but he was neither captain nor major in 1786. It is noticeable that the title 'To Major Logan' in the Laing transcript is in another hand than the text of the poem—his sister, and perhaps himself, would naturally prefer the senior title. Commentators—especially Chambers—have assumed the relation between Burns and Logan to have been one of friendship, but was it ever more than a chance meeting? 'Miss S. Logan' subscribed with Lieutenant Logan to the Edinburgh *Poems*, which edition includes an address *To Miss L - - - - with Beattie's Poems for a New-Year's Gift, Jan. 1, 1787*, a conventional copy of verses such as any eighteenth-century gentleman might address to any young lady on such an occasion, without any sign of familiarity. Scott Douglas (II, 45) identifies 'Sister Susie' as being the wife of one J. Thomson in December 1825, but the sister who sent the poem to Auld in August 1828 calls herself Mrs McKenzie. Were there two sisters, of whom Burns met only one? If so, he cannot have been a frequent visitor at Park. It is likeliest that Burns knew only that Logan was a half-pay officer, and the 'Captn.' of the holograph is the usual vague address to any 'military gent', and that Burns omitted it from his fair copy because he was not sure of it—he was always carefully correct in such matters. We have no record of a later meeting, nor of Logan's having mentioned—still less boasted like everyone who caught even a glimpse of Burns in the street—that he had known the much-talked-of poet. The poem is our only evidence of their meeting, and Mrs McKenzie is witness that it lay in a drawer for forty years.

This may seem to be contradicted by the familiarity of the style; but that familiarity was in the tradition of the verse epistle in Scots as Burns inherited it from Hamilton of Gilbertfield and Allan Ramsay. It was well known and well understood. It is improbable that Burns would call the Rev. Thomas Blacklock, D.D., 'my gude auld cockie' to his face, or address Mrs Blacklock—or Mrs Logan—as 'honest Lucky' over her tea-table; but he could do so in 'the crambo-jingle'.

One last point: why did Burns not publish this poem? He was never shy about revealing his own affairs and feelings, and he published worse ones. We may be allowed some conjecture. A week or two before he wrote this poem Burns had met Dugald Stewart, whose house at Catrine was only some three miles from Mossgiel. It was Stewart who drew him out of his depression, gave back his confidence, and encouraged him to visit Edinburgh and publish more of his work. Stewart might well ask whether Burns had been writing anything new, and be given the spoiled copy of this recent effort, which remained among his odd papers until a descendant gave them to the University. Burns had destroyed the rough draft, if there was one, and had no other copy, and, when he arranged for the collected edition, had no time to get Logan's copy from Ayr, or this one from Stewart at Catrine; or he did not care to ask for the return of his gifts; or he forgot; or he did not bother: any of which would be just like him.

[I am indebted to the late Dr L. W. Sharp and Dr Donaldson of Edinburgh University Library for valuable notes on Logan's military career.

The text which follows is a 'diplomatic' copy of the Stewart MS. which is worth printing not only for its variants, but as a specimen of Burns's variable orthography, especially in Scots, which he wrote by ear and not to any printer's house-style. It would be difficult to represent the differences of size and formation in his handwriting, some being equivalent to italics and some expressive of the emphasis he would give the words in recitation. His punctuation has always been disregarded by editors; this holograph at least shows that he had a better notion of the art than any of them.]

Epistle to Captn. Willm. Logan at Park.—Oct: 30th, 1786

Hail, thairm-inspirin, rattlin Willie!
Though Fortune's road be rough an' hilly
To ev'ry fiddling, rhyming billie,
We never heed;
But tak it like th' unbacked Fillie,
Proud o' her speed.

When idly goavin whyles we saunter,
Yirr, Fancy barks—awa we canter,
Uphill, down-brae, till some mishanter,
Some black Bog-hole,
Arreest us; then the skathe an' banter,
We're forc'd to thole.

Hale be your heart! Hale be your Fiddle!
Lang may your elbuck jink an' diddle,
To chear you through the weary widdle
O' this vile Warl:
Until ye on a cummock dridle,
A grey-hair'd Carl!

Come Wealth, come Poortith, late or soon,
Heav'n send your heart-strings ay in tune!
An' screw your temper-pins aboon,
A fifth or mair,
The melancholious, sairie croon
O' cankrie Care!

May still your Life, from day to day,
Nae lente largo, in the play,
But allegretto forte, gay,
Harmonious flow!
A sweeping, kindling, bauld Strathspey,
Encore! Bravo!

A' blessins on the cheary gang,
Wha dearly like a jig or sang;
An' never balance Right and Wrang
By square & rule,
But as the Clegs o' Feeling stang,
Are wise or fool!

My hand-wal'd Curse keep hard in chase
The harpy, hoodock, purse-proud Race,
Wha count on Poortith as disgrace!
Their tuneless hearts,
May fireside Discords jar a Bass
To a' their Parts.

But come—your hand—my careless brither—
I' th' tither Warld, if there's anither,
An' that there is, I've little swither
About the matter;
We cheek-for-chow shall jog thegither,
I'se ne'er bid better.

We've fauts an' failins; —granted clearly:
We're frail, backsliding Mortals meerly:
Eve's bonie squad, Priests wyte them sheerly,
For our grand fa':
But still—but still—I like them dearly;
God bless them a'.

Ochon! for poor Castalian Drinkers,
When they fa' foul o' earthly jinkers!
The witching, curst, delicious blinkers
~~Aft-pit us~~ **Hae put me** hyte;
An' gart ~~us~~ **me** weet ~~our~~ **my** waukrife winkers,
Wi' girnan spite.

But by yon Moon! an' that's high swearin;
An' every Star within my hearin!
An' by her een! wha was a dear ane,
I'll ne'er forget;
I hope to gie the jads a clearin
In fair play yet!

My loss I mourn, but not repent it:
I'll seek my pursie whare I tint it:
Ance to the Indies I were wonted,
Some cantraip hour,
By some sweet Elf I may be dinted,
Then, Vive l'amour!
Faites mes Baisemains ~~or I'll abuse-ye~~ **respectueuse**,
To sentimental Sister Susie,
An' honest Lucky; no to oose ye,
Ye may be proud,
That sic a couple Fate allows ye
To grace your blood.

Nae mair, at present, can I measure;
An' trowth my rhymin ware's nae treasure;
But when in Ayr, some halfhour's leisure,
Be't light, be't dark,
Sir Bard will do himsel the pleasure
To call at Park.

Thackeray's *Vanity Fair* Revisited: Fiction as Truth

HENRI A. TALON

I

VANITY Fair. When this title occurred to him, Thackeray burst out with joy,[1] as well he might, for, through its literary associations and the picture it conjures up, it is enough to express a whole outlook upon life. Involved as he was in the social activities of his time, Thackeray could nevertheless stand back and pass judgment. In the restless stir of many of his contemporaries he read their lack of a deep religious faith, the deterioration of their sense of values, and, as the crowning consequence of all, the futility of their desires. 'Everybody is striving for what is not worth the having', says the Marquis of Steyne.[2] In this remark of the old cynic (a man not given to long speeches but, for once, exceptionally articulate), occurring as it does in the course of an important chapter, I see one of the clues to the deeper significance of the novel.

And it tallies with another: Thackeray's declaration of intention to his mother: 'What I want is to make a set of people living without God

[1] Gordon N. Ray, *Thackeray. The Uses of Adversity* (London, 1955), p. 385.

[2] *Vanity Fair*, p. 601, Zephyr Books, Stockholm, 2 vols., being a reproduction of the Oxford University Press edition.

in the world.'[1] Had it received the credit it deserves many errors of interpretation would have been avoided. He would not have been reproached for being incapable of seeing 'the connexion between industrialism and the world of London finance', and for leaving out 'the whole world of industrial capitalism and labour'.[2] Such pre-occupations were beside his purpose.

It is true that he had little understanding of the complexity of the economic structure of the country but, as it happens, he was wise enough to think, like a famous logician of today: 'Whereof one cannot speak, thereof one must be silent.'

He had no wish to anatomize the world of big business. He wanted to give an idea of the mentality of certain groups of people in the upper strata of the middle class and the aristocracy. To him, economics were an unknown country. He is a psychologist and a moralist. The clash of forces at play in an expanding nation are beyond his ken; but how well he can see the most powerful drive in those men and women whose horizon is limited and whose destiny is determined by society! 'A set of people living without God in the world.' 'Faithless, Hopeless, Charityless.'[3]

This drive is envy, envy of those who, if I may put it so, live on the floor above them in the social edifice. Not only do they wish to reach them, but they also want to climb higher and become themselves the object of envy. They aim at gaining that 'invidious distinction' which, some fifty years later, Thorstein Veblen was to find at the heart of the American leisure class.

Are not such vulgarity and triviality of desire the essence of that snobbery which Thackeray has ceaselessly exposed? Taking it all in all, it seems as though he had written but one work, and that with a double title: *Vanity Fair. The Book of Snobs.* His integrity as an artist lies in his faithfulness to an obsessive vision which, in book after book, he sought to communicate.

For Bunyan's pilgrims, 'Vanity Fair' is the place of trial and suffering through which all men must go on their way to the Heavenly Jerusalem. It is a city built on either side of the high road, and they have no wish to stop. For Thackeray's characters, it is a walled-in universe where they walk in a circle with dreary pleasure.

[1] *The Letters and Private Papers of W. M. Thackeray*, ed. Gordon N. Ray (Cambridge, Mass., 1945), II, 309.

[2] Seymour Betsky, 'Society in Thackeray and Trollope', *Pelican Guide to English Literature* (London, 1958), VI, 145. (A very vigorous essay.)

[3] *V.F.*, p. 96.

Christian's faith gives him strength to scorn the rulers of the fair. Torment him they may, but never will he, or can he, recognize as valid the sentence they pass upon him. He has only one judge; and the model that inspires his action is not of this world.

On the contrary, Thackeray's personages, devoid of a true sense of transcendence, can seek a paradigm of conduct only in the society which closes them in. Christian's proud independence is unknown to them. They look at their fellow-men as so many judges, in whose eyes, as in a mirror, they watch for an image of themselves favourable or otherwise. And now they swell with complacency, now with impotent rage.

Christian's God is occasionally on their lips, but not in their hearts. Lordolatry prevails. Becky, George, Pitt, Jos, all try to ape the grandees with whom they long to hob-nob. In Thackeray's eyes, money itself, for which they all have a craving, is only the means of getting social promotion and honorific toys. Mammon seems to be their supreme idol, but, in fact, is merely a kind of go-between with power to open for them the sanctum of titled people. Through the property they covet, it is, strictly and yet ironically speaking, a 'metaphysical' desire they satisfy; for thus we can name their longing for an unreal distinction.[1] The petty world of bourgeois aspirations is the subject-matter of Thackeray's novel.

A pantomime sometimes, a shrill, grating comedy generally, such is the show of Vanity Fair which, for well over a hundred years, has been inviting critic after critic to look at the performance with a fresh mind.

For it *is* a show, a puppet-show (in a sense that this essay will attempt to make clear), with the stage manager exceptionally in the orchestra pit and not behind the scenes. Thackeray says so from the beginning, but there are none so deaf as those who won't hear. They take him to task for giving a warped picture of reality through omission or prejudice, or for making suspension of disbelief impossible through interference and commentary. They want levelness with life, a transfer-picture of the world they are familiar with, and lo! they are presented with fiction.[2] They demand a high-fidelity recording of

[1] See René Girard, *Mensonge romantique et vérité romanesque* (Paris, 1961), chapitre I 'le désir triangulaire'. It is a great pleasure and a duty to acknowledge my debt to M. Girard's remarkable book. Perhaps I owe him even more than I am aware of.

[2] If I am not mistaken, the only critic who has emphasized this characteristic is Joseph E. Baker in his fine article 'Vanity Fair and the celestial city', *N.C.F.* 1955, vol. X, No. 2.

experience, and the author bids them listen to a story and enjoy it, as La Fontaine said he would have enjoyed *Peau d'Ane*, had someone told him the tale.

A keen-sighted observer if ever there was one, gifted with a remarkable memory for all he had seen, Thackeray chooses nevertheless to remember only what serves his purpose. 'I want to make a set of people living without God in the world.' He is not interested in the endless book-keeping of existence. He selects and arranges his material. He has no wish to plunge us into the grey mist of daily routine, but to take us into a cosmos where bright light throws everything into relief: FABLELAND, as he calls it in *The Newcomes*.

But Fableland is not a universe where sheer gratuitousness holds sway, as the humorist would have us believe when he bids us farewell at the end of this great novel. 'Anything you like happens in Fableland', he says; but those who have read his letters know that it is not so. The fabulist can no more do what he likes with the characters he begets than the sorcerer's apprentice with the magic broom. Nothing is true in Fableland, and yet everything is true, for fancy itself is subject to the exigencies of a conception of life which cannot be tampered with.

To tell a story is Thackeray's way of sifting his experience and thereby understanding it better. For a writer, the *Lust zum fabulieren* of which Goethe has spoken is at once the aesthetic pleasure of drawing pictures and the intellectual pleasure of elucidating life through the image of it that he conjures up.

Thackeray's works belong to the *littérature d'images* which Balzac opposed to the *littérature d'idées*, not because its intellectual content is poorer, but because the thought that informs it is adequately expressed only through concrete illustration. Thus, whenever there is a discrepancy between the picture and the comment which Thackeray so readily supplies, trust the picture, not the comment.

In the process of elucidating experience through the fable, the fogginess of daily life disappears and a pattern is imposed upon formlessness. Becky, Old Osborne, Old Sir Pitt and all the others are consistently themselves as no human being ever is.[1] But this clarity of outline and this definition of character are precisely what the author has sought and what the fable-lover seeks in his turn. The course of Becky's life is not blurred, and at times indistinct, like that of most of us, but, as E. K. Brown puts it in his book, *Rhythm in the Novel*, 'her history

[1] Interesting remarks on the relation between fiction and life are to be found in an essay of the English Hegelian philosopher, T. H. Green, *Works* (London, 1888), III, 29.

has a beautiful circularity, which is the more satisfying since Becky at the end is exactly the same in impulse as she had been twenty years before. We are sure that she would like to hurl the prayer book ... and dash away.'[1]

The circularity of Becky's story contributes to bring out the significance of the whole fair which, as I have said, is a walled-in world where almost everyone keeps on repeating again and again the same mean performance, declaring himself well satisfied with it. But, monotonous though it be, the fair is a large one, extending from suburbia, where lower middle-class families occupy baby-houses in little streets off the Fulham Road, to the stronghold of the rich merchants and bankers in Bloomsbury, to the Anglo-Indian district of which Moira Place is the centre, and finally to the realm of the aristocracy in Mayfair.

Of so vast a ground we might well have caught but a very indistinct general view without Becky Sharp. She is not simply the agent who enables us to enter different milieux in her wake, she sums up in herself the mentality of the society which Thackeray wishes to study. She is the mirror in which the various aspects of the fair converge into a compact picture. Details scattered all over the large canvas and difficult to perceive become related and form a significant whole in the small-sized but clear-cut reflection. Thus, the architecture of the novel makes it possible to combine the somewhat confusing wealth and diversity of feature of a crowd with the strongly marked traits of a personality which towers above it. But, as Becky differs from the others merely by her superabundant vitality and boldness, a whole way of life can be judged in terms of her individual existence.

The sequence of her adventures constitutes the dynamic form of the novel. Whenever she goes off stage, not only does the tempo slow down, but some of the distinctness of meaning disappears; for surely some effort is required to see that the Amelia episodes are also subsumed under the theme of Godlessness in the world.

Try hard though he may, Professor Greig will never convince us that *Vanity Fair* is 'a novel with two heroines'.[2] Becky steals the whole show. She has so much pep, such a high potential of energy, she carries so far the snobbishness, hypocrisy and predatory instincts of all those with whom she associates, that she assumes a typical value. And great types make great novels—whether or not they are the hallmark of

[1] *Rhythm in the Novel* (Toronto, 1950), p. 19.
[2] J. Y. T. Greig, *Thackeray. A Reconsideration* (London, 1950), p. 105.

realism, as Georg Lukács has forcefully contended in several of his books.[1]

'The central category and criterion of realist literature', he writes, 'is the type, a peculiar synthesis which organically binds together the general and the particular both in characters and situations. What makes a type is not its average quality nor its mere individual being, however profoundly conceived; what makes it a type is that in it all the humanly and socially essential determinants are present on their highest level of development, in the ultimate unfolding of the possibilities latent in them, in extreme presentation of their extremes, rendering concrete the peaks and limits of men and epochs.'[2]

Becky has individuality enough and to spare, yet she is perhaps less interesting in her own right as an individual than as a typical representative of the society without which she 'could no more exist ... than an opium-eater without his dram'.[3] It is not for nothing that the book is called *Vanity Fair* rather than *Becky Sharp*.

Moreover, the allegorical overtones of a title lifted from Bunyan remind us of the paradox of fiction that I have stated: everything is true in the novel, and yet nothing is true. A person like Becky, who lives constantly in the superlative, has never walked the earth. In her are to be found a number of human traits brought to more than human intensity. That is why, from an aesthetic point of view, the question: 'Who were her prototypes?' is irrelevant. I am ready to believe that Thackeray was inspired by several women of mixed clay. Why try to unearth their names and secrets? When uniting to become the unrivalled Rebecca they lose their identity. A novel is a grave-yard, Proust has said. And from it there rise not men and women, but fictional personages: Old Pitt, Old Osborne, Joseph Sedley, etc.

That is why I rub my eyes in wonder when I come across some of the judgments that have been passed upon the book. Thus a good critic, W. C. Roscoe, writes: 'Many novelists have a world of their own. Thackeray thrusts his characters in among the moving every-day world in which we live. We don't say they are life-like characters. They are mere people.'[4] And Lady Eastlake, in her anonymous review of *Vanity Fair*: 'We almost long for a little exaggeration and

[1] And as Friedrich Engels was perhaps the first to remark in a letter to Miss Harkness, *circa* 1891.

[2] *Studies in European Realism* (London, 1950), p. 6.

[3] *V.F.*, p. 820.

[4] 'W. M. Thackeray, artist and novelist', *Poems and Essays*, ed. R. H. Hutton, 2 vols., 1860, II, 268.

improbability ... What are all the personages in *Vanity Fair* but feigned names for our own beloved friends and acquaintances?'[1]

For my part, I can see exaggeration displayed throughout the sixty-seven chapters of the book. And I relish it. However, if I were foolish enough to wish the novel other than it is, I would long rather for subdued light and muted voices, for occasional dotted lines instead of the constantly thick strokes, for some of the mystery that is as much part and parcel of my knowledge of friends and acquaintances as what I have learned about them.

But I never express such a wish because I never forget that I am at the show, in Fableland. It seems to me that the metamorphosis that reality has undergone is in the nature of a theatrical process. As Professor Geoffrey Tillotson has remarked, the 'scenic' character of the book is as strongly marked as the 'panoramic' vision which Percy Lubbock has emphasized.[2]

Indeed, when I cross the frontier of *Vanity Fair*, I bid adieu to the light of day. The actors perform on a brilliantly lit stage. They pass before the footlights in significant groupings,[3] with their faces made up as they would be today for television, not in order to conceal the wrinkles but to bring out every feature. As for the acoustics, they are so perfect as to make whispering out of the question, and even the thoughts of the characters can be overheard.

Whereas in *Henry Esmond*[4] Thackeray has recorded a long journey from appearance to reality, from the words that are spoken to the motives that are hidden, in *Vanity Fair* he simultaneously registers the thoughts and the words which belie them. And the deliberately facile devices are part of the fun.

By thus depriving his characters of almost all mystery, he has underscored the automatism of what psychologists call 'behavioural signals'.[5] In this respect alone they well deserve to be called puppets, for they are unwontedly transparent: all the strings of action are made visible. Puppetdom is our world, transformed by the glare of floodlight projectors and the vibrancy of microphones. Thackeray's show is a *son et*

[1] Quoted by G. Tillotson, *Thackeray, the Novelist* (Cambridge, 1954), p. 253.

[2] Ibid., p. 84. '... His novels are a string of scenes of all sizes. With his aspiration to hear his persons speak, how could it be otherwise? But even in a scene Thackeray is panoramic also, and he distances the picture and conversation by his commentary on them.'

[3] See Greig, op. cit., pp. 105–6.

[4] See my article 'Time and Memory in Thackeray's *Henry Esmond*', *R.E.S.*, May 1962.

[5] For a humorous study of this question, see Dr W. M. S. Russell's broadcast 'Signals and Shibboleths', *The Listener*, August 9th, 1962.

lumière, with the good and bad points of such productions. It brings about a *dépaysement*, and we see things as if for the first time. But once the spectacle is over, how welcome the silence and the night!

Puppets they are also because, as I have said, however strong their individuality, they ape one another. The gentry take their clues from the lords, as likewise do the rich businessmen; and the servants in their turn copy their masters. As we go down the ladder the simian performance becomes more and more ridiculous. It reaches a grotesque climax when Miss Horrocks rehearses the part of 'one as was to be a baronet's wife', rigged out in the first Lady Crawley's court-dresses, with always higher ribbons that must weigh as much as the head-dress of the Wyf of Bathe. What a rich meaningful comedy it all is! And how Thackeray enjoys it!

His commentaries show that he was the first to believe in his green-eyed, red-haired little crook, and in all the children of his imagination. These remarks of his, often banal, once or twice obviously mistaken,[1] are yet invaluable, for they reveal the keen delight of the creator in his creation. If only for this reason, I could not wish the showman to be silent. And, as pointed out before, his voice can never upset one who does not confuse truth and literalness. Professor Geoffrey Tillotson sums up the case admirably when he asks: 'What is it in the novels that we live into? ... Not into personages pure and simple. Rather it is into personages presented, mused over and judged.'[2]

After all, the very portrayal of the characters, the very relation of the events, are also a commentary, for Thackeray's descriptive style is always morally colourful. What may conveniently be called the 'facts' of the story come to us mediated through a highly personal language in which there inheres a whole set of values. The most innocent-looking epithet becomes instructively suspicious when the deadpan narrator affixes it to the ugly as if it were the beautiful, to a shabby reality as if it were perfection. To call Rebecca and Rawdon 'this worthy couple', to speak of 'the rural virtues' that are to be found at Queen's Crawley, or of 'the usual artlessness and candour' of Becky, indeed to call the book *Vanity Fair*, is to cast a personal judgment in the reader's teeth. It is commentary. To describe is to comment.

An ironical presentation of the people and occurrences tells us, as do the showman's remarks, that he is at once detached enough to

[1] Dorothy Van Ghent has vigorously pointed out the absurdity of one of Thackeray's comments in her essay on *Vanity Fair* in *The English Novel. Form and Function* (New York, 1953), p. 141.

[2] Op. cit., pp. 90–1.

laugh, and sufficiently involved to grieve. The fable and the commentary blend naturally and harmoniously because they both flow from a man who is hurt, but whose severity is ever tempered by charity. Snobbery, hypocrisy, dishonesty he finds hateful; yet he cannot bring himself to pronounce a final condemnation. It is not that his moral criteria are vague, but that he lacks subtlety of discrimination. Because he knows his own weaknesses so well, he shows a certain indulgence for his puppets. As if indeed his infirmities could be equated with their vices! This is sheer wrong-headed sentimentality.

However, there is also much wisdom in Thackeray, for instance in his recognition of that weakness in man's nature which makes vanity itself a vital necessity. The French philosopher Alain has said that we must indulge in short spells of vanity as we go out on to the doorstep for a breath of air and a little sunshine. Thackeray knows that what difference there is between his brand of vanity and that of his butts is one of degree, not of nature. He is 'one of themselves' and says so. He who laughs at others must also laugh at himself. His confession, which throws a bridge between the self and the other: the 'brother wearer of motley',[1] his confession, then, is not so much humility, as Chesterton suggests,[2] as clear-sightedness and honesty. Unless humility is precisely this: an awareness of one's kinship with those one derides, a half-melancholy, half-amused acceptance of one's shortcomings, indeed a form of self-love more difficult to achieve than self-hatred. All this colours Thackeray's satire and also leads to good-humoured chaff, as homely as Alain's simile:

> 'It is all vanity to be sure: but who will not own to liking a little of it? I should like to know what well-constituted mind, merely because it is transitory, dislikes roast-beef? That is vanity; but may every man who reads this, have a wholesome portion of it through life, I beg: aye, though my readers were five hundred thousand. Sit down, gentlemen, and fall to, with a good hearty appetite; the fat, the lean, the gravy, the horse-radish as you like it—don't spare it. Another glass of wine, Jones, my boy—a little bit of the Sunday side. Yes, let us eat our fill of the vain thing and be thankful therefor.'[3]

Passages like this have caused many readers to raise their eyebrows in scorn. They do not realize that this banter is not levity but comes as

[1] *V.F.*, p. 227: 'O brother wearers of motley.'

[2] ' .. he stood for the remains of Christian humility ... many others might have planned a Book of Snobs; it was Thackeray, and Thackeray alone, who wrote the great subtitle "By one of themselves".' Introduction to *The Book of Snobs* (London, 1911), p. ix.

[3] *V.F.*, p. 634.

the result of a hard-won victory over one's self, a victory that the comic writer must win before he can begin to write. He must get over his own infatuations. He must master and muffle the suffering and indignation that he has experienced personally. As a private citizen, Mr Thackeray is still in the fair; as showman he is no longer of it. Having, for the moment, transcended the vanity and snobbery of Mr Thackeray the man, Thackeray the author can smile. And since he has embodied his philosophy of life in his characters and fable,[1] he can even pretend that he has no head above his eyes ... and have his words taken at their face value; for, by all appearance, few are the readers who understand the process of irony and the wisdom of humility which characterize his work.

Having thus brought out what I consider the essential features of the novel, I now propose, through a more detailed study of the personages and occurrences, to elaborate the points I have made, and attempt to shed more light on Thackeray's insights into man and society.

II

I have said that Becky Sharp is perhaps less interesting in her own right as an individual than as a representative of the spirit of the society which she sums up and magnifies; but, of course, had she not an exceptional personality, she would offer little interest as a type. If it is true that no one like her ever walked the earth, it is no less true that she is alive as few real people ever are. It is not the schemer and the cheat that one sees first in her, but a woman possessed of an extraordinary *joie de vivre*. If she were only a calculating machine who would believe in her? But she is not. 'Hers is a wild and roving nature'[2] whose love of adventure is even stronger than her highly developed sense of lucre. Hence her buoyancy! No boarding-house at Boulogne, no garret in a Pumpernickel inn can damp her spirits, for there, as well as in Curzon Street, existence is an opportunity and a game.

Far from being the ever-discreet manager of her pleasures, she is sometimes carried away by them. 'Even our Becky has her weaknesses'[3] as the showman puts it. Much of the fascination that she exercises both upon her fellow-citizens in Fableland and upon us comes of this abounding enjoyment of existence. In this, she is indeed a-typical.

[1] In his excellent book *Thackeray, a Critical Portrait* (London, 1941), John W. Dodds rightly remarks: 'His thinking is fused thought, concrete, objectified in action', (p. 117).
[2] *V.F.*, p. 830. [3] *V.F.*, p. 600.

Hers is the only laughter that echoes, loud and free, through the fair. To her, life is new every morning. No mist of familiarity ever lessens its freshness. She is what Pitirim Sorokin calls 'the extreme sensual temporalist'[1] who gets all she can out of the present and yet is always full of projects.

In *Henry Esmond*, that novel of Thackeray's which in several respects is the antithesis of *Vanity Fair*, the hero feels the pulse of time in retrospection. Becky can only feel it in expectancy. To Esmond, time means the fullness of achievements. To Becky, time is today's plan for tomorrow as much as today's pleasures; it is the thing to do, the place to fill and the success to win. She hardly ever looks back, and then only very briefly. We cannot imagine her keeping a diary. Experience needs no second reading for one who is not interested in its significance. She asks herself no questions. She only wants to live herself out to the full. But however strong her zest for life, it never assumes the form of sexual desire. She enjoys kindling men's lust. She likes to feel her power over them, but in order to capitalize on it. There is method in her daring. She is always the shrewd manager of her attractiveness. A coquette must rouse her lovers' passion if only to deny it, and thus obtain more watches, jewels and money. I do not believe that she ever slept with Lord Steyne, or with any other man except her husband. Guilty she is, far more than Rawdon could understand, but in a different sense. In the sensual whirlpools she keeps her head the more easily since sexual temptation is not one she experiences. Thackeray, whose skill was great in the art of hinting at the things that he did not dare to show, not once—however obliquely—implies that she was sexually drawn to handsome young men like Rawdon and George.

Yet, in this particular instance, and perhaps in one or two others, one cannot be absolutely sure of what really happened. Becky is too much of the same thing ever to surprise the reader, but she can occasionally set him asking questions about her. What ambiguity there is in her behaviour testifies to the intense personal life with which she has been endowed.

But how can readers believe that she was serious when she said to herself: 'It isn't difficult to be a country gentleman's wife ... I think I could be a good woman if I had five thousand a year'?[2] Once wrenched out of its context a sentence is always susceptible of several interpretations; but, taking the passage as the close-knit whole that it is, we

[1] *Social and Cultural Dynamics* (London, 1957), p. 315. [2] *V.F.*, p. 532.

find Becky's visualization of a possible Arcadian life to be unmistakably humorous. Her knowledge of self is sufficient at least for her to entertain no illusion as to her qualifications for attending sick old paupers, counting the apricots on the wall, and picking off the dead leaves from the geraniums. Indeed, her very choice of rural virtues, homely occupations and quiet dullness, shows how well she knows herself. Thackeray's vocabulary does its job as well as ever, and, therefore, the comment that he tacked on to his delightful picture of Becky's daydream is a sad blemish.

He was too intimately acquainted with her to be taken in by her, but, sometimes, not only did the inspired creator of characters and the moralizing preacher fail to harmonize their tunes, but the latter gained the upper hand. Then, in all seriousness, Thackeray could examine whether there was truth in Becky's musing on the honest woman she might have been. Not only did he ask himself the question in the novel, but he also wrote to George Henry Lewes: 'If Becky had had five thousand a year I have no doubt in my mind that she would have been respectable.'[1] He forgot that she was a Bohemian at heart—very much her parents' daughter—to whom a 'life of humdrum virtue' would always grow 'tedious before long'.[2] He forgot that greed is always insatiable, and that her acquisitive desire, snobbery and love of excitement would always lead her into dubious relations with influential men, and shady transactions with any likely tools. Thackeray's remarks show that when a novelist comments upon characters who have grown independent of him, he is as likely to err as you or I. The creator, as Paul Valéry used to say, enjoys no privilege as a critic of his own work.

Becky is clever and quick-witted, but she has a small mind. She never thinks, she only contrives. Her life is not an enlargement of intellect, an expansion of being. It is an accretion of tricks and jugglings. And our final impression of her existence is one of sameness in multiplicity, distressing poverty in the very abundance which, at first, is so stimulating. In the fair, of which she is the epitome, movement leads nowhere. Although in one sense she is never young, evincing the dismal precocity of poverty as she does from the moment she enters the stage, yet, in another sense, she is always young, for she never changes. Her early shrewdness never ripens into wisdom. In the barbarian world where she lives and has her being, stunted growth is the rule rather than the exception. George Osborne, Jos Sedley, Miss

[1] *Letters*, vol. II, 6 March 1848, pp. 353–4. [2] *V.F.*, p. 819.

Briggs are infantile. Amelia and Miss Osborne are overgrown children. Nobody reaches that opening-out and balance of intelligence and sensibility which we call maturity. Becky's sprightliness cannot deceive us long: her limitations are of the same nature as those of everybody else in the fair.

At Miss Pinkerton's school—a scaled-down model of the society outside—Becky is taught both by personal experience and by observation that a good head or a good heart does not gain from others the respect which everyone wants. Paradoxically, this essential spiritual need of man can only be satisfied through the possession of material wealth. Thus begins the confusion of values that is responsible for all that happens in the fair. Let us remark here that, as the rhetoric of the novel[1] calls at once for repetition and contrast, Dobbin at school goes through the same trial as Becky, and draws from it a different—indeed exceptional—conclusion.

In a society where most men are bound to know humiliation through poverty, the individual is not urged by moral and intellectual emulation, but by the exigencies of practical competition. Money he must have. Becky learned this lesson early, as did Old Osborne. Vanity Fair is a game of grab, of which, however, Thackeray does not choose to give a complete picture.

He disregards the association between the world of finance and that of politics, the struggle of money for power, which fascinate Balzac.[2] It is on another facet of human ambition that he focuses his attention: the wish to attain prestige through one's connexions, the longing to find the assurance of one's merits in one's position of eminence. As Veblen did later, Thackeray traces the relation between the *appetitus divitiarum infinitas* and the insatiable desire to obtain a sense of being worthy. To Balzac, the principal substitute for a genuine religious faith is money. To Thackeray, it is what I have called the 'metaphysical desire': snobbery.

This craving for rank is a spur to action, but whereas it assumes an innocuous form in the weak, like Jos Sedley, in tougher natures, like Becky and Old Osborne, it rouses all the astuteness and ruthlessness they can command. The maxim they take to heart is expressed with

[1] I use the expression as does Wayne C. Booth in *The Rhetoric of Fiction* (Chicago, 1961).

[2] Several articles have been published on Balzac and Thackeray. The best is probably W. C. D. Pacey's in *M.L.R.*, 1941. The latest I have read, A. Carey Taylor's in *Revue de littérature comparée*, 1960, is very disappointing.

aphoristic brevity in *The Newcomes*: 'If your neighbour's foot obstructs you, stamp on it; and do you suppose he won't take it away?'[1] And yet this image gives no idea of the lengths to which they will go, given both the opportunity and the promise of sufficient booty. One of Steyne's cold-blooded, jeering remarks is more suggestive. To Becky's confession that she has ruined Miss Briggs he replies: 'Ruined her? Then why don't you turn her out?'[2] But even my Lord's grim humour can give no premonition of what is to follow: Jos Sedley's murder by Becky.

Old Osborne goes at it with peculiar brutality. At bottom probably not a very strong man, he has in compensation plenty of drive, a complete lack of consideration for others and a great capacity for kidding himself that he is right. Becky is a cynic who needs no reassurance, but Osborne could not give free rein to his predatory impulse without that sincere belief in one's own lies which Sartre has labelled 'mauvaise foi'. 'He firmly believed that everything he did was right, and that he ought on all occasions to have his own way.'[3] In order to trample forward without qualms, he must work himself up into a state of 'Godalmightiness', to use Jung's telling expression.[4] If dullness is to take the lead in the world, it cannot afford to have doubts about itself, as Thackeray remarks in a comment which places Osborne in the perspective of philistinism in general.

Lying to one's self, and to others, is a vital necessity for men like this old merchant, who wallow in muddy streams without having either intelligence or courage enough to face the ethical issues raised by their conduct. God is dead in their hearts, but they do not think of themselves as unbelievers. With great insight into men's souls Thackeray—this supposedly shallow observer of *mores*—shows that hypocrisy must rule the world if bullies are to live in spiritual comfort. The lies of the self-righteous philistine must change objective reality into the figure of his heart's desire.

> From a mere sense of consistency, a persecutor is bound to show that the fallen man is a villain—otherwise he, the persecutor, is a wretch himself.[5]

[1] See Ch. VIII. In the 1878 edition, p. 86.
[2] *V.F.*, p. 608. [3] *V.F.*, p. 444.
[4] Cf. Sir John William Kaye's essay 'Success' published in *The Cornhill Magazine* in 1860. '... To honour what has won success is worthy worship ... it is veneration for that type of manhood, which most nearly approaches the divine ... ' quoted by Walter E. Houghton, *The Victorian Frame of Mind* (London, 1957), p. 194.
[5] *V.F.*, p. 215.

The downfall of a man who was once his superior gives Osborne no small idea of his 'talents and genius', as he himself puts it with suppressed modesty,[1] but it is transitory. Only the admiration of those in his peer-group can provide constant self-satisfaction. And since, as Thackeray observed long before Veblen explained, worthiness is associated with money, extravagant expenditure is one of the exigencies of the fair. One of the best ways of proving to yourself who you *are* is through the display of what you *have*.

Thackeray is lavish of amusing instances of this, although none is perhaps so good as the one reported by Stendhal in his short story: 'Feder ou le mari d'argent'. And since—so far as I know—the names of these two novelists are never found together in Thackeray criticism (yet a comparison of them, different though they are in many respects, would be most rewarding), I shall sum up my compatriot's example rapidly before I give one or two from *Vanity Fair*.

Feder explains to a rich man, Boisseaux, how wealth can best provide the 'invidious distinction' which is so sweet to man's pride. Give a dinner party in February, says he, and supply green peas, off season.

> You send a five hundred pound note to the market, and everybody can see for himself those green peas on your festive board. The jealousy that a man like you naturally inspires in this age of Jacobinism cannot possibly deny the existence of those peas. I challenge your worst enemy to deny that this one course cost you a hundred crowns. You have an exceptional advantage: not five hundred people in the whole of Paris can vie with you.[2]

To Osborne, 'conspicuous consumption' and 'conspicuous waste' consist mainly in sumptuous meals and presents.

> When Mrs Frederick's first born, Frederick Augustus Howard Stanley Devereux Bullock, was born, old Osborne ... contented himself with sending the child a gold cup, with twenty guineas inside it for the nurse. 'That's more than any of your Lords will give *I'll* warrant.'[3]

Touches like this must have been what James Hannay had in mind when he said that Thackeray's satire 'is not employed upon the character, it is part of the character itself'.[4]

Whatever is costly is good, but how good no one can tell until the price tag is turned for everyone to see. Mr Jones, the American Journalist, was aware of this when he described one of Lord Steyne's parties, for the instruction of his New York readers. He depicted 'the service

[1] *V.F.*, p. 155.
[2] *Romans et Nouvelles* (Paris, 1928), II, 235.
[3] *V.F.*, p. 358.
[4] *Studies in Thackeray* (London, 1869), p. 42.

of the table; the size and costume of the servants', then he 'enumerated the dishes and wines served; the ornaments of the sideboard and the probable value of the plate. Such a dinner, he calculated, could not be dished up under fifteen or eighteen dollars per head'.[1]

A bourgeois whose pride it is to emulate aristocrats can therefore spend no less than they do. When the old merchant asked Jos and Dobbin to dinner, 'to a dinner the most splendid and stupid that perhaps ever Mr. Osborne gave, every inch of the family plate was exhibited'.[2] Every inch indeed! For, as Veblen has said humorously: 'the signature of one's pecuniary strength should be written in characters which he who runs may see.'[3]

Beati possidentes! Both in the mirror of the silver plate and in the eyes of their awed guests, they can catch an image of themselves most gratifying to their complacency. The dining table, a symbol of human fellowship in Flaubert's novels,[4] may well appear as having a symbolic meaning in *Vanity Fair* too. It is the symbol of the double failure of its inhabitants, at once incapable of bearing solitude and of achieving communion. Hence these constant gatherings without togetherness, which Thackeray calls, with obsessive repetition, 'dismal'.

However, Old Osborne cannot personally practise the most absurd forms of conspicuous waste. He must be content with vicarious enjoyment through his son and grandson. It is George alone who can indulge in such hobbies and vices as confer 'respectability':[5] horses and gambling. It is George alone who can taste what Thackeray has called felicitously 'otiose dignity'.[6] The old man's upbringing and hard-working habits do not allow him to know for himself the idleness that marks you a 'gentleman'. *Otium cum dignitate.*

The richer he grows the better-informed he is as regards the insignia of the aristocracy. Thackeray is careful to point out this growth of knowledge as he registers the increase in wealth.

> A few years before, he used to be savage, and inveigh against all parsons, scholars and the like,—declaring that they were a pack of humbugs and quacks ... He would mourn now, in a very solemn manner, that his own education had been neglected, and repeatedly point out, in pompous orations to Georgy, the necessity and excellence of classical requirements.[7]

[1] *V.F.*, p. 616. [2] *V.F.*, p. 776.
[3] *The Theory of the Leisure Class* (New York, 1953), p. 72.
[4] See J. P. Richard, *Littérature et sensation* (Paris, 1954).
[5] See Veblen, op. cit., for a highly humorous analysis of the same social comedy in America.
[6] *V.F.*, p. 765. [7] *V.F.*, p. 707–8.

Old Osborne's mind is too small to enable him to visualize the pleasures one may derive from the classics, but he is shrewd enough to understand that their very lack of practical utility makes them tokens of caste. For who but the rich can afford to pay for the unprofitable? Thackeray is content to give a series of pictures of all those processes the social scientists analyse: he leaves the reader to do the analysis for himself, if he likes ... and if he can; for one sometimes wonders whether those who see so little in this novel do not, thereby, reveal a paucity of experience that is a bar to appreciation.

Finally it is through both son and grandson that Osborne hopes to see his most exalted dreams come true: 'His blood boiled with honest British exultation, as he saw the name of Osborne ennobled in the person of his son, and he thought that he might be the progenitor of a glorious line of baronets.'[1] Osborne's snobbery is of the sort current in the late 1840s and after rather than in the early decades of the century. There was a time when, as Walter E. Houghton tells us, 'to be a merchant prince was a far finer thing than to be a gentleman'.[2] But when Thackeray came to write *Vanity Fair*, the age 'was even more distinctly one of snobs than it was of steam; you could get out of sight of a railway-line, but the snob was ubiquitous'.[3]

To further his ambition Old Osborne is ready to marry George to bejewelled and befeathered Miss Swartz. For in society as Thackeray saw it there was no clash between the cult of mammon and what Walter Bagehot has called the 'deferential principle'. On the contrary, worship of gold was so great because worship of the lords was supreme.

When parents utilize the sons and daughters they love as a means of relieving their own frustration, one may well ask, as the showman does, where is the hazy border-line between love and selfishness, and to what extent this perversion of order accounts for the infantilism of the children.

Thackeray shows the heart's affections caught and destroyed in the welter of money. Presents are used to make up for lack of love. George Osborne bids his wife 'buy laces, millinery, jewels and

[1] *V.F.*, p. 249. [2] Op. cit., p. 185.

[3] Esmé Wingfield Stratford, *The Making of a Gentleman* (London, 1938), Ch. XII, p. 274. 'The gentleman-conscious Victorians' is well worth reading. 'Men like John Bright and Cobden did honestly believe themselves to be ... on a level with any lord in the land. It might have been said that they were too proud to be gentlemen ... Of such were the Mr Bottles of Matthew Arnold and the immortal Mr Podsnap of Dickens', p. 273. These middle-class stalwarts were philistines, not snobs.

gimcracks of all sorts'.[1] Dobbin did not even attempt to make him understand that Amelia's happiness was not centred in turtle-soup.[2] The belief that objects are signs of worthiness shades into the conviction that they are as good as feelings, and thus Vanity Fair is crammed with things.

It is essentially an indoor, overfurnished, stuffy world. No one ever goes to a window to gaze at the scenery or the sky. The very setting conveys the absence of a spiritual outlook. Like Moll Flanders, Becky has watches numberless and 'her apartments were alive with their clicking'.[3] In the Osbornes' drawing-room 'the great Iphigenia clock which ticked and tolled with mournful loudness'[4] seems to be the symbol of the order in which they live. They hear the call of time. But no beyond is sought or dreamed of. Watch-time brings the schemes of one and all round and round with dreary monotony.

Of this sameness of the life in Vanity Fair the Osbornes' reception room—once again—may appear as the symbol. 'The great glass over the mantelpiece, faced by the other great console-glass at the opposite end of the room, increased and multiplied between them the brown holland bag in which the chandelier hung; until you saw these brown holland bags fading away in endless perspectives, and this apartment of Miss Osborne's seemed the centre of a system of drawing rooms.'[5] From mirror to mirror, ever the same image of the same small world closes in upon the reader who has entered Fableland and is caught in the illusion[6], shutting him in the prison of material interests where the Osbornes live.

In this large drawing-room, Miss Osborne is often alone, the victim of her father who, after driving all impecunious suitors away, 'wanted a woman to keep his house ... [and] did not choose that she should marry'.[7] Thackeray views the relations between parents and children from different angles and sees them vitiated everywhere, even when love is lavished upon the child, for it is a love that intelligence does not guide. Amelia, who dotes upon Georgy, starts the corrupting pro-

[1] *V.F.*, p. 341. [2] *V.F.*, p. 316. [3] *V.F.*, p. 369.

[4] *V.F.*, p. 539. Cf. p. 149: '... the utter silence in his genteel, well-furnished drawing-room was only interrupted by the alarmed ticking of the great French clock'.

[5] *V.F.*, p. 539. The description of Miss Osborne's drawing-room has also been analysed by G. Armour Craig in his brilliant essay, 'On the style of *Vanity Fair*', in *Style in Prose Fiction*, English Institute Essays, 1958 (New York, 1959). Mr Craig's conclusion and mine differ, but are complementary, not antagonistic.

[6] Huizinga reminds us that illusion is a pregnant word which means: 'in-play', from *inlusio, illudere, inludere*. *Homo Ludens* (London, 1949).

[7] *V.F.*, p. 540.

cess which his grandfather and aunt will carry on. Old Pitt, Mrs Bute Crawley, the Sedleys bring up their children stupidly or selfishly and make them the fools that they are.

Thus Becky as bad mother is no exception in Vanity Fair. In this respect, as in others, one of the strands in the skein of life is only more vividly conspicuous in her. Long before she had a child of her own, the showman could see that 'she had no soft maternal heart'.[1] She was not amused by the prattle of the little girls at school, nor did she feel inclined to comfort them and kiss their tears away. She confessed that she did not care a fig about her older pupils.[2] Indeed, the deliberate care of the artist is always apparent in Thackeray's study of a woman devoid of maternal instinct.

Far from being 'out of character', as some critics have contended, the box on her son's ears is a well-prepared climax. Good-humoured Becky can occasionally have a fit of temper like you and me. Thackeray's portrayal of Becky is faultless; it is his comment that goes wrong: that the child bores and annoys her as the showman says he does, nobody can doubt. That his presence in the house 'was a reproach and a pain to her',[3] I find impossible to believe. If Becky did feel such a pang of remorse before little Rawdon's innocent stare, she would be another woman. Thackeray gave a more exact expression of his knowledge of the world where Beckies prosper when he wrote: 'We grieve at being found out, and at the idea of shame or punishment; but the mere sense of wrong makes very few people unhappy in Vanity Fair.'[4] And least of all Miss Sharp.

The ultimate consequence of the parents' greed or snobbery, which they misname love of their children, is to be discovered in what Thackeray has called 'the marriage country'.[5] But as this question demands a whole book to itself, I can only indicate the recurring pattern of events: bartering rank against money, and money against rank leads to death-in-life. It must also be stated that this treatment of the theme loses much of its demonstrative force because, in any case, he can never see the 'marriage country' as a 'green and pleasant'[6] land, not even when it is love that has brought man and woman thither. *Vacuam sedem et inania arcana.*[7] This quotation from Tacitus (*Hist.* V, 9) is enough to show what is wrong with Thackeray's idea of love: he romantically conceived it as worship.

[1] *V.F.*, p. 19. [2] *V.F.*, p. 123. [3] *V.F.*, p. 562.
[4] *V.F.*, p. 534. [5] *V.F.*, p. 319. [6] *V.F.*, p. 319.
[7] Thackeray himself quotes Tacitus (inaccurately) in *Esmond*, Ch. VII.

Before we proceed further let us look back and see at a glance the whole prospect of the ground we have scrutinized point by point. Starting from Becky, we have studied what might be called the quality of time in *Vanity Fair*, the confusion of spiritual and material values, the link between the craving for rank and the love of money, the dialectics of predaciousness and self-righteousness, the urge to ostentation and the sense of being worthy, unbearable solitude and impossible communion, and the effect of snobbery and greed upon the life of the heart.

III

Of the various manifestations of 'Vanity Fair mentality' that we now propose to examine, Becky again is the best indicator. She solicits other people's friendship and praise as no one else does, and yet she remains self-sufficient. She basks in the warmth of men's and women's admiration but does not collapse when this fails her. This toughness strikes us the more since many people lack it today. Contrast reveals features once hardly apparent. Because the number of 'other-directed' people is large in the present world, we notice with greater interest the 'inner-direction' of bygone generations.[1]

Becky seeks friends to serve her own ends, to show off her charm and wit, and to indulge in play. Anyone amusing she enjoys, anyone useful she coaxes. Others she certainly needs, but as we need luxuries that give piquancy to life, not as necessities without which we die. She does all she can to be liked, for to be liked is fun and profit, but to her it is not a primary emotional exigency. The contempt shown for her by

[1] Is it necessary to say that the interest I take in David Riesman, in the several-times quoted Thorstein Veblen, or in any other social scientist, does not mean that I accept their views unreservedly and uncritically? Because truth is many-faced none can hope to see it whole, but I have learned much from them. 'There are books', writes an economist, Professor Kenneth Boulding, 'some of them rather bad books, after which the world is not quite the same again. Veblen, for instance, was not, I think, a great social scientist, and yet he invented an undying phrase: "conspicuous consumption". After reading Veblen, one can never quite see a university campus or an elaborate house in just the same light as before. In a similar vein, David Riesman's division of humanity into inner-directed and other-directed people is no doubt open to serious criticism by the methodologists. Nevertheless, after reading Riesman, one has a rather new view of the universe ... ' *The Image, Knowledge in Life and Society* (Ann Arbor, 1961), pp. 9–10. Indeed, one can never quite see the great novels of the nineteenth century in the same light either. The novelists' insights into man and society have been there all the time for us to study, but we can now understand them better than before and, it is not presumptuous to say, better than the novelists themselves.

the daughters of the local gentry at Queen's Crawley merely tickles her sense of humour. Great ladies may cut her or stare at her, but 'to stare Becky out of countenance required a severer glance than even the frigid old Bareacres could shoot out of her dismal eyes'. Her own estimation of herself is not dependent on other people's opinion of her. Nobody can mould her as she moulds Sir Pitt, for instance. This insecure prig becomes, to a large extent, what she suggests he should be. Desires that she instils into him he looks upon as spontaneous growth. His changes of front and reversals of opinion reveal the vacuum in his mind, whereas Becky's *volte-face* are but the expression of her singleness of purpose.

She likes her husband, but does not care if he is estranged from her. 'Indeed she did not miss him or anybody.'[1] We find magnified in her what may be called the 'extreme sociological singularism' prevailing in the fair; that is to say, in Pitirim Sorokin's words, 'that the individual is the only social reality ontologically'[2] and also that the only values are 'those of singularistic existence': the comfort, pleasures and happiness of the individual.

Becky, like practically all her fellow-citizens, is incapable of feeling *with* others. Nor is she ever *with* them, in the fullness of meaning that this humble preposition assumes for some people. She is *confronted by* them, or she *faces* them; she stands or sits *in front of* them, but always self-centred, self-possessed and unchanging.[3]

She likes men, but it never occurs to her that human beings may build something enduring in each other's hearts. Her time is always occupied, and yet her life is empty. Neither she nor any of the others will, when death comes, leave anything but money.

The idea of bankruptcy,[4] ever present on account of Old Pitt's unsuccessful lawsuits and speculations, of Sedley's insolvency and Becky's loss of money and jewels, calls to mind—to the mind of the reader and indeed to that of the showman—the thought of another failure—a spiritual failure. When he exclaims: 'All her lies and her schemes, all her selfishness and her wiles, all her wit and genius had come to this bankruptcy',[5] it is not only of her hundred rings, of watches, diamonds and bank notes he is thinking.

But inner-directed though she be, she is still a snob. She also—and

[1] *V.F.*, p. 659. [2] Op. cit., p. 337.
[3] Compare Georges Blin, *Stendhal et les problèmes de la personnalité* (Paris, 1958), p. 75.
[4] On bankruptcy in *Vanity Fair*, see also G. Armour Craig's article, op. cit., pp. 105–8.
[5] *V.F.*, p. 677.

indeed she more than any other—wants to pass for what she is not. She always contrives today to go one step higher than yesterday. To her, life means spatial motion and location, a constant climb, a repetition of gestures. Being ever tends—one should even say aspires—to seeming. It is because the gap between reality and appearance is so small that the narrator can record both at one go, as I explained before, bridging them together ironically. For instance, a parenthesis crudely inserted in a dialogue does the trick:

> Captain Crawley left me this morning as gay as if he were going to a hunting-party. What does he care? What do any of you care for the agonies and tortures of a poor forsaken woman? (I wonder whether he *could* really have been going to the troops this great lazy gourmand?) Oh! dear Mr. Sedley, I have come to you for comfort—for consolation.[1]

When being is almost reduced to seeming, when appearance fails to conceal what reality there is underneath, the characters do not, and cannot, develop, since development is ever greater radiance of the mind and spirit, greater definition and fullness of being. In the selfish, static world of Vanity Fair, therefore, time is denied its constructive power and spiritual significance. The clocks and watches tick away unavailingly, for the hands still point to the same hour, the hour of deceit.

Many readers complain that Thackeray has no sense of his characters' inner life and is content to stay on the surface of their existence. But when people ask themselves 'How do I look? What do I pass for?' not 'What am I?', when living is only scheming, when thought is mere calculation, there is little inner life. The novelist's technique is forced upon him by his choice of subject and *dramatis personae*. The personal life of his puppets tends to merge into their social life. On the relation between these two lives, any reader of modern psychology knows more today than Thackeray ever suspected, but one thing he saw very clearly: that the social life of the snobs is the expression of their inmost desire; that these arch-egoists, in one respect at least, evince little love of self, since they cramp it into a borrowed garment.

Thackeray's aim was to show the appalling impoverishment of existence when man's inborn sense of transcendence is degraded into the mere urge to outstrip his neighbour; when immense vitality is not accompanied by reverence for life; when fallow land extends where there should be harvest fields. He has realized his intentions so well

[1] *V.F.*, p. 379.

that his very success is counted to him for a fault or even for a sin. But this ironical fate would hardly have surprised this ironist, well used to disappointment and suffering, whose gaiety sparkles over such depths of wistfulness.

Grieved as we may be, we nevertheless enjoy the comedy that hypocrisy must put on, day after day, in Vanity Fair. Whether the actors are dullards like Pitt, clumsy through over-eagerness like Mrs Bute Crawley, or virtuosi in the art of lying like Becky, the show is always good, for there is something incongruous in the contortions that hypocrites must perform, something fundamentally absurd in the defacing of truth. The very sadness and contempt of the spectator find release in laughter.

And Becky is such 'a splendid actress!', as that connoisseur, the Marquis of Steyne, exclaims. She is one of the most brilliant liars in literature. A vice carried to such a height, with ever renewed brio and flourish, and an unfailing wealth of invention, seems so unreal that it ceases to be obnoxious.

But when everybody lies, mutual communication becomes a parody. It is said that the Emperor Che Houang-ti proudly declared, after the publication of his dictionary: 'I have brought order ... everything has a fitting name.' In Vanity Fair, apart from objects of daily use, nothing has its fitting name and disorder prevails. Rivalry is called friendship, unconcern love, honour 'd—d sentimentality'.[1] The characters are the counterfeiters of language, and language is between them like an insulator, not a conductor. Hence an extra thickness of solitude. The showman smiles a wry smile when he sees the degradation of a favourite word of his like 'gentleman'. To George and his peers, a gentleman is one who is 'worth' thousands of pounds, keeps his carriage, travels with servants, appreciates wines, etc. Because of his partiality for the rhetoric of contrast, Thackeray was moved to embody his own ideal of the gentleman in Major Dobbin. And yet his ironical portrayal of George made his conception very clear. Irony is a revealing paradox: it gives words fullness of meaning when it seems to be devaluating them. No one can miss the true significance of 'authenticity' when a letter of Becky's, which is a pack of lies, is called 'authentic'.[2] What heroism stands for is obvious when Jos is labelled a 'stout hero'.[3] Thus the ironical narrator restores to language the force and precision it loses through the characters' misuse of it. His rectitude serves as a foil to their crookedness, his sincerity to their hypocrisy. And his

[1] *V.F.*, p. 294. [2] *V.F.*, p. 311. [3] *V.F.*, p. 317.

style of presentation—in derisive counterpoint to their mendacious talk—rests on a delicate sense of the semantic value of language.

In the comedy of errors permanently acted on the stage of the fair, all the mistakes do not result from reciprocal lying. Many also arise from the selfishness that makes it impossible for anyone to understand anyone else, through lack of imaginative sympathy. Thus the tone of the comedy modulates from the farce of hypocrisy to the drama of solitude. Rawdon misunderstands Becky, Amelia George, Old Osborne his son, and—more humorously—Becky mistakes Miss Crawley, who never relents.

Between the characters, whose estrangement from one another is due to the several deep-rooted causes that I have analysed, there also stand the barriers that snobbery is for ever erecting. Two or three examples will suffice to provide material for discussion.

In the elation of her success at Gaunt House, Becky 'passed Lady Stunnington by with a look of scorn. She patronized Lady Gaunt and her astonished and mortified sister-in-law. She *écrasé*'d all her rival charmers.'[1]

At Brussels, in June 1815, people panted to be asked to a ball given by a duchess. Struggles, intrigues, prayers were used in turn. Becky 'vowed that it was a delightful ball; that there was everybody that everybody knew, and only a *very* few nobodies in the whole room'.[2]

Everyone is so much afraid of mixing with the people on the floor below that one's very family may prove embarrassing. Mrs Frederick Bullock, *née* Osborne, having married above her (so her husband's relatives believe) was therefore 'bound by superior pride and great care, in the composition of her visiting book, to make up for the defects of birth; and felt it her duty to see her father and sister as little as possible'.[3]

But the same 'Mrs Frederick Bullock ... would have gone on her knees from May Fair to Lombard street, if Lady Steyne and Lady Gaunt had been waiting in the city to raise her up, and say: "come to us next Friday" '.[4]

As for Old Osborne, who tyrannizes over his daughter, servants and clerks,

> Whenever he met a great man he grovelled before him and my-lorded him ... he came home and looked out his history in the *Peerage* ... he fell down prostrate and basked in him as a Neapolitan beggar does in the sun.[5]

[1] *V.F.*, p. 653. [2] *V.F.*, p. 356. [3] *V.F.*, p. 537.
[4] *V.F.*, p. 614. [5] *V.F.*, p. 154.

These are the manners observed by the showman in the fair, a symbolic pantomime of mastery on the one hand and of subservience on the other.[1] In this respect, Thackeray's vision is Hegelian. There are masters and slaves in Vanity Fair, but no *prochains*.

As usual, he selects and magnifies both incidents and behavioural characteristics; as usual, gestures stiffen, responses become more automatic, living persons are changed into the puppets of Fableland, and thereby one aspect of truth becomes glaring.

What he illustrates through comedy, John Stuart Mill, Ruskin and others have commented upon;[2] but Alexis de Tocqueville's analysis is perhaps the most illuminating.

> When it is birth alone [he writes], independent of wealth, which classes men in society, everyone knows exactly what his own position is upon the social scale; he does not seek to rise, he does not fear to sink. In a community thus organized, men of different castes communicate very little with each other; but if accident brings them together, they are ready to converse without hoping or fearing to lose their own position. Their intercourse is not upon a footing of equality but it is not constrained. When moneyed aristocracy succeeds to aristocracy of birth, the case is altered.
>
> The privileges of some are still extremely great, but the possibility of acquiring these privileges is open to all: whence it follows that those who possess them are constantly haunted by the apprehension of losing them ... ranks still exist but it is not easy clearly to distinguish at a glance those who respectively belong to them. Secret hostilities then arise in the community; one set of men endeavour by innumerable artifices to penetrate, or to appear to penetrate, among those who are above them; another set are constantly in arms against these usurpers of their rights; or rather the same individual does both at once, and while he seeks to raise himself in a higher circle, he is always on the defensive against the intrusion of those below him. Such is the condition of England at the present time.[3]

There had begun that endless artificial partitioning of society which was, and is, by no means limited to England. Stendhal and Proust, each with his own brand of irony, observed it in nineteenth- and

[1] Veblen, op. cit., p. 48.

[2] All relevant excerpts will be found in W. E. Houghton, op. cit., sections 'Respectability', 'the Bourgeois Dream'. One of my reasons for quoting Tocqueville—apart from its exceptional intrinsic interest—is that the passage is not given by Professor Houghton whose remarkable book is well-known to students of nineteenth-century English literature.

[3] *Democracy in America* (1835–40), abridged edition, 'World's Classics', pp. 436–7.

twentieth-century France. As René Girard points out,[1] in Marxist Russia as in capitalist America, social taboos have cropped up, new forms of alienation have superseded the old ones. Novelists and sociologists alike testify to the fears, restlessness and rivalries that vanity is for ever breeding.

> Ah! *Vanitas vanitatum*! Which of us is happy in this world? Which of us has his desire? Or, having it, is satisfied?

Just as Thackeray brackets together Thrifty and Thriftless who are equally selfish, he couples the aristocracy with the middle classes because, equally ignorant of the true nature of nobility, they judge one another on externals only. In this respect he agrees with Stendhal, who wrote to Balzac: all our aristocrats are ignoble (*in-nobilis*) 'parce qu'ils prisent la noblesse'[2] (as a caste, of course). Having no idea of what man's true worth is, having few, if any, moral and intellectual qualities, they must need emphasize trivial outside differences. The bourgeois and the lord have the same criteria. And these are nugatory. Old Osborne's sham coat of arms, Steyne's titles—First Lord of the Powder Closet and Groom of the Back Stairs—might stand as the symbols of the fake world of snobs.

Thackeray was as well aware as we are that such a view is excessive.[3] Fableland is like that motoring map of England, where only the major roads are charted. All is true there, but it is not the whole truth, as the unhappy motorist from the continent soon finds out. However, not even my better maps convey the friendliness of the hill's curve, or the peacefulness of a village clustering around its church. Due allowance being made, what the cartographer does for the natural scenery, the novelist does for man's land: he schematizes in order to bring out a meaning.[4] Of course, the comparison must not be pressed too far: the novel appeals to my sensitivity as well as to my intellect; but even its sensuous imagery, devised by an author who seeks to understand his experience, speaks first to the mind of the reader who seeks to understand truth. Moreover, the way in which the personages meet and associate in this novel (as in many others) gives it an exemplary,

[1] Op. cit., p. 226.

[2] Quoted by Girard, p. 127.

[3] 'God forbid that the world should be like it altogether.' *Letters*, II, 354.

[4] Cf. Georges Blin, *Stendhal et les problèmes du roman* (Paris, 1954), p. 11. In his profound book, M. Blin studies the problems of realism and truth in the novel at much greater length than I do here, and, indeed, in a different spirit; however, at times, his argumentation and mine are close to each other, and I am brought to wonder whether I have been influenced by him unawares.

therefore explanatory, character. Even if you believe that a woman like Becky, men like Steyne, Old Pitt and his son, Jos Sedley and all the others exist, you can hardly believe that 'such a collection was ever got together in one corner of the world'.[1]

When we think about the significance of the *dramatis personae*, we find that it is twofold. They convey their creator's judgment upon life by the very fact that he made them what they are. And the way in which they seek one another, in the autonomous world of the novel, is also a judgment upon life. A man's choice always tells how he views the world and what sort of a world he wants to promote. It always has an axiological meaning. And since the reader postulates that contingency, not determinism, prevails in Fableland, and that the characters are as free as we deem that man is, the fact that they all choose alike—money, careerism—is demonstrative in the highest degree.

As an artist, Thackeray knew how necessary is 'la fausseté de la perspective' as Flaubert calls it. As a man, he is sensitized to the sickness rather than to the health around him. Sickness is prominent in the fair. Old Pitt is an unbalanced lecher, my Lord Southdown is epileptic and simple-minded, Lord George Gaunt is insane, 'a living dead man'.[2] The narrator lays great emphasis upon this 'mysterious taint in the blood',[3] 'this awful ancestral curse',[4] which haunts that sadist and debauchee, Lord Steyne. However, the most conspicuous representative of the sickness of civilization is Jos Sedley, whose importance in the novel Dorothy Van Ghent was probably the first critic to underscore.[5]

Just as Becky's snobbery and ruthlessness are but the intensified images of the same traits in the others, Jos Sedley's gormandize, obesity and impotence are magnified characteristics of everyone. No one creates anything of value. For all, life is a race to win, not a work in which to put the best of one's self. Of this intellectual and spiritual sterility Jos's impotence is the symbol.

In that world, food assumes a monstrous importance, and the obesity of the body sets off the starvation of the mind and the heart. The wines, meats, fishes, fruits, spices, desserts mentioned, would make a handsome list even for a first-class caterer. Miss Crawley is fat, her horses are fat, her servants are fat, her spaniels are fat,[6] and she

[1] Adolphus Alfred Jack, *Thackeray, the Novelist* (London, 1895), p. 80.
[2] *V.F.*, p. 596. [3] *V.F.*, p. 595. [4] *V.F.*, p. 596.
[5] Op. cit., p. 146. Dorothy Van Ghent's study is very short but pertinent.
[6] *V.F.*, p. 118.

overeats herself to death. Old Osborne's biliousness is partly the result of overfeeding.[1] As for Jos's gluttony, it is one of the forms of compensation in which he indulges to forget his frustration and solitude, for he is as lonely in London as 'in his jungle at Boggly Wollah'.[2]

He belongs to the type of man that, in eighteenth-century France, was called by President de Brosses and others 'un Babilan', 'amoureux platonique par décret de la nature'.[3] Whether or not the glandular disorder to which Jos's adiposity testifies is a cause of physiological impotence, no one, not even Thackeray, could tell. But impotent he is, if only for psychological reasons.

What ambiguity there is in the portrayal is due to the author's inevitably very vague knowledge of this form of neurosis, as much as to the equally inevitable shyness that a nineteenth-century novelist felt when approaching ticklish subjects. Stendhal, too, was cramped, ill-at-ease, when he pictured Octave in *Armance* (1827).

Anyhow, clinical information would merely have hampered Thackeray. He had a sufficient stock of observations and even, after all, enough elbow-room to create one of the most interesting figures in the fair.

It is on Jos's effeminacy that Thackeray throws perhaps the most glaring light, describing his gaudy waistcoats, the 'profuse ornamentation of pins and jewellery about his person',[4] telling us that 'his toilet-table was covered with as many pomatums and essences as ever were displayed by an old beauty',[5] reporting the words of his father who has no patience 'with his dandified modesty. It is out-Josephing Joseph.'[6]

Jos is a figure of fun, but his pathos is not lost on the narrator who sees him as the loneliest puppet in a lonely crowd, at once separated from women, who 'frightened him beyond measure',[7] and to some extent from men, who laugh at him.

He can only carry on the business of life and living through his personal mythology. He forgets what he is in acting the part of somebody else, in effacing the borderline between the world of facts and that of imaginings, in living a wakeful dream. Jos is not himself, he is a stowaway,[8] attempting to sail through life concealed in the personality

[1] *V.F.*, p. 540. [2] *V.F.*, p. 27.
[3] See Henri Martineau, *L'œuvre de Stendhal* (Paris, 1945), p. 296.
[4] *V.F.*, p. 728. [5] *V.F.*, p. 28.
[6] *V.F.*, p. 36. [7] *V.F.*, p. 28.
[8] The metaphor is Karen Horney's, quoted by Louis Schneider in *The Freudian Psychology and Veblen's Social Theory* (New York, 1948), p. 196.

of an imaginary He-man. Thus he ogles the maidservants when they are at a safe distance, he affects a military appearance, sports a military coat, grows mustachios, forgets, in the highly coloured account he gives of it, the fear which almost killed him at a tiger-hunt, speaks of Waterloo as if he was partly responsible for the victory.

Every citizen of the fair is haunted by the thought of the others. Everyone is everybody else's hell or elusive promise of paradise. But Jos, too weak to bear such uneasiness and anxiety, finds an escape in fantasy.

With as much acuity as Flaubert, Thackeray has observed that disorder in man's personality which Flaubert's very perceptive critic, Jules de Gaultier,[1] has called 'le bovarysme'. In the interval that separates what a man is from what he thinks he is there is to be found all the comedy and all the tragedy of existence. We have both the fun and the drama in Thackeray's novel, and in Jos the comic and the pathetic are fused in one person. Even his vanity is at once grotesque and sad, for it is part of his neurotic self-delusion. His feeling of separateness makes him very shy and shyness, in turn, makes him very vain. Shyness is often the result of vanity,[2] as Thackeray says, but in Joseph's case, he probably mistook the effect for the cause: Joseph's vanity is the reverse side of his abnormal timidity.

He is vain of qualities he does not possess, proud of the man he is not. He has substituted a ghost for the self. And thus vanity saves him from himself as does also his snobbery. Indeed, he better than any other enables us to see snobbery as a sickness of the soul, in a world where man has become the idol of man. 'A set of people living without God.'

Of course, Jos is meant to make us laugh, but to miss his pathos is to miss the significance of one of Thackeray's most remarkable portraits, and some of the meaning of his picture of the fair.

On first reading the commentary on *Vanity Fair* that the novelist wrote to his mother,[3] one wonders if he had forgotten Amelia and

[1] Jules de Gaultier is primarily a philosopher. See *Le Bovarysme*, 2e édition (Paris, 1912), p. 16. Also *Le génie de Flaubert* (Paris, 1913). That Thackeray expressed his own 'Bovarysme' in his novels, and, to a certain extent, mastered it by expressing it, is certain but this is another story. Readers will find ample material in Thackeray's own letters, Gordon N. Ray's biography, Raymond Las Vergnas's psychological analysis in his book *W. M. Thackeray. L'homme, le penseur, le romancier* (Paris, 1932). See the section called 'Contradictions'.

[2] As Stendhal, among others, has testified time and again. 'S'il est excessivement timide c'est qu'il est excessivement prétentieux.' *Mémoires d'un touriste*, édition Champion, 4 vols., I, 45.

[3] See *supra*, p. 1.

Dobbin, if only for an instant. But the supposition is untenable. The careful construction of the book and the important role played by these two characters exclude the possibility of such forgetfulness. Yet Amelia does not live without God. We know that she prays, although her prayers are 'secrets out of the domain of Vanity Fair'.[1] The narrator does not scruple to describe the prayers of the household at Queen's Crawley, for this ceremony is one of the forms that cant assumes in society; but Amelia is sincere. She is in the fair like a 'lost wanderer in the great struggling crowds'.[2] What interests Thackeray is the plight of a woman caught in the worldly welter without any of the strength of Bunyan's pilgrims to steer her own course. Amelia initiates nothing. She only reverberates the decisions made by others. She is tossed about uncomprehending and unhappy. Professor Kathleen Tillotson[3] has pointed out how carefully her story is dovetailed into that of Becky, and she has made it clear, once for all, that Amelia cannot be shown out of the book as some would like. She is there to stay.

But does she not belong to the fair after all? Neither at home nor at school could she learn what religion is, faith living to the heart and strength renewed by trial. She is like the others in another respect too: she never was a woman of brain, and they have degraded their intellect by making it serve greed; the result is therefore the same, a life where mind has not its proper place. Faith should seek intelligence, but her share of intelligence is small. She is ready to sacrifice Dobbin, a life's friend, and let into her home Becky the destroyer, in accordance with what she thinks are 'the purest religious principles'.[4] The others' religion is lip service, or, at best, 'a sort of formal general assent in Christianity in the gross',[5] to use Wilberforce's words; hers is a very dim light indeed. As for her selfishness, I have mentioned it earlier.

W. C. Brownell has said that Amelia is not a simple character.[6] She certainly is not; neither is she unconvincing. But she is uninteresting: a milksop, as Thackeray wrote in a letter.[7] Much can be said, and has been said, to justify her presence. Gordon Ray contends that

[1] *V.F.*, p. 321. [2] *V.F.*, p. 319.

[3] In an essay that nobody interested in Thackeray can afford to miss, *Novels of the Eighteen-Forties* (Oxford, 1954), pp. 248–50.

[4] *V.F.*, p. 858.

[5] *A Practical View of the Prevailing Religious System of Professed Christians, etc.* The 1958 S.C.M. reprint (London), p. 55 (Ch. V, section I).

[6] *Victorian Prose Masters*, 1902, p. 31.

[7] *Letters*, II, 383: 'Arthur and his pretty amiable milksop Amelia sort of wife go to India this month.'

'even if Amelia's inadequacy is granted, however, one must still insist that to regard *Vanity Fair* as primarily the story of Becky Sharp is to place the novel in a false and impoverishing perspective'.[1] This is true. Careful study shows how necessary Amelia is to the economy of the novel, but she remains uninteresting all the same, because she fails to engage our aesthetic sympathies. The author's *a priori* conception of her character and role is sound, but it did not arouse his creative imagination to the full.

As for Dobbin, the very conception of his character is a mistake. You cannot make a man convincingly express your most deeply felt ideal of the gentleman, if you present him as 'a spoony'.[2] The rhetoric of contrast called for a fighter, a rugged representative of all that was best in the sons of the bourgeoisie, not for a Major Sugarplums and his 'bread-and-butter' paradise.[3] A choice had to be made that Thackeray did not make: either offer no alternative to the fair, or offer one that tallies with the seriousness of purpose that the satirical portraits and authorial comments imply. A novelist can play with his characters within limits. A little fun at the expense of a good man endears him to us, as all lovers of English literature know. His oddities and foibles humanize his virtues. But Thackeray went further. He allowed Dobbin to behave not like a man of fine sensibility tempered by lucidity of judgment, but like a sentimental fool. And thus he has degraded the ideal that Dobbin stands for. The Major belongs neither to the fair nor to a better world in which we can believe. His portrait is an error of judgment. If Thackeray had not made this mistake, if the Major was what both the form of the novel and its ethical significance led the reader to expect, the book would have an extra dimension, an opening on to the very light that guided the novelist as he drew his puppets and commented upon them.

The last part of my descriptive analysis has enabled me to sketch out a *rapprochement* between Thackeray and other eye-witnesses of the times. Because his picture is deliberately incomplete, the perspective is distorted, but what he chooses to look at he sees with extreme acuteness. Social analysts, among whom Tocqueville is prominent, testify to the essential truth of the image drawn by Thackeray; an image of the anxieties, struggles and ruthlessness of men, at the moment when the

[1] Op. cit., p. 425. On Amelia see Mark Spilka, 'A Note on Thackeray's Amelia', *N.C.F.*, December 1955, and Myron Taube, 'The Character of Amelia in the Meaning of *Vanity Fair*', *Victorian News Letter*, No. 18, 1960.

[2] *V.F.*, p. 844. [3] *V.F.*, p. 746.

old class lines are becoming blurred without being erased, and when ever-changing new barriers are being erected.

Like Stendhal, he dissects vanity and, with a sparkling sense of comedy, he studies the itch for unreal distinctions and the envy of trivial honours; he sees how the jealousy and rivalry between persons is mediated through the struggle for money, how, indeed, man's desire has a sort of triangular movement, from the self to the other through the object.

Like Flaubert, he is sensitive to the sickness in civilization as well as to the flaw in a man's personality that prompts him to conceive himself other than he is or can be.

In the comedy of errors that goes on uninterruptedly on the stage of Vanity Fair, egoism and the devaluation of language are seen playing the major roles. The inner life of the individual dwindles away. Temporal development, spiritual and intellectual creativeness dry up. Disbelief in God is unacknowledged, and indeed, unrealized, but Christianity has ceased to be an inspiration. Should there be more warmth of heart, religion could provide no sure guidance to people with small minds, as Amelia's story illustrates.

Both the highly stylized, ironical portrayal of the characters, and the technique of selective repetition and contrast, make for emphasis. It seems as though we heard strong beats only, and we are certainly not made aware of all the coils and thickness of life. This was the price Thackeray had to pay for the limitations imposed upon him, perhaps not so much by the theme of Godlessness in the world, as by the choice of people in whom it pleased him to see it at work. With force, brilliancy and an almost diagrammatic clarity, he brings out the features of certain territories in man's land, but he did not choose to portray it whole.

J. Middleton Murry

G. WILSON KNIGHT

WHEN after leaving Oxford I was groping for a way to express what I had to say about Shakespeare, Middleton Murry's articles in the monthly *Adelphi* magazine acted on me like an avatar; and to his writings of this period my debt remains. Here was someone who without reservations was proclaiming the religious importance of literature in a voice of authority.

After the death of Katherine Mansfield, Murry had had a mystical experience which he describes in *To the Unknown God* (1924; pp. 42–4) and *God* (1929; pp. 35–6). Here is his description, written soon after the experience:

> Then in the dark, in the dead, still house, I sat at the table facing the fire. I sat there motionless for hours, while I tried to face the truth that I was alone. As I had wanted to turn back, so now I longed to turn away. There was in me something that simply would not look, and, again and again, as it turned its eyes away, I took its head in my two hands and held its face towards what I had to see. Slowly and with an effort I made myself conscious that I was physically alone. Prompted by some instinct, I tried to force this consciousness into every part of my body. Slowly I succeeded. At last I had the sensation that I *was* in my hands and feet, that where they ended I also ended, as at a frontier of my being, and beyond that frontier stretched out the vast immensities, of space, of the universe, of the illimitable, something that was other than I. Where I ended, it began—

other, strange, terrible, menacing. It did not know me, would never acknowledge me, denied me utterly. Yet out upon this, from the fragile rampart of my own body, I found the courage to peer, to glance, at last to gaze steadily. And I became aware of myself as a little island against whose slender shores a cold, dark, boundless ocean lapped devouring. Somehow, in that moment, I knew I had reached a pinnacle of personal being. I was I, as I had never been before—and never should be again.

It is strange that I should have known that. But then I did know it, and it was not strange.

What happened then? If I could tell you that I should tell you a secret indeed. But a moment came when the darkness of that ocean changed to light, the cold to warmth; when it swept in one great wave over the shores and frontiers of my self; when it bathed me and I was renewed; when the room was filled with a presence, and I knew I was not alone—that I never could be alone any more, that the universe beyond held no menace, for I was part of it, that in some way for which I had sought in vain so many years, I *belonged*, and because I belonged, I was no longer I, but something different, which could never be afraid in the old ways, or cowardly with the old cowardice. And the love I had lost was still mine, but now more durable, being knit into the very substance of the universe I had feared. And the friends whose words had been so meaningless were bound to me, and I to them, for ever. And if it should prove that I had a work to do, or a part to play, I should no longer draw back at the last.

This experience had subsequently fused in his mind with his interests as a literary critic and in the *Adelphi* he was delivering a gospel based on that experience as corroborated by literature. His views at this period are covered by the volumes *To the Unknown God* (1924) and *Things to Come* (1928), most of which appeared originally in the *Adelphi*. These volumes I designate '*U.G.*' and '*T.C.*'.

The teaching is a teaching of soul-discovery through tragic experience and the final aim a 'change of consciousness' (*U.G.*, pp. 184, 191, 296). Through suffering and tragedy the soul is realized and such a realization conditions and empowers both the teaching of Jesus and the greatest literature. The interior and exterior worlds of human knowledge (*U.G.*, p. 220) are transcended: the more harmony there is in oneself the more harmony is discovered in the external order (*Adelphi*, IV, i; July 1926; p. 5). Jesus, says Murry, taught that there is a faculty attainable by which man can see beyond the apparent good and evil outside and within (*T.C.*, p. 170). Mind and heart may be unified to create this soul-sight:

The soul is simply the condition of the complete man. And to this

> completeness in the man, which is his soul, there corresponds a completeness and harmony of the world of his experience.
>
> (*T.C.*, p. 171)

That world now 'becomes God'; and the knowing of it is simultaneously a supernal love.

This state is achieved through loyalty to one's own experience (*U.G.*, pp. 9, 60). Great writers are authoritative only because the soul recognizes their authority. Truth is immediate and is recognized by the momentarily integrated man when

> through his whole being there comes a flash of sudden awareness of unity within him, and from some place that he scarcely knew leaps up a sense of knowledge and a sense of oneness in that which knows; when his deepest, unfamiliar self rises and takes possession of all that he is, body and mind and soul, and declares: *This is true* ...
>
> (*U.G.*, p. 75)

But what is experience cannot be easily defined. Intellect 'is the servant, not the master, of life' (*Adelphi*, IV, i; July 1926; p. 5); it cannot harmonize or create, but only elucidate (*T.C.*, p. 227). Again:

> To make artistic creation possible your knowledge *must* give way; you must resign yourself to the deep unconscious purpose that is in you, and 'let that which is creative create itself'. Purpose will declare itself in despite of all your philosophies, as it does in Hardy and Tchehov. But if you will not, or you cannot, do this, if you will *know* and know all the time, then there is an end. The books you write are dead, and you have slain the art you loved; and slain it when it would have saved you. For by its own operation the art of literature has power to recreate the sense of purpose in the soul.
>
> (*Adelphi*, IV, iii; September 1926; pp. 144–5)

This 'purpose' is 'prior to all its symbolisms, literature itself included' and 'religion depends upon it, not it upon religion' (*Adelphi*, IV, iii; September 1926; p. 145). Murry tends to avoid any detailed commitments. Great literature is a revelation of a harmony that *cannot be interpreted*:

> Art holds the place it does in our secret loyalties—so it seems to me—because it does reveal what cannot be uttered. That, and no other, is the test of its authenticity.
>
> (*U.G.*, p. 265)

Murry's attitude to 'God' is similar. He uses the term, but will not commit himself to a 'personal' God:

> The only record of the nature of God is history—the things that were and are. The inscrutable process of the universe, this is He; and man, in whom the great process knows itself for a moment, can know it is not in vain. Little enough indeed, yet enough, and more than enough. To know that there is a purpose, yet not to know the purpose—this is blessedness indeed. To see but a tiny inch into the million miles of the unknown future—this is not forlorn and despairing, as orthodoxy would persuade us, but an authentic *sursum* to the soul. To know the future—what utter weariness!
>
> (*T.C.*, p. 227)

In which there is a psychological truth to which we may respond.

Murry's position involved a conflict with religious orthodoxy. Christ is his supreme hero, but a hero as a man whose unrivalled perfection drove him to a tragic death. Official Christian dogma and doctrine are no longer acceptable (*U.G.*, pp. 135–7, 190–1, 193–203). Just as Murry rejects the 'intellectually premeditated' technique of James Joyce as a distortion of the creative impulse (*Adelphi*, IV, iii; September 1926; p. 140), so he distrusts dogma as a pandering to intellect. During this period he was engaged in a controversy with Mr T. S. Eliot as a romantic against classicism (*U.G.*, p. 134). Murry aligns Catholicism with classicism (*U.G.*, p. 136). His central tenet is this:

> When literature becomes a parlour-game and religion a church-mummery, they are alike only in their deadness. But between the literature that is real and the religion that is real the bond is close and unbreakable.
>
> (*U.G.*, p. 164)

For Murry orthodoxy was no longer 'real'. The Renaissance was the beginning of a new individualism, and it is useless to look back and 'sigh after a unity of religiousness that can never be ours' (*Adelphi*, IV, IV; October 1926; pp. 205–6. In discussing the Abbé Brémond's *Prière et Poésie* he will not allow that poetry aspires to the condition of prayer, putting it the other way round (*T.C.*, p. 217), and insisting on Eckhart's mysticism of descent, of a return to the actual, which is the concern of literature. Many today 'know that they are religious' and yet that 'the religion of today has no *meaning* for them'; while 'the words that have meaning for them are the words of the poets' (*T.C.*, p. 218).

Difficulties present themselves. Despite Murry's trust in poetry and his acute discussions of metaphor in *The Problem of Style* (1925), he rejects a personal God, saying that 'such metaphors', necessary in the past, are now dangerous (*T.C.*, p. 226). That may be, but it seems dangerous for an apostle of poetry to regard metaphor as in itself a limitation. Elsewhere he justly regards the doctrine of the Incarnation, which he personally rejects, as an example of the poetic process (*T.C.*, p. 209). We are really faced less with any rejection of dogma in the name of poetry than with the simple rejection of certain types of poetry in favour of others. He is thinking as a critic. He has every right to do this, but we must be aware of what he is doing.

In 1926 Murry accepted and published in the *Adelphi* two items of mine, one on Wordsworth's *Immortality Ode*, and another, which won a competition on a point of interpretation, on *Julius Caesar*. The second suited the *Adelphi*, but the first already contained the germ of a divergence, for in it I referred to spiritualism. My association with the *Adelphi* was for some years happy, and more Shakespeare pieces were printed in its quarterly successor *The New Adelphi*; but after a while Murry's reactions became less favourable. Simultaneously, my own Shakespearian investigations were becoming surprisingly successful. I found myself doing what I had expected Murry himself to do. New significances were seen unrolling in the tragedies and the plays of Shakespeare's final period. These insights were conditioned by the surmounting of the critical faculties and an acceptance of what was there, in detail and major outline alike. I looked at images and symbols as entities speaking in their own right, almost, one might say, out of context; and thrilled to the coming-alive of Hermione's statue as keenly as I responded to the death of Lear. My results countered what was generally supposed; but, in tune with Murry's own gospel, I refused to let the intellect interfere. And when I wrote *The Christian Renaissance* (1933), though I was myself as ill-at-ease with orthodoxy as Murry himself, I engaged in the same acceptance, and applied the same method, to the New Testament and Christian dogma.[1] To these discoveries I gave the name 'interpretation'.

Murry had himself regarded Shakespeare's last plays, except for their idyllic young persons and Prospero's 'cloud-capp'd towers', in terms of weariness and an 'idle weaving of words' (*U.G.*, p. 184; and see p. 287); and when my *Myth and Miracle* appeared in 1929 he reviewed it in *The Times Literary Supplement* unfavourably. His *Adelphi* review of *The Wheel of Fire* was also unfavourable. He was still friendly in correspondence but regarded me—he said so in one of his letters—as an 'intellectual'. Though I was at the time, and for some years after, surprised, thinking that I had been dropped just

[1] I am aware of a debt to Murry in the writing of this book, especially in my handling of the parables in the Gospels.

when I had found my direction, yet nowadays on rereading his letters I am struck by his kindness and regularity in correspondence with a younger man. His rejection was consistent. Interpretation in my sense he had never, except perhaps in his *Dostoevsky*, of which I reminded him, aimed at; and when he replied that Dostoevsky was different, the statement was in line with his earlier remark on him as 'the ultimate outpost of the attempt at an *intellectual* discovery of life' (my italics; *U.G.*, p. 128). As for *Keats and Shakespeare*, that was an interpretation of Keats's life and letters, not of the poetry.

Even so, he was nearer to my interpretations, or so I thought, than the opposing, 'classical', camp; and yet support was to come through the generosity of Mr T. S. Eliot, who recommended *The Wheel of Fire* for publication and wrote for it an invaluable introduction; and one of my most understanding reviews was written by Bonamy Dobrée in *The Criterion*.

While Murry was writing me off as an 'intellectual' I was becoming aware that he himself put too firm a reliance on the academic scholarship then current. In reviewing *Myth and Miracle* he regarded my emphasis on the Vision in *Cymbeline* as evidence of a lack in Shakespearian sensitivity. During my years in Canada I formulated certain criticisms of Murry's work, writing of his *God* in *The Canadian Journal of Religious Thought* (November–December 1931, pp. 364-9) that his system lacked 'the picture-language of imagination and the mystery of symbol', and that, while the dogmas of 'the early imagination of Christendom' were cast in 'the three-dimensional forms of figurative thought', like poetry, Murry's system, though seeming true, was only true on the lesser, intellectual level. In *The Canadian Forum* I reviewed his collection of the less mystical, literary-academic, essays of *Countries of the Mind* (1931), saying:

> He can be either rational, and, if we grant his critical premises, impersonal, or profound and personal; but not both at once. He refuses to formulate the deeper emotions with precision, probably because he is too much afraid of not telling the truth. But truth may be composed of a myriad of falsehoods, and the bold writer turns out one profound lie after another unashamedly.

I agreed with Murry's fears of intellect when autonomous but claimed nevertheless that it could be

> a glass through which we may focus reality; or as a prism to split the unsearchable golden fire into blending tints.

Murry renounced sharp and detonating statements in the name of truth. My conclusion was:

> Intellect, like the devil himself, is a dangerous master but an invaluable servant. Mr Murry will not make terms with the intellectual Mammon of unrighteousness. It therefore, in different ways, still dominates, instead of serving, his vision.
>
> (*The Canadian Forum*, pp. 107–8)

Observe that each had now charged the other with intellectualism. In reviewing Murry's *Shakespeare* (1936) in *Saturday Night* I attributed its delayed appearance to an 'inward uncertainty' of which signs were now also evident in the result. I concluded:

> The section on the final plays, though genuine profundities are scattered here and there, cannot be said to do more that flirt with the vast issues involved.
>
> (April 25th, 1936)

Which brings us to the heart of the disagreement.

As prophet Murry concentrated (i) on the tragic and (ii) on ineffable recognition in and through the tragic. What he refused was (iii) any attempt to formulate that recognition. Shakespeare's system of values, apparently so 'divorced from any faith in immortality', cannot be analysed: 'The order is there, but it is the inscrutable order of organic life' (*T.C.*, pp. 200–1). An analysis which revealed in Shakespeare intimations of immortality was for him suspect. Even had he been convinced, he would have been repelled, as he was by church dogma, fearing to be forced beyond his own experience.

He could himself write of 'a hidden universe' and 'a glimpse of what is beyond this mortal world', but such gleams could only be known through a man's 'deepest, unfamiliar self', through 'a new principle of authority in and through the deeper knowledge of the self' (*U.G.*, pp. 61, 240; 75, 182). Man's own experience is the one court of appeal: 'It lies in the very dignity of man to stand or fall by his own knowledge' (*U.G.*, p. 197). Those who accept religious dogmas only do it by achieving 'some sort of willing suspension of disbelief' (*U.G.*, p. 196). But what of Murry's own insistence that 'your knowledge must give way' (p. 151 above)? And is not this 'willing suspension of disbelief' the characteristic of what the Romantics meant by 'imagination'? My divergence from Murry, as a writer, was this: he wrote from his own spiritual experience, I from the imagination. My reading of Shakespeare's last plays originated from an acceptance of what others, and sometimes my own instinct, regarded as impossible. Imagination is precisely the faculty for apprehending and accepting what is *not* covered by one's own experience. It might be said to offer substitutes for the mystical experience, and such substitutes Murry would not accept. Shaw's *Saint Joan* aroused his admiration, but he rejected the Epilogue (*U.G.*, p. 242), that wonderful composite of spirit-life and astral travelling, as irrelevant. Christ's tragic suffering was to him authoritative (e.g. *Adelphi*, IV, x; April 1927; pp. 593–4), but the resurrection, at least as stated, impossible (*T.C.*, p. 95). Neither, anyway, were *needed*; Murry received all he wanted from tragedy as tragedy. And yet Sophocles has his *Oedipus Coloneus*, and all great dramatists push beyond tragedy. If tragedy becomes an end in itself, it ceases to be greatly tragic. Its majesty, the dark majesty of death, is the shadow cast on our minds by a presence that is not dark.

Writing of the contemplation of Christ's death, Murry is himself forced into a symbolism beyond tragedy:

> And then, suddenly, strangely, out of the chaos, the despair, the agony of this contemplation, rises a voice like the singing of a solitary bird after the terror of the storm. Some mysterious song of triumph rises and swells within our darkened souls ...
>
> (*Adelphi*, IV, x; April 1927; p. 594)

But this can only come, he says, through an absolute acceptance of death as death: 'Life, spelled with a capital, is life *and* death'; and that 'Life', says Murry, 'goes on' and it is for us to 'serve' it through 'acceptance' of 'death' (*Adelphi*, IV, iv; October 1926; p. 209). Neither 'life' nor 'death' are complete; they are 'partial manifestations of one hidden, living and eternal reality' (*U.G.*, p. 63). We must not 'strive to overcome death, by striving to believe in personal immortality', for 'this is not to overcome death' but simply to 'falsify' it by trying to 'change death into life' (*U.G.*, p. 298). Those who believe in 'personal immortality' make death 'the plaything of life', so wronging its 'majesty'. The 'magnificent opposition' of life and death '*must* be a formulation of that which is beyond them, and is one' (*U.G.*, p. 299; and see *T.C.*., pp. 119–20). Theosophy, Rudolf Steiner, Gourdjiev and Madam Blavatsky are scornfully dismissed (*U.G.*, pp. 279–80). There is worse:

> The prying spiritualism, the muck-raking of eternity, into which even men of science have lately fallen in [is ?] a degradation of human dignity; and the instinctive nobility of the human soul turns away from it in pity

and disgust. In our hearts we know better than that; we know how to choose between these sordid affronts to the majesty of an event that fills us with awe and wonder ...

(*U.G.*, p. 299)

The venom, so unusual for Murry, is a symptom of unease, and perhaps fear.

One must, he again argues, at all costs preserve intact the 'glory' of death's 'substantial mystery' (*U.G.*, p. 300); and of that 'greater thing' which encloses both life and death 'we can *say* nothing', though we can be 'aware of' and even 'know' it (*U.G.*, pp. 300–1). Death is central in Murry's argument: the opposition of life and death, he says, includes all other oppositions (*U.G.*, pp. 302–3). The mystery of death is not, however, likely to be quite so easily dissolved as he fears. Nor is it only scientists who have involved themselves in this 'degradation of human dignity'. A study of the relation of literary genius to spiritualism during the last hundred years would involve a dazzling list of names. But at any point when the relation becomes assertive, Murry would be likely to condemn it, as he condemned the Epilogue to *Saint Joan*.

His uncompromising denial of personal immortality elicited an interesting rejoinder from William Archer, who was dying. Archer pointed out the evidence of spiritualism:

If there is one thing I am certain of in this world, it is that there is *something* which we do not begin to understand behind the phenomena which we loosely describe as spiritualistic.

(*T.C.*, p. 66)

This, he said, is something 'which science must, so to speak, fathom and assimilate, on pain of wilfully living in an incomplete universe' (*T.C.*, p. 67); and he proceeded to give as good a summary as I know of regarding what spiritualism demonstrates, and what interpretations are open to us. He wrote from actual experience.

In answer Murry assured him that though he rejected '*personal* immortality', he yet believed that 'something survives' and 'most emphatically' did not believe in 'annihilation' (*T.C.*, p. 69). Archer died. Murry composed a fictional dialogue (*T.C.*, pp. 70–7) such as, in his opinion, there might have been between him and Archer, in which he describes the birth of a 'spark' which 'knows, and is, your self and is something quite other than yourself'; this is the 'soul'. At which the fictional Archer shakes his head, saying that it means nothing to him. Murry explains that if the soul 'exists out of time and space and belongs to another order of reality' it would be 'wrong', 'vulgar' and 'belittling' to speak of 'personal survival'; the soul 'eternally is', 'in another mode of being, which neither our senses not our mind but our soul alone can comprehend'. To 'reimpose personality upon the soul which is the triumph over personality' would be 'strange'. But if the soul is not born during life, then, says Murry, it may be born in death, and at death perhaps 'we do indeed put on this incorruptible', everyone, 'saint or sinner, wise man or fool'; and this would explain Archer's spiritualistic convictions.

Murry is here in retreat so far as the central beliefs of spiritualism are concerned, but he still argues that we should win our souls through death-conquest and avoid communication. The dead 'live indeed, but not with our life'; one must not 'seek to compel' them—the usual error, drawn from the Faust tradition, of those who have no first-hand knowledge of spiritualism—to return. Asked if he condemns communication, he now says 'I condemn nothing'. But he insists that we should attain a condition which realizes that real communication is impossible. When Archer insists in reply that he has himself had an obviously genuine communication, Murry—not to be outdone—replies: 'So have I, though I did not seek it.' It told him, too, that there was 'something there'. He concludes well:

> The knowledge that 'something is there' may come to a man by many ways; but to know the something that is there—to that, I believe, there is but a single way.
>
> (*T.C.*, p. 77)

He has admitted Archer's contention, while denying its value.

His phraseology has been dangerously confusing. The denial of personal immortality turns out to be, pretty nearly, its opposite. In an essay 'Personality and Immortality' he attempts a clarification:

> The immortality of this personality is a contradiction in terms: the mere fact of immortality would make this personality quite unrecognizable.
>
> (*T.C.*, p. 82)

If by 'personality' we mean 'that which does not survive', it is true that its survival will be inconceivable; but the statement merely wastes ink.

Murry replaces the word 'personality' by the word 'soul': 'a man has a self that is beyond and hidden from his self of every-day' and this 'hidden and higher self' is the 'soul' (*T.C.*, pp. 80–1). His earlier phraseology had said as much: the soul was the 'highest' and 'unawakened' part of us, whose language is great poetry (*T.C.*, p. 29); and he has used the phrase '*non omnis moriar*' (*U.G.*, p. 155). He is not being inconsistent; he is merely being unfair to the reader. Our 'reality', we are told, lies deeper than the phenomenal 'I' and 'personality' is a 'veil' only (*T.C.*, p. 83). This reality he neatly relates to the children's angels beholding God in the New Testament (*T.C.*, pp. 264–5). But if this soul-reality is after all immortal, then much of our previous heart-searching has been in vain; for achieving one's soul makes one, in Murry's system, 'in the truest and highest sense, an individual' (*T.C.*, p. 31); the soul 'is ourselves in a new wholeness, without division' (*T.C.*, p. 173); and if this 'wholeness' is what survives, that is surely enough to satisfy the most demanding of us. If at death we first, irrespective of our deserts, achieve a state of complete integration, and then enter on our immortal heritage, what could be better? The suggestion far surpasses the most optimistic expectations of spiritualism.

So when Murry is attacked by a theologian for offering mankind an immortality 'less than personal' he rightly replies that what he is offering is not less but 'more' than personal (*T.C.*, p. 87). On the conflicting accounts of the resurrection in the New Testament and on the Church's dogma of the resurrection of the body he registers some telling hits. He is nevertheless willing to believe that Jesus' followers had an *experience* of his existence after dying, and that soul may make contact with soul across the barrier, as did Saint Paul (*T.C.*, pp. 95–6). The theologian makes a good point too:

> The poet's vision, no doubt, is untranslatable into argument, but so is a pain in one's finger. Theologians attempt to explain one kind of experience, physiologists another. The best of their theories or 'dogmas' may be no more than shadows; but, as long as men are afflicted with rationality, so long will such theories continue to appear.
>
> (*T.C.*, p. 91)

That is a statement I would myself apply to poetic interpretation.

Our confusions can only be resolved by some such intermediate link as the etheric or astral body known to esoteric tradition from ancient times and announced today by spirit-communications. This was the line taken by Saint Paul when he defined the resurrected body as a 'spiritual' body (1 *Corinthians*, XV, 42–9). Spiritualist accounts give doctrines such as Murry's concerning a supernal reality their proper place, while explaining that it cannot be achieved in one leap by so simple a process as dying: there are intermediate planes.

These accounts, the accounts I mean delivered by high spirit personalities through trance mediumship or the direct voice, have, moreover, certain advantages to be distinguished from the mystic experience. Some of us have never had such an experience, and those who have may pass through moods when they distrust it. Objective evidence appealing to the prosaic consciousness is surely not to be despised. Similarly my poetic interpretations depend not at all on any spiritual experiences of my own, but are only valid in so far as the patterns exposed are there for all to see. Murry put sole faith in his own mystical experience. That was his final authority, and if great literature, or interpretations of it, or spiritualist communications, countered, or even added to, his central intuition, he tended to oppose them. The tendency aligned itself naturally with his profession as literary critic, for whereas such esoteric matters are regularly the concern of creative writers, they are with equal regularity ignored by the academic scholar and the literary critic. The school of criticism which, as it were, took over from Murry's *Adelphi*, replacing prophecy by its own astringent doctrine, was that of *Scrutiny*; and the writers of *Scrutiny* shirked occult categories. To this extent criticism and works of genius remain divided. When they are no longer divided, criticism as we know it will have ceased to exist, being conditioned by interpretation.

Murry, mainly interested in his religious experience, and finding himself now cut off, by his own rejections and perhaps also by my own interpretations, from his moorings in literature, proceeded to apply his insights on a variety of fronts, writing in favour of communism, pacifism, democracy, British patriotism and finally of the necessity for a war of prevention against Russia. He came near to taking orders. He once thought of becoming a Catholic. His story is told in Mr F. A. Lea's excellent biography. We may be tempted to smile at these shifting allegiances, but there was a single conviction running through them, and in the process he shed light on each in turn. His community farm had been adumbrated as early as 1924 when he had dreamed of a small community 'shaping some fragment' of the external world 'into harmony with the world within' (*U.G.*, p. 222). There is pattern in Murry's story. His life and writings form a unique commentary on the thought-confusions of his generation.

He was a man of brilliant critical intellect who had had, and tried frantically to remain true to, a mystical experience; and the interaction of mysticism and intellect produced many apparent contradictions and seeming insincerities. He had, however, few of the characteristics usually associated with literary genius in the Renaissance era. Of these, I here emphasize two: the first, involvement, as though by instinct, with the Faustian and spiritualistic fields, and, second, sexual abnormality, sometimes pushed, perhaps with humour, to obscenity. Murry reacted against both: all his prophetic writing remained well within the conventions of twentieth-century respectability. His 'pity and scorn' for spiritualistic investigators we have already noticed. In the sexual field he was brought up against D. H. Lawrence whom he denounced for a perverted sexuality. Murry was, as I have recently shown ('Lawrence, Joyce and Powys', *Essays in Criticism*, XI, IV; October 1961), right; and those who have tried to build up Lawrence as in any normal sense a moral counsellor in sexual affairs while criticizing Murry for his attacks in *Son of Woman* (1931) and *Reminiscences of D. H. Lawrence* (1933), falsify the facts. Murry's subsequent soft-pedalling of Lawrence's sexual abnormalities may perhaps be attributed to consideration for his widow. Murry comes out of it well.

In this relations with Lawrence Murry acted as a man of sound British normality and common sense; but he was not acting as an interpreter of genius, nor even being true to the loneliness of genius, so excellently handled in his treatment of Jesus (*U.G.*, p. 199). His *Adam and Eve* (1944), one of his best later books, is a study of sex-relations from a normal viewpoint.

The problem was raised again by his admirable *Jonathan Swift*, published in 1954. In my review of it for the *Yorkshire Post* on May 26th, 1954, high praise was countered by a reservation:

> While honestly trying to face the challenge of genius, he has always been reluctant to depart too far from traditional valuations in either religion or the psychology of sex; and that is not so easy.

Murry recognized Swift's genius but was antagonized by his neurotic disgusts. My answer, referring to men of genius, was

> Had these men been sexually normal, would they have composed their greatest works? And should we still be writing books about them? What, then, is the secret of their enduring appeal?—of this strange *malaise* which proves more vital than health?

After praising the book highly I concluded my review with the suggestion that 'it will be for others, should they choose, to delve deeper'.

I sent Murry the review. I had written to him only twice since 1929 and had on each occasion received kind replies. I now received, in his old exquisitely neat handwriting, this answer, dated May 31st, 1954, from Thelnetham:

Dear Wilson Knight,

Thank you very much for sending me the *Y.P.* review. I had seen it, and *had* wondered what you meant by yr. last sentence.

I have lately been reading some of your Shakespeare books which had escaped me—nearly 12 years farming puts one well behind; but now, being practically retired, I have begun to pick up the threads again. I was particularly concerned with yr. *Crown of Life*, because of its argument for the entire authenticity of *Henry VIII*, in which I have never been able to believe.

I am afraid you did not convince me. But you must put that down to the excessive 'normality' of my mind. Though I had not realized that my mind was a very normal one, I think it is probably true. I am abnormally normal, so to speak: at least that seems a fair description of a man whose literary criticism ends up by putting him in charge of a co-operative farm. (I mean this literally: my farming is the direct consequence of my effort in literary criticism.)

Or, to put it differently, my mysticism is a mysticism of descent. Yours isn't. And I get lost in your high speculations as applied to Shakespeare. I was acutely conscious of this divergence as long ago as *Myth and Miracle*, though it came out at a time when I was distracted with domestic anxiety and was unable to set out the reasons of my disagreement with the fullness that initial essay of yours deserved.

However, I am in a very small minority—not perhaps a minority of one as I used to think, but very near it. My normality is therefore (as I said) peculiar.

On the particular question of Swift, you may well be right in thinking that the appalling power of Gulliver IV derives from Swift's 'unhealthy and unreasoned disgust'. But that does not justify you in generalising that supreme literary power is, in general, derivative from sexual abnormality. Indeed, I should say that the specific literary genius is utterly independent of sexual constitution, though that will certainly play an important part in the particular *manifestation* of literary genius. And, again, literary genius at the highest is not exempt from moral judgment; —though the moral judgment to which it is amenable is not the facile judgment of moral convention, but one based on the deepest philosophy (or religion) of which the critic is capable.

Yours sincerely,

J. Middleton Murry

That is a fair statement, though I would lay no personal claim to 'mysticism'; and what there is in my writing is, surely, 'a mysticism of descent', in that I have preferred the multi-coloured qualities of literature to the one soul-centre on which Murry concentrated. I have been more drawn to Shakespeare, Pope and Byron than to Donne and Blake.

More important is it to note Murry's conclusion. At the limit he writes not as an interpreter of genius but as a critic; the final court of appeal is his own judgment. But, it may be said, so is everyone's; and it would then be merely a question as to where to draw the line. Should not I myself be antagonized by a work deliberately counselling sadistic cruelties? My reply would be this: in so far as the imagination has ratified a work of literature, the critical intellect must be silenced. Sadistic horrors, if extreme and approved, would not have been ratified by the imagination, within which certain moral valuations appear to be contained. But the imagination has, in myself and others, already ratified the life-work of Swift. We sense in him a supreme importance: and therefore the approach must be interpretative. However far we may be, in normal life, from approving it all, there yet may be *something which our normal thinking has left out of account*. That is why an imaginative interpretation may be needed.

Murry's life-work may be defined as a continuous attempt to remain true to his one great experience. This experience he tried desperately to align with his love of literature and for a while, and within limits, succeeded magnificently. When a divergence was forced he followed the law of his own greater 'self', or 'soul', going his own wandering way. The choice was honourable.

II

Poems

The Maker

Unmarried, near-sighted, rather deaf,
This anonymous dwarf,
The legendary ancestor
Of Gunsmiths to His Majesty
And other bespoke houses,
Every museum visitor knows him.

Excluded by his cave
From weather and events, he reckons
Days by the job done and at night
Dreams of the Perfect Object, war to him
A scarcity of bronze, the fall of princes
A change of customer.

Not a musician: songs
Encourage labouring demes, amuse the idle,
But would distract a self-appointed worker
From listening to a hammer's dactyl.
And not an orator: sophists
Don't do metallurgy.

His prices are high and if he doesn't like you
He won't oblige: the Quality
Are made to learn their charm is useless,
A threat fatal. He will deliver
In his good time, not yours: he has no rival
And he knows you know it.

His love, embodied in each useful wonder,
Can't save them in our world from insult
But may avenge it: beware, then, maladroit
Thumb-sucking children of all ages,
Lest on your mangled bodies the court verdict
Be Death by Misadventure.

W. H. AUDEN

Teaching Wordsworth

I'm paid to speak, and money glosses
Irrelevance: to keep their places
Students are paid and so the burden
Is lightened of our mutual boredom,
And if the gain's not much, the damage
Is also slight within this college.

'Since for the most part it's subjective,
Verse is not anything you might have
In hand or a bank—although it is
Important to some—it is on our syllabus—
Concerned with life's outgoing towards death,
Such as our theme today, the poet, Wordsworth,

Who, since not alive still, I disinter
For the sake of a question you will answer,
For the sake also of the vagrant lives
He was concerned with, and the wind when it raves
Round such unmarketable places as Scawfell.
An unsociable man and often dull,

He lived for a long time posthumous
To the flashing shield, to the great poet he was,
Busy for the most part, with pedestrian exercise.
However you will not be questioned on those days
Only the decade when with stone footfall
Crags followed him, winds blew through his long skull.

That of course is known as the 'Great Period'
Though one hesitates to apply the word 'God'
To a poet's theme, it is so manhandled,
Gentlemen, I can offer you nothing instead.

If he himself never applied it to what occurred
When 'the light of sense' went out, this useful word,
Though inaccurate will cut my lecture short
Being the fullstop which ends thought,

And consequently for our purpose useful;
For its brevity you should be grateful,
Anyway for those who knew what the man meant,
My words are—thanks to God—irrelevant.
'Take notes', is the advice I bequeath the rest,
It is a question of self interest,

Of being as Shakespeare says to oneself true
For the right marks will certainly benefit you.
After all in the teaching world exam and thesis
For the better posts provide a useful basis
And in this sense poems are as good as money.
This man's life was a strange journey.

Early deprived of both father and mother
To the rocks he turned, to lapping water,
With a sense by deprivation made so acute
That he heard grass speak and the word in a stone's throat;
Many of course to silence address their prayer
But in his case when he called it chose to answer;

And he wrote down, after a certain time lag,
Their conversation. It is a dialogue
Almost unique in any literature
And a positive goldmine to the commentator,
For although these poems mention what silence said
It can almost any way be interpreted,

Since to find a yardstick by which the occult
Language of stones can be measured is difficult.
Also that 'something far more deeply interfused',
Will be belittled by critiques if not abused,
There being no instrument by which to measure
This origin of terms and formula,

Which together with the birth and deathward aim
Of the life in us and things was this man's theme
As he grew, then dwindled into a worse
End of life—as regards verse.
My conclusion is most words do violence
To what he said—listen to silence.

THOMAS BLACKBURN

Reflections on an Exilic Theme

Little boy, little boy, where was thou born?
Far away in Lancashire under a thorn
Where they sup sour milk in a ram's horn.

Clouds and a spire, the geometric sun
With compass legs, thin light, brown air, chill wind,
A child sees this composed under a thorn.

A life to work the composition out
Falls to the lucky, to the unlucky comes
A composition that devours the life.

That steely landscape is the truer home:
Home is too grossly palpable, too dense,
Too rough, too warm, sedate, imperious.

Home is the pudding in the belly, guilt,
Furry upon the tongue, phlegm, bile, tears,
The thud of anger: here are domestic sweets.

Trapped in the landscape we are free to wander
And snared within the looking-glass of summer
The hurt of exile ratifies our choice.

Supping sour milk out of a ram's horn
I drowsed beneath the hedge and in my dream
I saw that landscape yellow on the page.

It was the heart's honey and disease,
The sweet-and-sour of youth, the rust of age,
The rage of argument and the cure of lust.

When Doré wrote his name upon a cloud
The cloud became a cloud, the intrepid spire
Drew all its thrust from the engraver's tool.

Only the light, the wind, were natural gifts
And in their nature gave the fiction power
And in the giving drew the nature out.

Child of the artifice, the choice was sealed
When Irwell sweetly ran and from the tower
They watched the driven hart in the white field

Far away in Lancashire where I was born.

J. M. CAMERON

Saints

The saints of older times had sharp firm lines
And face today's inquisitors all in one piece.
They stand, their backs braced by cathedral stone,
Centuries clipt of Janus tendencies.
One aspect alone inspires their neophytes
Radiance undimmed by recent questionings.

Saints of today can certainly be found
Through all vicissitudes, carved in the round.
Their backsides are exposed, no splendid screen
Defends their poverty. They must stand free
So all may peer, rotate and judge their worth.
Surely the centuries will furnish more.

Saints of past times, Saints of a latter day
Fold us to your hearts. We who seldom pray
Must learn our tasks, make straight our dubious way,
Glad that you guard that ancient heritage, the Rock,
Sad in our present part to entertain we know not what,
Twice sad to journey on and never see you plain.

VALENTINE DOBRÉE

To Bonamy Dobrée because he likes it

For the Indian Soldiers who Died in Africa

A man's destination is his own village,
His own fire, and his wife's cooking;
To sit in front of his own door at sunset
And see his grandson, and his neighbour's grandson
    Playing in the dust together.

Scarred but secure, he has many memories
Which return at the hour of conversation
(The warm or the cool hour, according to the climate),
Of foreign men, who fought in foreign places,
    Foreign to each other.

A man's destination is not his destiny,
Every country is home to one man
And exile to another. Where a man dies bravely
At one with his destiny, that soil is his.
    Let his village remember.

This was not your land, or ours: but a village in
                                        the Midlands,
And one in the Five Rivers, may have the same graveyard.
Let those who go home tell the same story of you:
Of action with a common purpose, action
None the less fruitful if neither you nor I
Know, until the moment after death,
    What is the fruit of action.

T. S. ELIOT

Wemyss Cottage, 1956

A street of battered laisser faire
Leads to the house: past its parterre
Blushes the bogus-Georgian of
The borough council's awful love.
Thus the twin shadows of the State
Fall upon stucco, lawn and slate
And on the Afric god who smiles
Across the little Flemish tiles
To where a painter keeps alive
By helping with the spade. Birds strive
Against a clarinet's long curl
Swayed by the breathing of a girl.
From the professor peeps a slim
Volume of poetry—for him
Neither the best nor past's enough:
He really buys the newest stuff,
Indulgent with the private dream
Though longing for a public theme.
So often since that former song
Corporate decisions have been wrong.
Committees set to make a choice
Have mostly raised a stupid voice.
Now it's a marvel that there still
Remain good things for groups to kill.
Before such ambiguities
The poet only murmurs his,
Revulsed by almost every faction
And quite incapable of action.
Moved by the emblems here, his pen
Writes of the obvious again.
Magnolias offer on dead wood

Their tiny lip-sticked cups; the good
Inherent in briar starts to show
And what the tag says soon will blow.
The mistress of the house imparts
Nurture to soil in which the arts
Extend: the tendrils of a tune
Creep up the windows: in the noon
Hues leap from beds; and, ordered by
A critical hand, the shrubbery
Of verse (that flowers on gloomy caves)
Reminds this sense of all that raves.
The guest must take his leave at last
By the unequal way that's past
Or through the future's juster hell.
Precarious happiness, farewell!

ROY FULLER

Douanier Rousseau

In jungles dark and bright of the Middle Ages,
Signs and images creeper'd, cramped with meanings;
In those deep thickets where liana-muscles
Bind all creatures close in strife and kinship;
There, one tropic day,
Though I had seen the medieval vision
Flame out of shadow, I was dark and lost.

And yet—
Was it not there in the dreaming thickets
I met you, found you at home, Douanier Rousseau?
There, purged of sophistication,
Saw ringed eyes of your fearful ingenuous tigers
Scare the sleek foliage, they in thick ambush
Fixed immutable? And you yourself,
You yourself were there in your black homespun
Totally unconcerned, and I like a child
Who from the sticky smell of his Noah's Ark
Dreams back to the Flood.

G. ROSTREVOR HAMILTON

A Ballad of Mozart and Salieri

(NOTE: In justice to Salieri it must be said that there appears to be no foundation for the legend that he poisoned Mozart; though, according to Russian sources, further evidence on this point has recently come to light.)

Salieri encountered Mozart;
    Took him friendly by the arm,
And smiled a thin-lipped ambiguous smile.
    This was Italian charm.

Mozart observed the smile of Salieri
    But was not enough observant
(For the Angel of Death had called already
    In the guise of an upper servant).

And the mind of Mozart was dazed and fuddled
    With the shame of his poverty,
Unhonoured promises, unpaid bills,
    And the music that struggled to be.

'Maestro,' said Salieri 'Dear Maestro,
    It is happy that we met.'
('We'll end this smart boy's tricks,' he thought
    'He'll not get by—not yet!')

'And as for that post of kapellmeister
    We'll do what we can do.'
But something black within him whispered:
    'He is greater, is greater than you.

'He is great enough to oust you, one day,
And take your place at Court.'
('Not if Salieri is Salieri,'
Salieri thought.)

'It is happy that we met,' said Salieri
'I wish I could ask you to dine—
But I have, alas, a pressing engagement.
You will stay for a glass of wine?'

* * *

No one carried Mozart to nobody's grave
And the skies were glazed and dim
With a spatter of out-of-season rain
(Or the tears of the Seraphim.)

Then two stern angels stood by that grave
Saying: 'Infidel, Freemason,
We are taking your soul where it willed to be judged
At the throne of Ultimate Reason.'

But the Queen of the Night in coloratura
Horrors trilled at the sun,
For she looked at the soul of Wolfgang Amadeus
And she knew she had not won.

They lifted that soul where the great musicians
In contrapuntal fires
Through unlimited heavens of order and energy
Augment the supernal choirs.

And the spirit of Johann Sebastian, harrowed
With abstract darts of love,
Escorted the terrible child Mozart
Through courteous mansions above.

And hundred-fisted Handel erected
Great baroque arches of song
As the Cherubim and the Seraphim
Bandied Mozart along.

But Mozart looked back again in compassion
Below the vault of the stars
To where the body of Beethoven battered
Its soul against the bars.

* * *

Successful Salieri lay dying—
The priest had blessed him and gone—
In a chamber well-fitted with Louis Seize furniture
But dying, dying alone.

Then two small devils, like surpliced choirboys,
Like salamanders in black and red,
Extracted themselves from the dying firelight
And stood beside the bed.

And they sang to him in two-part harmony,
With their little, eunuchoid voices:
'You have a pressing engagement, Salieri,
In the place of no more choices.'

So they hauled up his soul and put it away
In a little cushioned cell
With stereophonic gramophones built into the walls—
And he knew that this must be Hell.

Salieri sat there under the arc-lights
(But never the sun or the moon)
With nothing to listen to from eternity to eternity
But his own little tinkling tune.

JOHN HEATH-STUBBS

Men are a Mockery of Angels

i.m. Tommaso Campanella, priest and poet

Some days a shadow through
The high window shares my
Prison. I watch a slug
Scale the glinting pit-side
Of its own slime. The cries
As they come are mine; then
God's: my justice, wounds, love,
Derisive light, bread, filth.

To lie here in my strange
Flesh while glutted Torment
Sleeps, stained with its prompt food,
Is a joy past all care
Of the world, for a time.
But we are commanded
To rise, when, in silence,
I would compose my voice.

GEOFFREY HILL

Wodwo

What am I? Nosing here, turning leaves over
following a faint stain on the air to the river's edge
I enter water. What am I to split
The glassy grain of water looking upward I see the bed
of the river above me upside down very clear
what am I doing here in mid-air? Why do I find
this frog so interesting as I inspect its most secret
interior and make it my own? Do these weeds
know me and name me to each other have they
seen me before, do I fit in their world? I seem
separate from the ground and not rooted but dropped
out of nothing casually I've no threads
fastening me to anything I can go anywhere
I seem to have been given the freedom
of this place what am I then? And picking
bits of bark off this rotten stump gives me
no pleasure and it's no use so why do I do it
me and doing that have coincided very queerly
But what shall I be called am I the first
have I an owner what shape am I what
shape am I am I huge if I go
to the end of this way past these trees and past these trees
till I get tired that's touching one wall of me
for the moment if I sit still how everything
stops to watch me I suppose I am the exact centre
but there's all this what is it roots
roots roots roots and here's the water
again very queer but I'll go on looking

TED HUGHES

Ten Pure Sonnets

The sacred springtime, season that never
Changes, alters morning's diurnal blood
And my awakening crepuscular
Excitements fade like autumn, angular
And moody in the hesitating sun,
The brilliant strong triangle the air
Tingling in the mammoth of the lung
Levels in the grim theodolite the gun
The apparatus of removal, bang
And birth; elusive are the villagers,
The four infrequent birds, the messengers
That steam their letters open in the clouds
And sometimes give the answer in a long
Audition. And the cerements are nouns.

The circular caressive downs the brine
Of flowers hissing in essential soil
Envelope anything and on the stile
Erected at the edge, the vantage-point
Of any precipice, the fathers climb
Enthusiastic and are killed. On high
Perilous posts the children are devoid
The rising sap recapturing their voice
Enfolds them, fastens them like flags or leaves
On these, the summits of potential trees
While mothers pivot round the leafy masts
Of merchantmen whose holds are black and stark
With strange lovers in the possessive dark
That passes through the rigging to the past.

Implicated, urgent, the vindictive
Branches spend their telescopic fervours
Irretrievably in any corner
That the leaves pattern with the zest of love
The clouds are gliding through the gothic nave
In archways megaliths and phantoms move
The sun's galvanic axis strikes the hour
Violently in the cool humming choir
Once is enough for the rendered anthem
O the hyacinths are through in the school
The floors are in emotion and the hymn
Creeps round the lichened profile of a girl
Like ivy tightening upon the heart's
Expanding trellis. In the shaking park.

The episodic statuary throws
Disturbing shadows on the entrances
The vertical divisions and the home
Of emperors, upon the vacant grass
Forbidden angels move with granite oars
That grind the marble oceans in the dome
Of light, the rock of silence and the stone
Of space revolving with phrenetic force.
The ardours of the nyctitropic flower
The figures in the distance and the sail
That pedestals girate to follow, all
Begin at this horizon. It is there
The nightingale the aromatic bird
The wind is poured into its sudden urn.

Those who are rivers who are fountains' ears
Run in the rain to them the sky is loud
With terror and the vehicle of hours
Immovable is centred in a bead
That burdens them with error and the void:
Caressive, vigilant eternities
The number the remembered pyramid
Is measured out in terms of wilderness.
The garden where the magnifying lakes
Expended versions of infinity

And were expanded, the magnetic oaks
That polarized mythology, the bed
Whose lilies hesitated to be plucked
Are liberated by their agony.

Exit the corrective to importance
Regulates the antlered paralytics
The excessive parallels of entrance
Unlocks the clustered genitals the brain
Conceals accelerations, equinox
Inside its crenellated horror dawn
The high incessant bird has just begun
To creep into the zenith of the lakes:
Trumpet lighted column of insistence
Trees are flame the call is incandescence
Love is a hiatus in the midlands
Resounding canopies of heat proclaim
Resistance waterfalls electric hands
Shoot, thirst, scream, hunger, love, and no response.

The sad foreigners have come to stay
The summerhouses and the birdcage trees
Are darkened with their visitors. The shy
Pilgrims memorize the land's open screen
Mysteriously and are kind to me.
And I can not define the timid hands
Memorial shells in auditory
Shores whose stilled palms are orifices stunned
By strangeness and the greatness of the wave.
In the narrow country they are gathered
While the winter's masonry shadows
Portraits framed in silence and cemented
To the grave's one hallucinated rose
That lifts an index in the anteroom.

The extra voices reassemble in
The valley and upon a certain night
Entire forests reappear and dim
A distant scaffolding with intricate
Revivals and a visitant refrain

Of indigo and green intensified
And structured on the reredos of death,
The relics of a formal winter day
That hallowed fields and river like a wraith.
All through the shrinking tributary house
The veins are laid the cerements are loosed
The temporary stranger moves his head
And on the stairways all the invalid
Deliriums sink in the miracle.

O iron heart, when sleep is on the wall
To which the lonely mourner turns in vain
For eyes, and feels the phantom of his brain
Abandon him; o heart, the anchor-chains
Untwist, the interim of iron rain
Extends into the ocean of the dawn;
In the forests ships await the call
Of mariners, the flying fields prepare
Their home for wanderers, and at the thaw
A latent promise beacons to the hill
The sleepless maniac of snow, the sound
Of spirit leaves exhilarates a wind
Whose stars breathe ether in the foliage
That hovers like the outline of a wave.

The symptomatic dawn is on the edge
Disfigured like a fall of parapets
Upon an antique shore. The sun, pharos
Swollen with rotations in the rapid
Ballroom of the clouds the hidden spaces
Meditate an answer to the solid
Sequence of disaster, and are nameless
Shaken and unaltered. In the dark breast
Of doves or in a momentary lull
In his obscure finale is contained
Perhaps one answer to the oracle
Of love. Though none silently can travel
Homewards with a question in his head
To satisfy the springtime of the blood.

JAMES KIRKUP

Processes

Not flesh; and spirit is
One part of this.

It is a softness not easily abraded;
Whose play, a slipping out of the summer's fingers,
Detains me.

If it were
Your kiss fixed on my body
Not all of that
Would suffice.

Something than can be thought.
Though that smelted into
Mind's cold, yet
Upon the fingers.

Its pressures sink onto
The man inside the flesh
Who gropes after union.

So that the manifold thing
Is like the body which
Poor Plato whirled about in
Sick as war.

And you can feel that what
I'm speaking of is love.

I touch you; but mostly those
Charges your smile grows from

Until you are a gathering of forms:

The rose in mildews
Whose trenchant whorls
Of felt shape self-perfectingly
Caused to char inwards.

The idea itself, perishing
Against its will, like a man
Enlisted to fight
War's contradictions.

It is these things you seem like:
All of them:

Even the man.

The fatherless body melts
Of its enormous wounds.

Though if we'd bent over
This dying man, such care
Would be, like the adult's finger
Closed over by the child's hand.

A form of permanence.
But he has turned apart.

JON SILKIN

A Slice of Lemon

A slice of lemon in my tea, a sun
made by the pale crayon in the drawing book
whose colours outrun uniforms,
whose smiles
extend beyond the faces of their rhymes;

there colours spill out: scribbled free and red,
the mouth escapes the face as if it knew
the passion to transgress,
or how to fit
its clownishness to every passing kiss,

like kissing petals on a black wet road
one hollow hour between breath and breath
when Nothing makes its pass;
at three o'clock
the phone: crashed head on, and a total loss.

At Belle Fourche, South Dakota, the huge hearse
took us from the automobile graveyard
down to the wide street's haze;
'Hell of a hearse',
the man said in the back, 'No Goddam ash-trays!'

A slice of lemon in my cup, a moon
slit from the sour round of those moral tales
that brought rags riches:
foolishness is dead,
red silks of blood under November hedges.

A slice of lemon souring up the mouth:
her skin was greasy and coarse, her jawbone long,
her lipstick the wrong tone;
amendment died
in the dust-clogged grass of a badly cambered lane.

'Hell of a hearse' the man said at Belle Fourche,
'No Goddam ash-trays,' fingering the velvet,
the dusty ebony, the brass;
we drove
along Fifth Avenue on one of those

surrendered empty mornings when the sun
is lemon yellow, shadows sharp and strong,
and memory empty as the sky;
it seemed
if we had anything, we had the time.

A tartness in the mouth, a yellow sun,
a lemon-yellow moon, spin in her cup
whose eyes are blind as fur,
whose blood has run
dark through the stiffening dusts to which we turn

in time, from time. 'Hell of a hearse', he said.
We rode Fifth Avenue to the store, and felt
like Lazarus. We lived
whoever died.
I pin this on her leaden coverlid.

ROBIN SKELTON

Lothar

In 1929 we drove out to
The marshlands, where the thatched roofs make
Nests, under nests of storks.
In the artist's white new house we lay
On mats, where the June evening
Poured in one line of Mozart through a flute.
Lothar lit a log fire in the yard,
And Irma came out on the balcony
Gown billowing round the unborn child.
The fire was golden brooches in her eyes,
Sparks floated up in flakes around her skirt.
Suddenly in the heat a pimple burst
On the art critic's nose. Lothar said
That while the child was being born he'd take
His bicycle and ride along white roads
Flat all the way to Holland.
I thought of him
Pedalling unendingly leaning over
The handle bars, his boxy head thrust forward
From which the blonde hair jutted back: and in his eyes
That prairie look reflected from the fire.

STEPHEN SPENDER

III

Personalia

Bonamy Dobrée: Teacher and Patron of Young Men

RICHARD HOGGART

I

I IMAGINE that others will write about Bonamy Dobrée's scholarly work. I shall write about him as a teacher and patron of young men. This essay must be a very personal thing, therefore, since it is about a relationship. Bonamy Dobrée was one of the major influences on my own development.

I suppose he came to Leeds University in about 1935. I remember that those of us who were then sixth-formers in the city's grammar schools and hoping to read English heard about the rather strange new professor the University had acquired. I went up in 1936, on a local scholarship. He must then have been about forty-eight.

On the opening days of session, the registration days, the University ran what used to be called the 'Freshers' Bazaar'. The Great Hall did look as much as anything like a parish festival or church bazaar; it is a Victorian Gothic building and resembles many a big chapel interior in the North. There were great numbers of society stalls and club stalls; and there were tables for each department, manned by members of the academic staff, where you signed on for your Honours or Subsidiary courses and in your confusion sought whatever advice was available.

Bonamy was presiding at the English table when I reached it. I remember being struck straight away by his 'style', though I wouldn't have then described it like that to anyone else or even to myself. He was unusually upright and brought to mind all sorts of words and phrases which were still just in currency then but now seem dated, such as: 'a military-looking man' who 'bears himself well'. He had a heavy well-clipped moustache, rather like those worn by decent majors in films about the 1914 war. He was slightly tweedy, and smelt of pipe-tobacco.

So far I have made him sound a little too heavy. He also had a sort of brightness. His hair was quite thick and long and brushed well back, but already was almost completely silver. He had a bright and bird-like eye and a quick crinkly smile which he used freely, partly to put you at your ease but also because he did enjoy being with students. To a Leeds youth his voice was the most remarkable thing about him. It was light and very high-pitched; and when it rose with enthusiasm took on what one can best call a feminine ring. It was a mannered voice, and in drab old Woodhouse Lane—the English department was in a Victorian terrace house there—as exotic as a flamingo. I have a bad ear, but I suppose it was compounded of southern upper-class, Haileybury, the regular army—and then laced with the peculiar Cambridge slightly nasal sing-song.

It is plain that I found him interesting from the start. I felt he was rather grand, of course, as undergraduates used to feel about professors; for a long time I was immensely impressed by the number of books he owned and had read, by the range of his other affairs and by the brisk speed with which he handled them. So I was fascinated by the whole person or by as much of it as I saw. I do not remember ever seeking to imitate him or be like him, except in some professional particulars; there was a lot in his 'image' which seemed a little dubious to a Yorkshire adolescent. But he was always interesting: he had a sort of style or shine, as I've said. And—though the city had compensatory virtues—those qualities were very rarely seen in so elegant a form in Leeds.

I imagine he began to notice me, as a 'promising' student, towards the end of my first year. Somewhere about that time he stopped me and said he wanted a word. By now I have forgotten what it was about, though I seem to remember, and this would be entirely in character, that he wanted to give me advice based on a knowledge of some particular need I was in. I do clearly remember a small circumstance in that meeting which may as well be recounted as the first indication of what will be a continuing theme in this essay—the contrasting play of social habits which were brought out in the friendship. We had run into each other on the half-landing and after stopping me he said: 'Hang on a minute. I must go in here for a pee.' I remember my double reaction. First, my respectable-working-class mind was slightly shocked; then my 'wide' teenager's mind took over and asked: 'What's up? Is he trying to show that he's unconventional?'

After the second session had started he began rather more deliberately to pay attention to me, to include me in the cluster who were loosely under his wing. Inevitably, since I was at that point the junior, the other Dobrée protégés seemed grand and suave to me. There was I. F. Porter who sounded organ-voiced, magisterial and assured. He was said to have London literary and intellectual connections. He went to lecture in a central or eastern European university, and Bonamy kept in touch. I think he eventually came back to join the Foreign Office. There was Kenneth Young, who now edits the *Yorkshire Post.* He seemed both a literary man of affairs and an intellectual maverick. My own favourite was Tom Hodgson, a beautiful and intelligent young man with a sharp and dry but charitable wit which won me over. He went to St John's, Cambridge, to work for a Ph.D., which was never finished. He was killed in a bomber over Germany. I still have some of his Cambridge letters and a small Faber volume of poems, *This Life, This Death.*

Each year Bonamy seemed to pick one or perhaps two students to keep an eye on. We were probably the brightest, in both the good and bad senses of that word. We were intelligent but also likely to be quirky and offbeat, rather than steady and reliable. At our weakest we were bright rather than deep. I think some other members of staff gave an eye to other students according to their interests. Bonamy always had more time for the creatively untidy than for the steadily reliable. Though I must add that I was on the whole a reliably hard worker and not particularly creative; but in general the distinction is true.

This is not to say that he encouraged a sloppy bohemianism, as some members of staff in other departments were said to think. He was almost always something of a disciplinarian. It wasn't only in his carriage that you could still see the marks of the regular officer. He never withheld saying what he thought was the right thing for fear of hurting your feelings. I suppose his principle was that feelings soon recover, but bad advice can affect a lifetime.

It was in this way that he slapped me down at the second-year bazaar day. Standing at the trestle table, I asked to be allowed to read psychology as my new supplementary subject. He may have thought me a promising student but he had a fairly clear sense of my weaknesses. Quite shortly, he refused permission: I needed all my spare time, he said, to develop my English studies. I suppose this implied that I would have spent too much time on an exciting new subject like psychology. The rebuff stung badly and I still feel eighteen when I remember it. I think now that it was good for me to be hit sharply on the chin at that point. I was a hubristic hurdler—always halving my hurdles in advance—and he had realized that. 'Don't make Aunt Sallies of your enemies, Richard,' he said later, after listening to one of my tutorial essays, 'it's bad intellectually and tactically.'

This essay is proving even more personal than I said at the start it would. But only in this way can I bring out the particular nature and manner of expression of Bonamy Dobrée's interest in his group of undergraduates. I do not know if I was a more than usually raw and uncertain character (I had been an orphan for ten years, living with my grandmother. She died at Christmas in my first year.) I certainly *was* raw and uncertain—and proud, and perky. The combination made for some silly but not trivial difficulties and seemed to attract Bonamy's charismatic nature. Obviously he had to make most of the going, and he was patient and relaxed enough to be willing to do so.

So I began to see more of him, outside the University. I can best recall the variety of attention he gave, and some of what seem interesting elements in the relationship, by recounting a few incidents: they differ a good deal but all are typical.

One morning at about 8.15 there was a knock on my door. I was then living in a university hostel because of my grandmother's death, and was very hard up. I was still in pyjamas, unshaved and dreary from a very late night's reading. Bonamy came in, smelling freshly as usual. He had driven up there, out of the road that took him to the University, to tell me that there were hopes of some extra grant, and would I go to see the Registrar's department as soon as possible. I hadn't known that he was doing anything on my behalf.

On another occasion I was being taken by him to the house he and Valentine had built on the Wharfe at Collingham. It was mid-afternoon and we were in his cheap boxy Ford—an early Anglia, perhaps it was. He stopped before a confectioner's in Woodhouse Lane and said he ought to get some cakes, since there would be other visitors at home.

'Come in and help me choose,' he said. I knew at a glance, with that finely attuned register the poor have, that this wasn't 'a good shop'. I do not mean that it wasn't a Fortnum & Mason among confectioners; obviously it wasn't. But there are good cheap shops and bad cheap shops, and this was a bad cheap shop. In fact it was a late-'thirties chain-confectioners, and a member of the respectable poor could tell at a glance that its stuff was 'all show and no body'. Bonamy, with a high-pitched cheerful politeness which dazzled the assistants, bought a garish and ersatz-looking cake. He carried it out with panache; I tagged along feeling altogether older and unillusioned. Ironically, he liked sometimes to show that he had both feet on the ground, that he shrewdly knew a hawk from a handsaw. He used to say, with a proud practicality, that he would always buy only the cheapest serviceable car; it was simply a means of getting quickly from here to there. Early in the war he pedantically and proudly explained how he had learned to save petrol by switching off and disengaging the engine at various points on his way home.

On the afternoon he bought the cake the house seemed full of visitors, though indeed there were often some people there—especially writers and painters. It was all heady and—in small-minded self-defence—one was sometimes tempted to join those who sneered at it as self-conscious salon-making in the North, with a few selected undergraduates being allowed to mix. But he—they—did not *have* to take that kind of trouble with students; the conversation among their company was intellectually quite tough and honest. I was not used, any more than are most youths with my background, to much intellectual directness and toughness. In my world you tended to sheer away from arguments and especially from abstract argument: partly because you were not used to handling general ideas, but also because such arguments as you did have might well end in blows or 'bad blood'.

On Bonamy Dobrée's upper-class intellectual's directness was superimposed a touch of the professional army officer, with a no-nonsense approach and a quick mind. Sometimes a little too quick. Once, just after the war, we were walking down the corridors of the old university building at Leeds. For me it was the first visit since 1940 and by then that seemed a whole generation ago. My nose caught the smell of institutional polish, a smell which would always be associated with walking on those corridors to lectures. I remarked that the smell brought everything back—perhaps a little too nostalgically, for Bonamy came back smartly with: 'Mustn't look back, Richard—soon become sentimental.' He was right in one sense, of course; but I think he rather too quickly dismissed a fragment of experience.

On another occasion I was out at Collingham for dinner, on my own. We had a gin-and-something before the meal. It was probably the first gin I had ever had. Then he said: 'Drink up, Richard. Dinner's ready.' I drank and put down my glass, leaving—without thought—about half a teaspoonful in my glass. That is to say, I did not tip back the glass to drain it. Why? I suppose it was a habit. In my district you did not, for instance, drain your tea to the dregs. It was considered more polite to leave a little in the cup bottom. You also reduced the risk of getting tea-leaves in your mouth. More, I suppose this attitude was inspired both by a fear of seeming vulgar (we didn't want to look like rough workmen who put their heads back and drain a pint) and by a defensive pride (to show that we were not so hard up as to need to drink the *last* dregs of anything).

Bonamy was not attuned to all this, of course. His proprieties were different. He was onto me like a flash. 'Come, Richard, drink up. Gin costs a lot and is a good drink anyway. Why should we leave any in the bottom of the glass?' It was all said quite directly and with a laugh. But I was slightly disconcerted. I was more disconcerted on another evening. Again, we had just had a before-dinner drink (this makes it sound like a habit, but in fact the total number of such occasions was not large. He had many other demands on him). We were standing in the drawing-room, I think. As we rose to go I thoughtlessly put my glass on a shining mahogany table. 'Ah, Richard,' said Bonamy, 'you'll mark the surface.' He picked up the glass. There was indeed a rim of gin on the table. He drew out a large clean white handkerchief and carefully wiped it dry.

At this point I suspect that I am overemphasizing the slightly directorial air. But I have almost done with such aspects by now. And my excuse is that here there came into play most strongly that friction between different notions of conduct and manners which I have already mentioned.

To come back to that glass of gin. Of course, Bonamy's attitude—and mine—are not wholly to be explained in terms of our environments. But still they have a social point. In my world the equivalent to the error with the gin would have been, say, putting a cup of hot tea on the polished sideboard. We would no more have drawn a visitor's attention to such a mistake, as we would say, 'than fly'. We would have been too anxious not to hurt him, as I was hurt then (though my embarrassment was increased because I also felt grubby-finger-nail'd again). Even today, many years after I have left my original neighbourhood, I could not bring myself to tell a guest about such an error. I would be worried about the table; and I would probably be mad that he had put down his glass so thoughtlessly as to leave a mark —and madder still because I was inhibited from doing anything about it. I might have clumsily run back once he had left the room and furtively wiped the table. But whatever the urgency I would not have spoken to him.

It may well be that behind the hesitancy of our kind of people in such a situation there is a sort of gentleness and niceness, a subtle and extensive desire not to hurt another's feelings. On the other hand it is possible to be excessively nesh and to let relationships bog down in gentle evasions. If a table or sideboard really is likely to be marked unless something is done quickly it seems a pity that we can't be direct enough to say so and take the saying. Obviously each social group respects and stresses certain attitudes more than others and I certainly do not want to set up a pecking order of attitudes by classes. But one thing I have come to admire, in *some* upper- or upper-middle-class training, is this particular kind of directness. I admire it, that is to say, if it is reasonably integrated with other decencies and disciplines. I still hate it smoulderingly where it is merely a vestigial, socially acquired habit in people who are otherwise evasive and inefficient. Then it tends only to be used *downwards* and is boss-classy and enough to make any workman or clerk feel thoroughly bloody-minded. But I still cannot act in that way myself except in some limited and well-defined situations, such as academic discussions.

My last word on Bonamy as a firm teacher of young people. One day he swept in (the over-used verb fits here) for one of his weekly lectures, looking very angry indeed. He then upbraided us because we did not go to the public lectures which the University occasionally arranged. The previous evening Sir Ronald Storrs had been talking about Lawrence's Arabian campaigns. The hall must have been half empty and Bonamy, looking round, had seen few of his own undergraduates there. This had got him, as the Americans say, where he lived. He admired men of action; for himself, he tried not to be a sedentary bookworm; he respected a man of affairs who was also an intellectual and a soldier. At that stage in the term his teacher's charity was probably becoming worn, as it does with all of us. So perhaps he saw us that day as another man might have seen us for much of the time—as a bunch of rather weedy, pasty, plodding, cautious, calculating unexpectants, derisive and small-minded about the celebration of courage as about that of patriotism; main-chancers, insurers, play-safers. We might laugh at the public schools and the professional army, but with what justification? They might as justly call us little grey worms who—like the traders in Conrad's *Heart of Darkness*—would not recognize the heights to which men might be called or, for that matter, the depths to which they might fall. We were Dante's middle range of people, fit neither to be saved nor thoroughly to be damned. Not that he said anything like all this, and I do not believe that much of it went through his mind. I am interpreting. But I think that something like this was driving him at that moment, and he made no bones about saying how little he thought of us for cautiously refusing to put out our imaginative necks so as to feel a more challenging air.

But it was Bonamy Dobrée who—alone or almost alone among the professors—would regularly push into the noisy and crowded Union coffee bar to sit and talk with undergraduates. His attitude towards his northern students was obviously a complex one and no doubt it changed a good deal in the twenty odd years he was at Leeds. I knew it intensively only in the earlier years. I think he did recognize some of the peculiar strengths these students can show—a sort of awkward pawky pushing at the truth, a refusal, as he would say in testimonials for people of whom he approved, 'to take anything at second-hand', and especially a refusal to join the 'posh club' of the knowing intelligentsia, a stubborn and unstylish search for the light that would really serve their condition. He saw that kind of thing. But I have the impression that much else in the deeper grain of northern life—good and bad—passed him by. It would probably have needed altogether too much of an effort at that age and across that gap, and in any case he had other preoccupations. But he could sometimes walk across the deep water of those differences simply by pretending that they did not exist—and in one sense, though not in others, they then did not exist.

He did not romanticize the North in the usual cliché-ridden way. He was not one of those southern-trained, ruminatively pipe-smoking professors whose fortune has placed them in northern universities for a quarter of a century, and who have become hammy experts on the wit of the Lancashire man or the dry salty humour of the Geordie. Grey, dirty and damp—physically Leeds is, or used to be, like a large, tough old mongrel whom only the family could love. The contrast with Bonamy's native Channel Islands or with Cairo or London must have been acute. Yet I never heard him grumble about being in the North, as I have heard many assistant lecturers grumble at length; nor did he speak with nostalgia about Cambridge. He seemed to enjoy being there, to feel challenged and determined to put his best into it.

One side of him, slightly romantically, saw himself bringing a little more sweetness and light to the benighted North. And he did have, as I have said more than once, a certain style; he was more colourful than most Leeds professors, and more cosmopolitan. He was particularly fluent in French and belonged to that intensely Francophile generation which came to maturity just before the First World War. My own generation is not, as older people sometimes say, Francophobe and arrogantly insular. But we think some British provincial strengths have been underestimated; in our day France has not given the best of democratic examples; and when we look outward we tend to be especially interested in the United States, as a country whose virtues we discovered for ourselves when most of our teachers were still ritualistically talking about 'Coca Cola civilization'.

If Leeds seemed drab to Bonamy, he naturally seemed strange to Leeds. The *Yorkshire Post* knew it could usually get a quotable reaction from him on North *v.* South issues, and he in his turn enjoyed giving them a good run for their money. I remember one minor newspaper storm when he refused to pay his dues to one of the great Yorkshire gods. We talked too much about the splendours of roast beef and Yorkshire pudding, he said; there *were* other good dishes but Yorkshire seemed hardly to have heard of them.

He liked (how one is inclined to use rather Edwardian phrases) to cut a bit of a dash, to shock the bourgeoisie. Among his many ancestors one of the most obvious was Lytton Strachey. He liked to be a little odd and uncustomary. I came in to his room one day and found him smoking as usual over his work. The smell was strange, though, like something wafted over damp meadows in autumn. 'Get out your pipe, Richard,' he said, 'have a fill.' It was herbal mixture—'bucketful for half a crown, you know'—mixed with his Dobie's Four Square. He was childishly pleased at the discovery and the economy. I do not know how long he smoked the mixture, but I used it for years afterwards.

Or he could be frivolous and boyish, especially when he was anxious to shake someone out of 'stuffiness'. 'Stuffy' was one of the most potent words in his dictionary of dislikes. Our students' English Society 'socials' usually brought this side out. We had at those times no visiting speaker to deliver a paper, and we had few social arts. We tended to sit or bump around, uneasy because we were out of the context within which we had grown used to one another—that of a competitive Honours group or 'year'. At such a party Bonamy once, sitting between two particularly phlegmatic girls, ate a high tea backwards (from 'sweet' to 'savoury') because it was 'less dull, more interesting you know'. On another occasion he came in, in evening dress, when the social had reached the party-game stage. He had been to an official dinner at the University, and we soon noted that he had drunk well. We were then playing—at this stage we always seemed to be playing them—literary games. Bonamy didn't at all like that kind of shop talk. Within minutes he was on his back, balancing a glass of water on his chin and trying to do something complicated with it. Two or three of us brooded irritably; who did he think he was anyway, jollying people along; we would work our own way through our own awkwardnesses; this wasn't a Duke of York's camp for clean-nosed apprentices.

He enjoyed a fight, and could be mischievous at times. I have seen him running downstairs on his way to Senate with his tail flicking between his legs in the expectation of a battle. I knew little except from hearsay about his part in the inevitable larger struggles within the University. I knew about more marginal matters, such as his support for the famous but controversial Eric Gill relief, or his continuous barrage about the badness of university food, or his fights to get some decent contemporary pictures for the University or to save as many trees as possible in the massive rebuilding. But I have heard that he was regarded as a nuisance by some on Senate, and probably they had some justification in feeling like that. I expect that some felt—again not altogether without grounds—that he could be dashingly unwise; and that he made them feel like stolid, inhibited, stiff-necked provincials. But the fair-minded would also recognize that he was never contentious in a mean way and never a calculator.

The same vivacity informed his lectures. They were exciting and stimulating rather than comprehensive or exhaustive. He deliberately moved across the formal boundaries of specialisms. He laced his lectures with side-comments, odd *aperçus* from other disciplines, sudden changes of level, irruptions into contemporary affairs. I can trace the origins of some of my own less formal literary-and-social interests to incidental comments he threw out—on Faulkner and violence in literature, for instance.

He was, as he still is, an immensely hard worker. But he would have regarded it as a weakness to complain or even to show the effects markedly. You should carry your load lightly; after all, you had made your own choices. But to get through all he got through—and pay dues to the personal values and teacher's values he respected—he must have imposed a hard discipline on himself, in distinguishing the light-hearted which deserves time from the trivial which wastes it, and in distinguishing solid work which demands steady application from the merely drudging.

When I was a student he was in what could be called his early prime, and at that time was producing—heaven knows how—about two books a year. They varied in depth, and in subject ranged 'dangerously' widely. But they all bore witness to his dream of literature. I need to stress this because, inevitably, some people called him a butterfly. He had some butterfly qualities, it is true; and butterflies are so bright that we ought perhaps to be glad to see them more often in universities. But at bottom his manner and his range were fed from deeper sources than that tag implies.

We all have our images of what we admire and would like to aspire to. Bonamy Dobrée had a dream of 'the man of letters'—a widely read man, a good scholar who yet wore his scholarship easily (but anyone who has seen him at work on a thesis or a manuscript will think twice before they talk lightly of butterflies; he is a stickler for detail, very well informed, pertinacious and severe). But still his ideal man of letters will *carry* his scholarship well, will not be borne down by it. He won't be musty or dusty, not one of the 'bald heads forgetful of their sins/Old, learned, respectable bald heads'. He will have one foot always in the foul rag-and-bone shop of the heart, or at least in the untidy garrets where literature is often written. In his school of English he stressed less the steady grind of historical or textual scholarship (though these had their due) than the sense that literature came out of living men who put their hopes and pain into the making and the meaning of it. This, I suspect, was what decided which students he took special care of, why he would prop up an unstable poet before patting a steady worker's back, seek out the surprising impressionist before the reliable or predictable. As a result he occasionally enlisted very odd characters for his department—whether staff or students—as well as for his friends. But the special quality of the Leeds school was that you never lost the feeling that the study of literature was different in kind from the study of most other academic subjects. It had its history and its scholarship, yes; but its raw material was alive, was made out of the stresses of individual lives ... lives not necessarily ordered or respectable or earnest.

II

I have stressed throughout that my undergraduate relations with Bonamy had a number of subterranean cross-currents (he told me later that he had been, and is, much less aware of them than I am). So this is a peculiarly subjective essay and risks a peculiar irrelevance, that it may reveal more about its author than its subject. Naturally I have tried not to let that happen. But, partly as a result of these cross-currents, I was always a little inhibited with him. He may have felt this underneath. Or perhaps he decided that I had more the caution of a critical than the dash of a creative mind. At any rate he unbuttoned himself more, dropped the stance of the teacher more, with those who had more of a flair or who approached him more uncomplicatedly. I remember a much younger protégé telling me that Bonamy, in a pub one night, had run over his life and achievement very frankly and ended by saying: 'But, you see, I have to recognize that I have a second-class mind.' I was touched to hear again the voice of the old straight Bonamy, but also slightly hurt (and ashamed) that he had never in my own early acquaintance with him been so frank, been able so to relax his role.

This is a crablike movement to a conclusion. Before I try to sum all up I want to mention two qualities which were more quietly exercised than others but were important parts of the texture. He was, then, extremely courteous, and careful not to give offence where he felt someone needed special care or wasn't strong enough to take direct contradiction. In his courtesy towards women he was slightly old-fashioned, even slightly gallant. I suppose he had lived for most of the years up to his early manhood in a predominantly male society (as I had lived in the woman-centred living-room of a working-class home). So I was particularly struck by the formality and attentiveness of his courtesy towards women. I remember once that my wife (as she is now is) and I were walking with him in his garden. I grew very interested in the conversation and Mary fell back for a moment, perhaps to look at some flowers. I knew she had fallen back but kept on walking—partly because I was very interested and partly because I simply expected her to catch up. Bonamy cut straight across my talk and, slightly quirky, said: 'Shall we wait for Mary?'

Second, there were the simple kindnesses; kindnesses which had no show about them, which went well beyond the line of duty or normal acquaintanceship, and implied a good deal of steady and precise thought. They were—and I hardly expected ever to quote these lines—'little, nameless, unremembered, acts/Of kindness and of love'. Many young writers waiting for a commission knew he was always good for five pounds. I do not suppose anyone can tease out the extent and ramifications of all this help. I had best mention some of his particular thoughtful kindnesses towards me, from quite small to large ones. Thus, on our degree day, when T. S. Eliot was given an honorary degree, he took care to tell Eliot a little about me and steer him across to meet me since I was more than usually interested in Eliot's work. After we had both joined the Army he sent me some good khaki socks, saying he had more than he needed and knew that recruits in basic training were never flush. Earlier, in fact in my third year, he said suddenly one day: 'Richard, I want you to go down to the *Yorkshire Post* offices at 11 tomorrow morning. I've arranged for you to have an interview with Arthur Mann.' Mann was the formidable editor of the *Post* at that time. Bonamy had, of course, acted autocratically in deciding that I might make a good journalist on a good paper, and in arranging the interview without asking me. I reacted true to type, by being a little put out yet not telling him so. But I was put out less because he had acted without speaking to me than because he had decided that I would make a journalist. Starry-eyed about the academic life, I was hurt that he had not thought of me as—and only as—a fit candidate for its ranks. Last (of these instances): just before the Easter of my Finals year Bonamy happened to be sitting next to the Director of Education for Leeds at a public dinner. He knew that the Director, an idiosyncratic and independent man, had given me an impromptu £30 nearly two years before so that I could go abroad for the first time. They spoke of me and Bonamy said that I had a good chance of getting a First a couple of months later. But I was overstrained and needed a break. There was no money for a holiday. Wouldn't this be a good opportunity for the Director to repeat his earlier inspired kindness? Bonamy called me in a day or so later and told me with a typical mixture of warmth, briskness and perkiness—he really loved to bring rabbits out of a hat—that the money would be there if I would go straight away to the Education Offices near the Town Hall. I spent Easter in Venice.

He was, it is plain, in many respects a substitute father for me, at a particularly difficult time. But he kept the relationship taut and challenging, well-brushed and swept, not indulgent. And this I liked too: here the working-class nonconformist chimed with the upper-middle-class professional and military man. But I am again too quickly making the social point to the neglect of the personal. Others with his background would not necessarily have acted as he did. In spite of all I have said, the basis of our friendship was affection for each other as persons; and in my case a great *respect* for him, a respect which overrode considerations of social class. He showed me in action (though I cannot claim to have learned from them all) qualities such as these: hard work and thoroughness, a detailed attention to whatever job was in hand; a complex teacher's care; a touch of the happy warrior, an attack and gaiety; a disinclination to calculate and a refusal to sentimentalize, a kind of stiff dignity, courtesy and magnanimity.

All these have been brought out in the long and severe illness of Valentine which has so far overshadowed the years of their retirement (and which she has borne with a similar courage and grace). The last time I saw them at Blackheath was in an interval between two of Valentine's painful operations. She had insisted that they get a leg of lamb, and stayed up for a while. We talked over the meal, domestically and seriously and lightly, and later Bonamy took me to the tube-station and—now with an openness not snagged by little unknown eddies—we talked of his work and his life in retirement. As the train moved off, he gave his familiar radiant smile, and I remembered with sudden force Yeats's line about 'gaiety transfiguring all that dread'. So I salute him more strongly than ever now, understanding much better the puzzling social interactions which used to go on in our relationship, still full of respect for him—as a pupil for his best master; but, overwhelmingly, feeling love for the man.

The Art of Collaboration

HERBERT READ

THERE are several ways of working together on a literary project, but to guarantee success there must be a marriage of true minds. Even then it can be a marriage of convenience in which each partner is assigned a separate sphere and is united to the other only on public occasions. Or one partner can do all the basic work and the other can add to it or revise it. I leave on one side creative collaboration, of which there are relatively few examples. Experts claim to disentangle the respective parts of Beaumont and Fletcher with ease; but no one would make the same claim for the work of that neglected poet, Michael Field (not entirely neglected—Yeats chose eight of his (their) poems for the *Oxford Book of Modern Verse*). The kind of collaboration I undertook with Bonamy Dobrée on the *London Book of English Prose* and the *London Book of English Verse* was of none of these kinds, but nevertheless the truest kind of all. It might be compared to the building of a tower, to which each partner brings his loads of stones, but only those are used that fit a preconceived plan. The plan may be modified by the builders' experience, but it guides the choice of every separate stone.

The plan, therefore, was the thing, and to it we must have devoted a considerable amount of preliminary discussion. This discussion of the principles of selection to be adopted first took place in the editing of the prose anthology in 1930–31, but we soon realized, when we undertook a verse anthology thirteen years later, that very different applications of our principles were involved for the two media. In November 1929, when Bonamy first agreed to collaborate with me on the prose anthology, he wrote in a still extant letter:

> There are two things I would like to urge. The first is that the anthology should take the form of ... division into intent. The second is that it should be suitable for schools, the motive for this being entirely financial, and pure of all thought for that dismal affair we call Education. The first is the more important point. For me, the whole interest of the business lies in that. What is good prose for one purpose, is not good prose for another. Think of a military despatch written in the prose of Donne!

I agreed, and the prose anthology that we then made has a functional design—its aim, we said in the Introduction, is to examine prose as an instrument, to take the various purposes for which prose is written, and to see if any principle of writing will emerge. We divided prose into three categories (narrative, scientific, emotive) and found no difficulty in subdividing these categories into stylistic types determined by the purpose the writer had in mind. As for the principle of writing that was to emerge, this was purely pragmatic. 'There is no mystery about good prose', we concluded; 'it is not a question of inspiration, or even of education ... But equally, good prose is not a question of simplicity alone; that way lies monotony. Prose is as various as mankind itself; it only ceases to be of interest when it expresses, not the man himself, but a convention, or a confusion, or an unresolved impression.'

Little of the correspondence we exchanged in editing the prose anthology has survived, but by good fortune practically all the letters we exchanged when editing the verse anthology still exist, and they show step by step how the book took shape. Correspondence was forced on us by our respective locations, Bonamy in Leeds, myself near London. There were, of course, occasional meetings at which some questions may have been discussed verbally, but they do not sensibly interrupt the critical exchange, which continued for three years, from the first tentative outlines of a plan in October 1944 until the correction of the final proofs in November 1947. In the aftermath of war there was considerable delay in production; the first edition is dated 1949.

Having agreed to take the plunge, the first difficulty was to draw up the plan. I began with one firm conviction—that there is a strict correspondence between modes of expression and psychological types, and that our divisions of verse should be based on the best available analysis of psychological types, which I believed to be Jung's. I therefore began with Jung's four basic psychological functions—thinking, feeling, sensation and intuition—and by multiplying these by the two 'mechanisms', introversion and extraversion. I had eight possible categories. I added a ninth for those rarer forms of poetry that might seem to transcend all categories, unitary verse, which finally I called 'the symphonic poem', and still another category for satirical verse, which though it belonged to the extraverted thinking type of expression, was self-critical and detached and also, in its own way, transcended all categories.

All this psychological structure was to be disguised when it came to the actual presentation of the poems, and I never thought of it as more than a scaffolding for our building. But for Bonamy it did not have even that virtue. 'I don't think it matters how we categorize,' he wrote to me, 'because however illuminating our plan will be, every poem will defeat us. Practically all poetry tries to convey an emotion, and a sentiment, and to express a philosophy. I thought of narrative too: but was Coleridge trying to tell a story in *The Ancient Mariner*, or convey an emotion, or express a philosophy, or convey a lesson? Where do we put *To his Coy Mistress*? Is Tennyson's *Ulysses* narrative or philosophic? Is *In Memoriam* intended to convey a philosophy or an emotion? What is the first chorus in *Atalanta*? And where oh where in the hell is *A World within a War*? This is a far more complicated business than the prose—and I'm sure that we shall find the objective categories made by literary naturalists the only workable ones. However, I'm willing to have a try at anything.'

To which I replied: 'Of course there will be hybrids of all sorts and sizes, but I think we shall find that most poems have a bias somewhere, and sometimes indicated by the poet himself in his correspondence, etc. *The Ancient Mariner* I should have thought was a narrative poem: it is a ballad. *In Memoriam* definitely philosophical—an emotion can't last so long. Swinburne's chorus is incantation.

'I think it is hopeless to start with the specimens and try to invent a pigeon-hole for each one. The right way is to build a nice neat pigeoncote and then pop the birds in the appropriate holes. I don't believe poets go outside the psychological categories. It would be too boring and academic to start with psych. cats. but I think we shall arrive at a scheme which approximates to them.'

I continued to refine and stretch my categories and Bonamy continued to criticize them, sometimes furiously, and the argument had one good effect—it compelled us to think about the nature of the poems we hurled into the argument. For example: I had suggested Occasional as a category and quoted Goethe (all real poetry is *occasional*) in justification.

> His dictum seems to me meaningless, unless you stretch the word 'occasion' to include a long series of mental events. You can't call *King Lear* an occasional poem, nor *Paradise Lost*, nor *The Prelude*, nor *The Ancient Mariner*, nor *Four Quartets*. I dare say very often some occasion started the poet off on something, but unless we knew the occasion we couldn't do anything about it; and if we did, it would only make confusion worse confounded. What do you suppose was the occasion of *The Phoenix and Turtle*? There are, of course, occasional poems: *Agincourt*, *Jenny kissed me*, *Waterloo*, *Rose crossed the road*, *The Wreck of the Deutschland* The idea simply doesn't help.

I continued to press my categories and cried 'back to essentials'—the essentials being 'physical and psychological facts'. 'I don't want to introduce an unusual spate of psychic jargon into this affair, but one can have a framework of steel and then cover it with beautiful slabs of polished marble.'

Finally, on December 7th, 1944, Bonamy agreed. 'Yes, I think the scheme will do. Any extravagations we can regard as ramifications, as long as we don't take it too scientifically and Teutonically. I don't think really we can treat poetry by the method of analytic perception, but we must adopt a more intuitive mode (see *Education through Art* and *Science and the Modern World* passim et ubique).'

There were further preliminaries to settle—the length of the anthology, where to begin and where to end, whether to include translations or extracts from plays, practical questions of spellings, standard texts and copyright. These are of no general interest. The fun began when we began to make our selections. Our tastes were to a large extent complementary—or perhaps I should say that our prejudices cancelled out. Mine were for the Romantics, and Bonamy's for the Augustans. At least I thought so, but I find him protesting (February 21st, 1945): 'What d'you mean by my period. I take all Eng. Lit. that is not O.E. or M.E. for my parish. I have written on the 17th C and am doing a book of 1700–1740—but as for 1763 etc: to hell with it. Am I not struggling with Akenside, and have I not suffered from the Wartons? And don't I think Gray a dull dog, & Goldsmith very small beer?' Some of his suggestions I must have successfully resisted—for example, the Wartons, 'very much harbingers of the Romantic Revival, and we ought to work in one of them if we can'. He suggested 'a nice little eight line thing inscribed on a grotto' by Tom Junior, but it did not survive the scrutiny. As the possibles accumulated we had to be severe—we considered and scrapped Cunningham, Somerville, Thomas Watson (and Sir William), and many such like poets, and of course many individual poems—for example, I find myself pleading for more than one poem of Shenstone's—'I think we ought to have "My banks they are furnished with bees" ', but in vain. Perhaps the full flavour of our procedure can best be indicated by two complete letters—short ones, for most of them are too long.

H.R. to B.D. 5:3:45

This is a mere stop-gap, anticipating your upbraidings. I have had a bad week or two—page proofs of my old rag-bag (360 pages) and the arrest of four of my anarchist friends, and much consequent activity (letters to the press, formation of a defence ctee, etc. Really our Gestapo is overreaching itself and a stand must be made. I suppose, if the worst comes, I could continue from Brixton—The Brixton Book of English Verse would be a good title).

I enclose lists for DIXON (which you have seen), COLERIDGE, SPENSER and HOPKINS. Also two poems of Nat Wanley's. I will copy out in full the one of which you have sent me about half—if you don't like the Psalm (the first two stanzas are miraculous) we can take the Resurrection (your piece).

Now about Coleridge. I may be going mental, but I cannot now read either Christabel or the Hoary Old Mariner without feeling considerably restive. The things are terrific tours de force, but essentially meretricious. Fancy doing that sort of thing now ... It is Wardour Street romanticism, compact Ossian, fustian, phoney, but of course hypnotic. But apart from this shocking spate of heresy, the poems are both too long for the space at our disposal, and that need be our only avowed excuse—we can't conceivably give STC more than 15 pp, and I don't see anything on my list that can be spared.

Will answer LBEV 9/10/11 [we numbered our letters] in the course of the week. Meanwhile I have had a look out of turn at Bridges. Please consider London Snow, On a Dead Child, The Winnowers and 'I shall never love the snow again' and a poem called Noel which I can't find in my edition (1914).

I have been through your Blake notes and mostly agree, but will comment later.

To which this answer came:

DIXON. I leave to you, though I confess I regret losing The Less and the More, which I think has something queer and distinctive. [It was restored to the list and appears in the anthology.]

COLERIDGE. It may astonish you to see me say so, but I have always thought the Ancient Mariner an over-rated poem, except for children. Also that I feel your dis-ease over Christabel. So I will not quarrel with your general position. I think I shall agree completely, but I would like to look through my Coleridge first. It is at the University—where most things are.

SPENSER. Infernally difficult. I'm not quite happy about this. First your arithmetic. 1 takes 2½; 2 takes 3½; 3 takes 5, and 4 takes 12. I think I am right. This makes still greater the very heavy weighting towards the marriage poems. I agree to 1 and 2; very good high lights. As to 5, I wish we could have a whole Calendar. I wish we could have Astrophel. I wish we could have a section of The Tears of the Muses, or one of the Fowre Hymnes. I feel that in your list there is so much of the same kind of Spenser and though I agree that we don't want to show all sides of a man, but only what is good poetry, practically all Spenser is. I am dubious about your 6. We have, after all, to think of schools. The Bower of Bliss is supposed to be part of a moral tale; Coming to kiss her lips is not—though it is marvellous. Would there be room for a section from Daphnaida? Say Part II of the plaint?

HOPKINS. Yes, though I wish we could find room, and cash, for Heaven-Haven, even though Q has it. That change of rhythm in the last line is breath-lifting.

BRIDGES. We ought to consider:

1. Splendid Ship, which Q has.
2. London Snow.
3. On a Dead Child.
4. Winnowers.
5. I never shall love the snow again.
6. Noel.
7. Who has not walked upon the shore.

Let us agree to leave out 1. 2 is very good, and special attention is drawn to it in Dobrée and Batho's admirable Introduction to Victorian Lit. But I am not sure that it doesn't mark the change from his lyric capacity to the tedious pedantry of The Testament of Beauty. 3 is good: I get a little chilled by 'thee' and 'wert thou; —alas! no longer'. I don't much like 'wondrous' joy. St 3 is bad, with the horrible sound of 'Dost thou with a turn or gesture *anon respond*'. I dislike anon anyhow, except when an author. I don't much like 'the last little bed'. I quite like 4, but I think we can do better pastorals than that. Still, it is good: I prefer it to 3. I don't altogether like 'oversprent', nor 'what time of year', nor 'thresh'd', nor 'gat us'. His archaisms tend to spoil him. I don't very much like 5. I feel it's rather made up. I dislike 'with rime bedight'. And why on earth did they bring back Maurice with a flower in his hand? No, I think this is below the others. As to 6, my edition is 1912, but I have Last Poems or summat at the University of Botherem, and will look it up. I now put forward 7 as a candidate. It has good vivid imagery, and imagination. It is evocative, as very little Victorian poetry is. I like 'The horses of the strong south-west Are pastured round his tropic tent'. I like the clouds breaking into phalanx; I like the shadows leaping sheer off the cliff into the sea, and I like the final vision. It is also a musical poem. I don't altogether like the ships laughing, and I dislike 'drave'.

[In the end we included Low Barometer, London Snow, and After the Gale, the poem referred to above as 'Who has not walked upon the shore'.]

We shall soon have to begin to think of proportion. How are we getting on for pastoral? for instance. We ought to have Barnfield's 'As it fell upon a day', and we could alter Daniel a bit if you liked; it would give you an argument for 'Now each creature joys the other', and I very much like his 'O, happy, golden age!' but that would be about 2 pp. We must also consider the poet A. W. whoever he may have been. When I come to do Sidney, I should like to put in 'The lad Philisides', but it will come to about 4 pp.

And aren't we rather short of narrative? Only Chaucer straight narrative, as far as I remember. Shall we have that story I told Thomas the other night? Gower, about 5½? I shall try to choose a short Crabbe. I suppose we must have Crabbe. A dull parsonical dog for the most part.

Dare I confess that Spenser *cloys* me a little?

And so it went on for many more letters. The one quoted is No. 14; the last I numbered is 105, and then Bonamy began to number his derisively 2436, etc. I sent the anthology to Douglas Jerrold (Eyre & Spottiswoode) 'ready for the press' on December 30th, 1946. It was passed to Graham Greene (who was then working in the editorial department of Eyre & Spottiswoode), who made some minor criticisms, mainly about our Introduction. These were easily met. Then followed, six months later, the tedious business of correcting the proofs, which involved many problems of spelling, glosses, and some rearrangement. A few poems were withdrawn in the process, others inserted. It seems to me now that our publishers were very tolerant—the cost of the proof corrections must have been outrageous. Endless queries arose in connection with the Notes—no wonder it took a year to see the volume through the press. I have no note of the exact date of publication. It was printed on 'economy' paper (one forgets how the effects of the war were prolonged), but the large edition was exhausted in three years and subsequent editions were printed on decent paper and otherwise improved. I might mention, as a curiosity of literature, that even after the second edition had appeared, with all possible care devoted to corrections, we received a letter from a retired gentleman in the south of London (it may have been Brixton!) submitting a considerable number of further errors that had escaped all our scrutinies. In spite of our inquiries he remained anonymous, or at least inaccessible, and did not acknowledge our abject gratitude.

It had been a great experience, and I think no one of the many people who have reason, as colleagues and pupils of Bonamy Dobrée, to be grateful to him for his many virtues can have such an intimate knowledge of them as I possess as a result of this experience. His scholarship is evident in many fields; his enthusiasm may have affected others in an equal degree. What I experienced was a tolerance, a wit and a gaiety that carried us through a long and arduous task that without these qualities might have endangered a friendship founded on affection.

A Selected List of the Published Writings of Bonamy Dobrée

compiled by

MARGARET BRITTON, B.A.

This list includes all books and important essays and periodical articles published between 1919 and 1962. The following have been excluded: minor contributions to periodicals, including letters to editors, book and theatre reviews, except when they discuss several works and take the form of a 'critical essay', Prefaces and Forewords, except when editorial work was also involved, and a few works published outside the United Kingdom.

1919

1. Drama and Values. *New Statesman.* Vol. XIV, no. 344, pp. 161–2.
2. Episode. [Short story.] *English Review.* Vol. XXIX, pp. 517–22.

1920

3. What is 'Dramatic'? *New Statesman.* Vol. XIV, no. 351, pp. 379–80.
4. Elizabethan Drama on the Modern Stage. *London Mercury.* Vol. II, no. 10, pp. 420—33.

1924

5. RESTORATION COMEDY 1660–1720. Oxford: Clarendon Press. Reprinted 1938.

1925

6. HISTRIOPHONE: A DIALOGUE ON DRAMATIC DICTION. London: Leonard and Virginia Woolf at the Hogarth Press. [The Hogarth Essays, 5.]
7. ESSAYS IN BIOGRAPHY. London: Humphrey Milford (O.U.P.). [Contains essays on Sir George Etherege, Sir John Vanbrugh and Joseph Addison.]
8. TIMOTHEUS: THE FUTURE OF THE THEATRE. London: Kegan Paul, Trench, Trubner & Co. Ltd. [Series 'Today and Tomorrow'. A satirical essay on theatres in A.D. 2100.]
9. COMEDIES BY WILLIAM CONGREVE, edited with introduction and notes by B. D. London: Humphrey Milford (O.U.P.). [World's Classics, no. 276.]

1926

10. ROCHESTER. A CONVERSATION BETWEEN SIR GEORGE ETHEREGE AND MR. FITZJAMES. London: Leonard and Virginia Woolf at the Hogarth Press. [The Hogarth Essays, series 2, no. 2.]
11. Sir John Denham: a conversation between Bishop Henry King and Edmund Waller, at the Palace, Chichester, March 1669. *The New Criterion*, Vol. IV, no. 3, pp. 454–64.
12. Young Voltaire: a conversation between William Congreve and Alexander Pope, Twickenham, September 1726. *The Nation and Athenaeum*. Vol. XL, no. 5, pp. 179–80.

1927

13. SIR JOHN DENHAM: A CONVERSATION BETWEEN BISHOP HENRY KING AND EDMUND WALLER, AT THE PALACE, CHICHESTER, MARCH 1669. Kensington: At the Cayme Press. [Cayme Press Pamphlet no. 8. Limited edition. Reprinted from *The New Criterion.*]
14. SARAH CHURCHILL, DUCHESS OF MARLBOROUGH. London, Gerald Howe. [Representative Women.]
15. SIR JOHN VANBRUGH: COMPLETE WORKS, the plays edited by B. D., the letters edited by Geoffrey Webb. Bloomsbury: Nonesuch Press. 4 vols. [Vol. I contains a biographical essay by B. D. Limited edition.]
16. THE SOFA: A MORAL TALE BY CRÉBILLON FILS (CLAUDE PROSPER JOLYOT), translated with an introduction by B. D. London: Routledge. [The Broadway Library of XVIII Century French Literature.] Reprinted 1951, republished by the Folio Society 1952.
17. The World of Dean Inge. [A critical essay.] *The New Criterion*. Vol. V, no. 1, pp. 109–14.
18. Thomas Otway. *T.L.S.* No. 1309, pp. 133–4. [Unsigned].
19. Rudyard Kipling. *The Monthly Criterion*. Vol. VI, no. 6, pp. 499–515.
20. George Savile, Lord Halifax. *T.L.S.* No. 1350, pp. 941–2. [Unsigned.]

1928

21. FIVE RESTORATION TRAGEDIES, edited with introduction by B. D. London: Humphrey Milford (O.U.P.). [World's Classics, no. 313.] Reprinted 1935.
22. THE MOURNING BRIDE, POEMS AND MISCELLANIES BY WILLIAM CONGREVE, edited with introduction by B. D. London: Humphrey Milford (O.U.P.) [World's Classics, no. 277.]
23. William Congreve: a conversation between Swift and Gay at the house of the Duke of Queensberry, near London, June 1730. *The Criterion.* Vol. VII, no. 4, pp. 7–17.
24. Cleopatra and 'That criticall warr.' *T.L.S.* No. 1393, pp. 717–18. [Unsigned.]

1929

25. THE LAMP AND THE LUTE: STUDIES IN SIX MODERN AUTHORS. Oxford: Clarendon Press. [Contains studies of Ibsen, Hardy, Kipling, Forster, D. H. Lawrence and T. S. Eliot. The study of Kipling was reprinted from *The Monthly Criterion.*]
26. Dryden and Artificial Tragedy. *T.L.S.* No. 1437, pp. 629–30. [Unsigned.]
27. Richard Steele: died September 1, 1729. *T.L.S.* No. 1439, pp. 657–8. [Unsigned.]
28. RESTORATION TRAGEDY 1660–1720. Oxford: Clarendon Press. [Contains some of the same material as *Five Restoration Tragedies*; the chapters on Cleopatra, Dryden and Otway are based on articles in the *T.L.S.*]

1930

29. Robert Smith Surtees. *T.L.S.* No. 1469, pp. 257–8. [Unsigned.]
30. The Future of Criticism. *Spectator*. Vol. CXLIV, No. 5302, p. 189.
31. Achigar. Translated from the Basque by B. D. [Short story.] *The Criterion.* Vol. IX, no. 25, pp. 476–81.

1931

32. THE LONDON BOOK OF ENGLISH PROSE, selected and ordered by Herbert Read and B. D. London: Eyre & Spottiswoode. 2nd revised edition, 1949.
33. John Dryden, August 9, 1631–May 1, 1700. *T.L.S.* No. 1540, pp. 601–2. [Unsigned.]

1932

34. ST MARTIN'S SUMMER. [A novel.] London: Leonard and Virginia Woolf at the Hogarth Press.

35. VARIETY OF WAYS: DISCUSSIONS ON SIX AUTHORS. Oxford: Clarendon Press. [Contains essays on Dryden, Savile and Steele, reprinted from the *T.L.S.*; on Bunyan's *Badman* and Congreve, reprinted from the World's Classics series; and on Mandeville's *Fable of the Bees.*]
36. WILLIAM PENN, QUAKER AND PIONEER. London: Constable.
37. THE LETTERS OF PHILIP DORMER STANHOPE, edited with an introduction by B. D. London: Eyre & Spottiswoode. [6 vols. Limited edition.]
38. Lord Chesterfield: a conversation between the Hon. Horace Walpole and Dr Matthew Maty (Principal Librarian at the British Museum) at Strawberry Hill, 1776. *The Criterion*, Vol. II, no. 43, pp. 198–208.
39. The Duke of Newcastle: a conversation between Lord Chesterfield and Lieut.-General Irwine, 1769. *Nineteenth Century and After*. Vol. CXI, no. 659, pp. 106–14.
40. Some Novels of Meredith. *National Review*. Vol. XCVIII, pp. 255–63.
41. Modern Biography. *National Review*. Vol. XCIX, pp. 121–9.

1933

42. GIACOMO CASANOVA, CHEVALIER DE SEINGALT, etc. London: Peter Davies. Republished by Thomas Nelson & Sons, 1938. [Short Biographies, no. 3.]
43. JOHN WESLEY. London: Duckworth. [Great Lives, vol. IV.]
44. ENGLISH CRITICAL ESSAYS, TWENTIETH CENTURY, selected with an introduction by Phyllis M. Jones. [Contains 'Thomas Hardy' by B.D.]
45. THE POST-VICTORIANS, with an introduction by the Very Rev. W. R. Inge. [Contains 'Lytton Strachey 1880–1932' by B. D.]
46. Government, a conversation between Robert Harley (soon afterwards Earl of Oxford) and William Penn: October 7, 1710. *Nineteenth Century and After*. Vol. CXIII, no. 672, pp. 253–6.
47. Samuel Pepys: February 23rd, 1633–May 26th, 1703. *Spectator*. Vol. CL, no. 5460, pp. 210–11.
48. Novels and Subject Criticism. *National Review*. Vol. C, pp. 561–8.
49. Macaulay. *The Criterion*. Vol. XII, no. 49, pp. 593–604.
50. Back to Mediaevalism? [A critical essay.] *Nineteenth Century and After*. Vol. CXIV, no. 678, pp. 247–56.
51. The Duchess of Marlborough: a conversation between Alexander Pope and William Pulteney, recently created Earl of Bath. In the Grotto, Twickenham, 1742. *Life and Letters*. Vol. IX, no. 50, pp. 347–59.
52. AS THEIR FRIENDS SAW THEM: BIOGRAPHICAL CONVERSATIONS. London: Jonathan Cape. [Contains studies of Sir John Denham, Congreve and Lord Chesterfield reprinted from *The Criterion*; of Voltaire, reprinted from *The Nation*; of the Duchess of Marlborough, reprinted from *Life and Letters*; of the Duke of Newcastle, reprinted from

Nineteenth Century and After, and of Lord Rochester reprinted from The Hogarth Essays, series 2, no. 2.]

1934

53. MODERN PROSE STYLE. Oxford: Clarendon Press.
54. POEMS OF JOHN DRYDEN, selected with an introduction by B. D. London: J. M. Dent. [Everyman's Library.] Reprinted 1954.
55. A COMPANION TO SHAKESPEARE STUDIES, edited by Harley Granville-Barker and G. B. Harrison. [Contains 'Shakespeare and the Drama of his Time' by B. D.]
56. The Novel: Has it a Function Today? *National Review*. Vol. CIII, no. 620, pp. 530–7.
57. ESSAYS BY DIVERS HANDS, being the transactions of the Royal Society of Literature of the United Kingdom. New series, vol. XIII, edited by W. B. Maxwell. [Contains 'The Novel: Has it a Function Today?' reprinted from the *National Review*.]
58. Contemporary English Drama. *Queen's Quarterly*. Vol. XLI, pp. 397–404.
59. An Experiment with Rhyme. *Life and Letters*. Vol. X, no. 52, pp. 66–72.
60. Modern Prose Style (a Public Lecture delivered at Leeds University). *The Criterion*. Vol. XIII, no. 53, pp. 561–76.
61. The Shavian Situation. *Spectator*. Vol. CLIII, no. 5533, p. 46.

1935

62. THE FLOATING REPUBLIC: AN ACCOUNT OF THE MUTINIES AT SPITHEAD AND THE NORE IN 1797. By G. E. Manwaring and B. D. London: Geoffrey Bles. Reprinted 1937.
63. AN OPEN LETTER TO A PROFESSIONAL MAN. London: Stanley Nott. [Pamphlets on the New Economics, no. 14.] Republished in *The Social Credit Pamphleteer*, 1935.
64. THE LETTERS OF KING GEORGE III, edited by B. D. London: Cassell.

1936

65. THE ENGLISH NOVELISTS: A SURVEY OF THE NOVEL BY TWENTY CONTEMPORARY NOVELISTS, edited by Derek Verschoyle. [Contains 'George Meredith' by B. D., reprinted from the *National Review*.]
66. Milton and Dryden: a comparison and contrast in poetic ideas and poetic method. [Lecture given before the Tudor and Stuart Club. December 11th, 1935.] *English Literary History*. Vol. III, no. 1, pp. 83–100.

1937

67. ENGLISH REVOLTS. London, Herbert Joseph.
68. FROM ANNE TO VICTORIA: ESSAYS BY VARIOUS HANDS, edited by B. D. No. 16. LORD CHESTERFIELD (1694–1773), by B. D., pp. 241–51. London: Cassell.
69. The Plays of Eugene O'Neill. *Southern Review*. Vol. II, pp. 435–46.
70. A Basque Wedding. *Spectator*, Vol. CLIX, no. 5714, pp. 1174–5.

1938

71. INTRODUCTIONS TO ENGLISH LITERATURE, edited by B. D. VOLUME IV. THE VICTORIANS AND AFTER 1830–1914, by Edith Batho and B. D. London: The Cresset Press. Reprinted 1950, revised edition of whole series, 1952.
72. SHAKESPEARE: TROILUS AND CRESSIDA, edited by B. D., with introduction, notes, essay on Shakespeare's verse, glossary, etc. London: Blackie & Son. [The Warwick Shakespeare.]
73. Basque Sport: Urzoak. *Spectator*. Vol. CLX, no. 5724, p. 424.

1939

74. Poetic Drama in England Today. *Southern Review*. Vol. IV, pp. 581–99.

1940

75. George Bryan Brummell (died March 30th, 1840.) *Spectator*. Vol. CLXIV, no. 5831, pp. 445–6.
76. Then and Now: a comparison of thoughts and emotions in 1915 and 1940. *Political Quarterly*. Vol. XI, pp. 314–21.

1941

77. The Dynasts. *Southern Review*. Vol. VI, pp. 109–24.

1942

78. THE UNACKNOWLEDGED LEGISLATOR: CONVERSATION ON LITERATURE AND POLITICS IN A WARDENS' POST, 1941. London: G. Allen & Unwin. [P.E.N. Books.]
79. A.B.C.A. Gets Going. *Spectator*. Vol. CLXVIII, no. 5925, pp. 55–56. [Article on the Army Bureau of Current Affairs.]

1943

80. THE UNIVERSITIES AND REGIONAL LIFE. King's College, Newcastle upon Tyne: Twenty-fifth Earl Grey Memorial Lecture, 1943.

1944

81. Arts Faculties in Modern Universities. *Political Quarterly*. Vol. XV, pp. 341–52.

1945

82. SCIENCE, THE UNIVERSITIES AND THE MODERN CRISIS. Memoirs and proceedings of the Manchester Literary and Philosophical Society, vol. CLXXXVI, sessions 1943–45. [Contains a paper by B. D., 'The Janus Heads of Knowledge'.]

1946

83. ENGLISH ESSAYISTS: London: Collins. [Britain in Pictures, no. 106.]
84. Daniel Defoe. A lecture delivered at Amsterdam to the Allard-Pierson Stichting, Afdeling voor Moderne Literatuurwetenschap. *Neophilologus*. Vol. XXX, pp. 97–106.

1947

85. ALEXANDER POPE. London: Sylvan Press. Reprinted 1951.
86. THE AMATEUR AND THE THEATRE. London: Hogarth Press. [The Hogarth Essays, series 3, no. 1. A lecture held at the Summer School at the Civic Playhouse, Bradford, July 1945.]
87. HENRI ALAIN-FOURNIER: THE WANDERER (LE GRAND MEAULNES), translated by Françoise Delisle, illustrated by John Minton, with an introduction by B. D. London: Paul Elek.
88. A Minor Restoration Poet [B. D. on Rochester.] *The Listener*. Vol. XXVII, no. 957, p. 594.

1948

89. ALEXANDRE BELJAME: MEN OF LETTERS AND THE ENGLISH PUBLIC IN THE EIGHTEENTH CENTURY, 1660–1744, etc., edited with an introduction and notes by B. D., translated by E. O. Lorimer. London: Kegan Paul, Trench, Trubner & Co. [International Library of Sociology and Social Reconstruction.]
90. Mr O'Neill's Latest Play [i.e. *The Iceman Cometh*. A critical essay.] *Sewanee Review*. Vol. LVI, pp. 118–26.

1949

91. THE LONDON BOOK OF ENGLISH VERSE, selected by Herbert Read and B.D. London: Eyre & Spottiswoode. 2nd revised edition, 1952.
92. POPE AND HIS CONTEMPORARIES: ESSAYS PRESENTED TO G. SHERBURN, edited by J. L. Clifford and L. A. Landa. [Contains 'Some Aspects of Defoe's Prose' by B. D.]
93. The Theme of Patriotism in the Poetry of the Early Eighteenth Century. [Warton Lecture on English Poetry, read February 16th, 1949.] *Proceedings of the British Academy*. Vol. XXV, pp. 49–65.

1951

94. RUDYARD KIPLING. London: Longmans, Green & Co. [British Council: Bibliographical series of supplements to *British Book News*. B. D. took over the editorship from T. O. Beachcroft in 1954. Contains material from an article published in *The Criterion* and in *The Lamp and the Lute*.]
95. ENGLISH STUDIES TODAY: PAPERS READ AT THE INTERNATIONAL CONFERENCE OF UNIVERSITY PROFESSORS OF ENGLISH HELD IN MAGDALEN COLLEGE, OXFORD, AUGUST 1950, edited by C. L. Wrenn and G. Bullough. [Contains 'What is "Literature" for?' by B. D.]
96. Chesterfield and France. *English Miscellany*, 2, pp, 107–24.
97. The Matter-of-fact Novelist [B. D. on Daniel Defoe]. *Listener*. Vol. XLV, no. 1151, pp. 468–9.

1952

98. ENGLISH ASSOCIATION: ESSAYS AND STUDIES. New series, Vol. V. [Contains 'The Tempest' by B. D.]
99. Rudyard Kipling, a New Aspect [B. D. on 'The Breaking Strain']. *The Listener*, Vol. XLVII, no. 1215, pp. 967–8.

1953

100. Science and Poetry in England. [A critical essay.] *Sewanee Review*. Vol. LXI, pp. 658–64.
101. Berkeley as a Man of Letters. *Hermathena*. No. LXXXII, pp. 49–75.

1954

102. THE BROKEN CISTERN. The Clark Lectures 1952–53. London, Cohen & West.
103. BERNARD DE MANDEVILLE: A LETTER TO DION, edited by B. D. Liverpool: University Press. [Liverpool Reprints, no. 10.]
104. The Confidential Clerk. [A critical essay.] *Sewanee Review*. Vol. LXII, pp. 117–31.
105. English Poets Today: The Younger Generation. *Sewanee Review*. Vol. LXII, pp. 598–620.

1955

106. Some London Plays. [A critical essay.] *Sewanee Review*. Vol. LXIII, pp. 270–80.
107. Some Remarks on Prose in England Today. [A critical essay.] *Sewanee Review*. Vol. LXIII, pp. 631–46.

1956

108. JOHN DRYDEN. London: Longmans, Green & Co. [British Council: Writers and Their Work, no. 70.] Revised edition, 1961.

109. ALEXANDER POPE: COLLECTED POEMS, edited with an introduction by B. D. London: Dent. [Everyman's Library, no. 760.]
110. POETRY AND CHILDREN, BY THE CENTRAL COMMITTEE ON THE TEACHING OF ENGLISH IN THE EAST AND WEST RIDINGS OF YORKSHIRE. [Essay-foreword by B. D.] London: Methuen.
111. ENGLISH ASSOCIATION: ESSAYS AND STUDIES. New series, vol. IX. Jubilee volume. [Contains 'On (not) enjoying Shakespeare: an un-buttoned conversation in a study' by B. D.]
112. Drama in England. [A critical essay.] *Sewanee Review*. Vol. LXIV, pp. 470–84.
113. Some Literary Autobiographies of the Present Age. [A critical essay.] *Sewanee Review*. Vol. LXIV, pp. 689–706.

1957

114. No Man's Land. [A critical essay.] *Sewanee Review*. Vol. LXV, pp. 309–26.

1958

115. NEW POEMS 1958, edited by B. D., Louis MacNiece, Philip Larkin. London: Michael Joseph. [Seventh P.E.N. anthology.]
116. The London Theater 1957. The Melting-pot. [A critical essay.] *Sewanee Review*. Vol. LXVI, pp. 146–60.
117. Some Recent London Plays. [A critical essay.] *Sewanee Review*. Vol. LXVI, pp. 649–56.

1959

118. OXFORD HISTORY OF ENGLISH LITERATURE, edited by F. P. Wilson and B. D. VOLUME SEVEN. ENGLISH LITERATURE IN THE EARLY EIGHTEENTH CENTURY, 1700–1740, by B. D. Oxford: Clarendon Press.
119. The London Stage. [A critical essay.] *Sewanee Review*. Vol. LXVII, pp. 109–17.
120. Dryden's Poems. [A critical essay.] *Sewanee Review*. Vol. LXVII, pp. 519–26.

1960

121. FIVE HEROIC PLAYS, edited with an introduction by B. D. London: Oxford University Press. [World's Classics, no. 576.]
122. THE LIVING SHAKESPEARE, edited by Robert Gittings. [Contains a chapter: 'The Last Plays' by B. D.]
123. The Writing of Daniel Defoe. [The Peter Le Neve Foster Lecture, delivered April 27th, 1960.] *Journal of the Royal Society of Arts*. Vol. CVIII, no. 5050, pp. 730–42.

1961

124. SWINBURNE: POEMS, selected and introduced by B. D. Harmondsworth: Penguin Books.
125. Durrell's Alexandrian Series. [A critical essay.] *Sewanee Review.* Vol. LXVIX, no. 1, pp. 61–79.
126. William Hazlitt, 1778–1830. *Review of English Literature.* Vol. II, no. 1, pp. 30–7.

1962

127. THREE EIGHTEENTH-CENTURY FIGURES: SARAH CHURCHILL, JOHN WESLEY, GIACOMO CASANOVA. London: Oxford University Press. [Reprinted from separate works published in 1927 and 1933.]
128. BYRON'S DRAMAS. Nottingham: University Press. [Byron Foundation Lectures, 1962.]

Subscribers

The Library, Aberdeen University
Ronald Ayling

Patricia M. Ball
Martin Banham
C. L. Barber
Bedford College for Women
Department of English,
University of Birmingham
R. F. Brissenden
G. L. Brook

E. F. Caldin
J. M. Cameron
A. C. Cawley
C. B. Cox

M. Bryn Davies

J. O. Ekpenyong

Ian Fletcher

Helen Gardner
W. H. Gardner
B. C. Gillinson
Desmond Graham

Bernard Harris
John W. Harvey
Rayner Heppenstall
Richard Hoggart
R. G. Howarth

Ian Jack
D. W. Jefferson
John D. Jump

The Library, Karnatak University

Arnold Kettle
R. W. Ketton-Cremer
John Killham
L. C. Knights

Clifford Leech
The Library, University of Leicester
W. J. Lucas

The Library, University of Malaya
Michael Millgate

Mrs. A. M. Oliver
G. A. Over

A. C. Partridge
Cecil Price

The Library, Queen Mary College,
London

The Quaestor and Factor,
University of St Andrews
The Library, Sheffield University
J. McH. Sinclair
A. H. Smith
Raymond Southall
Walter Stein

G. and K. Tillotson

The Library, University College,
London

P. F. Vernon

Mrs G. Watson
Basil Willey
George Wing

Index